Grass Roots
Peacemakers

Gary Barnell

Grass Roots Peacemakers

The Free World Wake-Up Call

Gary Bowell

Library of Congress Cataloging-in-Publication Data

This book was printed in the United States of America.

To order additional copies of this book, contact:
Xlibris Corporation
888-795-4274
www.xlibris.com
orders@xlibris.com
22400

Contents

Appendices

M   Statement by John Polanyi, Canadian University Professor, Nobel Laureate, Chemistry, 1986—"Stupidity is the Enemy; Idealism is Our Only Hope."

*To our children, grandchildren,
and great-grandchildren, whose lives will be
governed by the actions of today's generation to
build a more peaceful, just, and humane world.*

About the Author

Gordon (Gary) Bowell was born in 1918 in Vancouver, British Columbia, Canada, and grew up in Nelson, a small town in the West Kootenay mountain region of B.C. He has a B.A. in economics and history from Queen's University, Canada, a Rhodes scholarship, and a Harvard M.B.A. He was editor for several years of a small newspaper, followed by four years in Europe, in the Canadian Artillery during World War Two. Major Bowell was awarded the M.B.E. (member of the Order of the British Empire) for his wartime services. He was CEO of two leading Canadian forest products companies, and lectured frequently across Canada on his industry.

He has had a life-long interest in writing; in study to find a new approach to peacemaking; in the lives of the Nobel Peace Laureates; in the United Nations; and in the failures of state government peacemaking throughout the twentieth century. He and his wife Frances (née Webb) live in Vancouver, and have traveled frequently, meeting the citizens of many countries.

Grass Roots Peacemakers

What is happening to mankind, now facing increasing threats of warfare, dire poverty, disease, terrorism, and weapons of mass destruction? Governments have failed completely to ensure peace. The grass roots must now find recruits to energize public opinion and become peacemaking partners with governments and the United Nations.

An impossible dream? Read how fourteen unemployed young activists started Greenpeace in a church basement in Vancouver, Canada. Read the stories of 110 Nobel Peace Laureates, including Woodrow Wilson, Mikhail Gorbachev, Willy Brandt, Mother Teresa, Yitzhak Rabin, Martin Luther King Jr., and Nelson Mandela. Learn about the seventeen Nobel peace organizations, such as Amnesty International, Red Cross, and Doctors Without Borders, who are dedicated to work to find a different road to peace—the only alternative to preventing a repetition of the carnage of the twentieth century.

The author states the case for an understanding of the increasing threats to peace. He calls for a different approach, an *Action Now Campaign* with a new commitment of the grass roots to become a significant power working for peace.

This book is of vital interest to anyone concerned about world peace—educators, university students, civic-minded professionals, humanitarians engaged in helping the poor, political leaders, environmental activists, countless volunteers in non-governmental peace organizations, and workers in all management ranks of state governments and the United Nations.

It is a treasure-house of quotations for any speaker on world peace, democracy, politics, the social free enterprise system, technology, business, the environment, current history, world social conditions, and human rights.

The complex issues of the obstacles to peace and the necessary foundations to build an enduring world peace are presented, both with the wide-ranging fundamentals and the detail that brings a sharp focus on the specific issues.

An assessment of recent progress and failures of the leading organizations responsible to build world peace is presented, along with the track records of state governments, the United Nations, and non-governmental organizations. The book also deals with the all-important linkages of peace with democracy and the social free enterprise or market economy system, and with the importance for these institutions to become more reforming and committed to their public relationships and responsibilities.

A new approach to peacemaking raises many difficult questions and a search for answers, building toward the primary purpose of this book—to help volunteers find the key steps to taking action to become peacemakers. There are specific examples of the start-up of small peacemaking teams and a wide range of potential projects for new peacemakers groups.

The conclusions of this book touch all lives, and spell out a wake-up call for all citizens, young and old, who want to help in the work for peace. The author hopes that *Grass Roots Peacemakers* will plant the seeds to grow many small teams of peacemakers working to create a peaceful world for all humanity and for future generations.

"Blessed are the peacemakers, for they shall be called the children of God."

The Holy Bible

"Then if they should be inclined to make peace, do thou incline towards it also, and put thy trust in Allah."

The Holy Koran

"Do not unto others what you would not have them do unto you."

Confucianism

"What is hateful to you, do not do to your fellow man. That is the law."

Judaism

"This is the sum of duty: do not unto others that which would cause you pain if done to you."

Hinduism

"Living a good life with honesty, love, compassion, and unselfishness will lead you to nirvana."

Buddhism

Epigraph

There is a record of an experiment with a frog, placed in warm wetlands water in a deep bowl, above a small heater on the grass. As the water temperature rose slowly, the frog made no effort to jump to freedom. The hotter the water, the more relaxed the frog. When almost asleep it realized its discomfort, but was now too weak to manage more than a few feeble jumps, and died in the bowl.

Acknowledgments

The Norwegian Nobel Institute, Oslo, Norway, has granted permission to use extracts from the lectures given by the Peace Laureates at the annual award presentation of the Nobel Peace Prize, and from the speeches of the Norwegian Nobel Committee on this occasion.

Permission has been given, or is pending, to use information from the following sources: *The Nobel Peace Prize and the Laureates,* and *The Words of Peace* by Irwin Abrams; *Challenges to the United Nations* by Erskine Childers; *The Economist,* London, U.K.; article in *The Globe and Mail,* Toronto, Canada, 3 January, 2002, by Michael Edwards; *Encyclopaedia Britannica Inc.,* Chicago, U.S.; *Champions of Peace* by Tony Gray; *An Enquiry Into The Human Prospect* by Robert Heilbroner; *The State, War, and the State of War* by Kalevi Holsti; *The Age of Extremes* by Eric Hobsbawm; *Warriors of the Rainbow* by Robert Hunter; *Wilson's Ghost* by Robert McNamara and James Blight; *Power and Prosperity* by Mancur Olson; *Stupidity is the Enemy, Idealism Is Our Only Hope,* statement by John Polanyi, Nobel Laureate; *Out of My Life And Thought,* by Albert Schweitzer, Nobel Laureate; *Earth Time: Essays* by David Suzuki; *The Future of Capitalism* by Lester Thurow; articles in *The Vancouver Sun,* Canada; and *Future Positive,* by Michael Edwards.

Generous assistance has also been given by the following: Head Librarian Anne C. Kjelling of the Nobel Institute Library, Oslo, Norway; Dr. Jennifer Allen Simons, President, The Simons Foundation, Vancouver, Canada, and Elaine Hynes, Assistant to the President; Dr. Patrick Moore, Greenspirit Enterprises Ltd., Vancouver, Canada; Dr. R. K. Carty, Head of Department of Political Science, University of British Columbia, Vancouver, Canada; Erika Becker, for a German translation of the award ceremony lecture by Willy Brandt, Nobel Laureate; Rhidian Gatrill for cover artwork; Molly O'Callaghan, and

Joanna O'Callaghan for computer research assistance; Jasper Gatrill for computer assistance; and to my grandson, Kevin O'Callaghan, for many constructive discussions on his generation's point of view, resourceful fact-finding, and editing.

My special thanks to Diana P. H. Gatrill, who at all times was a patient and skilled secretary, work organizer, and helpful critic.

Abbreviations
And Acronyms

ABM	Anti-Ballistic Missile Treaty
AEC	Atomic Energy Commission (U.S.)
AIDS	Acquired Immune Deficiency Syndrome
ANC	African National Congress
Appx.	Appendix
B.C.	British Columbia
Cdn.	Canadian
CEO	Chief Executive Officer
CIDA	Canadian International Development Agency
CTBT	Comprehensive Test Ban Treaty
DPI	Department of Public Information (UN)
EC	European Community
ECOSOC	Economic and Social Council (UN)
EEC	European Economic Community
EU	European Union
GATT	General Agreement on Tariffs and Trade
G.B.	Great Britain
GDP	Gross Domestic Product
G8	Group of Eight
FAO	Food and Agriculture Organization (UN)
HIV	Human Immunodeficiency Virus
HR	Human Rights
IANSA	International Action Network on Small Arms
ICBL	International Campaign to Ban Landmines
ICBM	Intercontinental Ballistic Missile
ILO	International Labor Organization (UN)

IMF	International Monetary Fund
INF	Intermediate-Range Nuclear Forces Treaty
Int'l.	International
IPPNW	International Physicians for the Prevention of Nuclear War
MSF	Médicins Sans Frontières/Doctors Without Borders
NATO	North Atlantic Treaty Organization
NGOs	Non-governmental Organizations
NPT	Nuclear Non-Proliferation Treaty
Ont.	Ontario
PLO	Palestine Liberation Organization
RCMP	Royal Canadian Mounted Police
SALT	I, II Strategic Arms Limitation Talks
START	I, II Strategic Arms Reduction Treaty
U.K.	United Kingdom (Great Britain)
UN	United Nations
UNCTAD	UN Conference on Trade and Development
UNDRO	UN Disaster and Relief Organization
UNESCO	UN Educational, Scientific and Cultural Organization
UNHCR	UN High Commissioner for Refugees
UNICEF	UN Children's Emergency Fund
UNRRA	UN Relief and Rehabilitation Administration
U.S. or U.S.A.	United States of America
U.S.S.R.	Union of Soviet Socialist Republics (now Russia)
WHO	World Health Organization (UN)
WTO	World Trade Organization
YMCA	Young Men's Christian Association
YWCA	Young Women's Christian Association

Preface

Many persons today feel that the happiness and confidence of the human spirit is not as abundant as it was in their parents' time, and see many disturbing signs of growing anxiety about the prospect for the future of mankind. Our streets, schools, homes, and public meeting places are not safe. The gap between the rich and the poor is widening, both within wealthy nations and between rich and poor nations. Barbaric armed warfare and terrorism have continued in many parts of the world since the Second World War, and have increased during the past twenty years. The threats of terrorism and weapons of mass destruction, over-expanding populations, and a closing environmental vise continue. Recently, there has been continuing slaughter in Palestine/Israel, terrorist killings in Bali, North Korea's statement that it will continue to develop nuclear weapons, and the U.S. and coalition force's war in Iraq. The present world is one of increasing instability and inhumanity, with the failure of both the citizenry and national political leaders to find the road to peace. The advances in the twentieth century, in technology, health care, women's equality, human rights, education, economic efficiency and democracy will not be enough to reverse current trends toward deterioration of the human prospect unless mankind takes a new approach to peacemaking. Living in peace among nations means not only the cessation of wars, but also ensuring for all peoples the rule of law, security, equal human rights, and a sharing of economic opportunity to provide a good standard of living.

The first Nobel Peace Prize was awarded in 1901. The Nobel Peace Laureates were a group of outstanding men and women who dedicated their wisdom and lives as workers for world peace. Why did the world not listen to them? Why did the statesmen fail to learn the lessons of two tragic World Wars and hundreds of wars since? Why is world peace further away today than it was in 1901? I wrestled with these questions and decided that there were six major flaws respecting peace and war in governmental systems since 1900. First: the primary aim of most ruling classes was the aggrandizement of their power and the power of the state, not the *welfare of the citizens*. Second: *there was a disconnection* between the aims and policies of state authorities and the interests of the grass roots of society, who had left state authorities in charge of decisions of peace or war. Third: *the citizens did not produce the leadership, nor the mass popular support, that would enable them to be partners with the state authorities in matters of war and peace*. Fourth: the citizens did not understand that they had the final responsibility for war or peace, *requiring communication both up and down between the citizens and the state*, and not communication only from the top down, as was the practice. Fifth: *the democratic process failed repeatedly*. Democratic governments did not understand that, while co-operative international relations between states were essential for peace and economic prosperity, repeated warfare was inevitable in any system whereby state sovereignty viewed protection against invasion as the pre-eminent concern, secured if necessary by dishonoring international commitments. When there is a system of non-co-operating sovereign states, the price is permanent insecurity, competitive arms build-up, and inevitable warfare. Sixth: *many democracies have still not learned that world peace depends on states joining in a collective and co-operating international defense organization in which all nations honor their international commitments*. It has taken hundreds of years for most democratic states to build a mature democracy. All of the ex-colonial and ex-dictatorship states will need several generations for peace-loving families to train children and young adults in the ways of peace and democracy.

This analysis leads to the conclusion that the individual citizen needs to understand the urgency of the problem and develop the will to do something about it. Many persons under sixty do not remember the Second World War, and have not been seriously concerned about understanding the conflicts and failures of peacemaking since 1945. An awakening to the reality of the many crises of 2003 is now a priority. How do today's generation learn about the failure of the present system and the urgency to try something new? A book is needed, one that leads to discussions among friends, to decisions to form small groups of peacemakers and to develop an action program to work at the grass roots level for peace.

Most young people today are very busy with jobs and families. I felt that a book to propose a new force for peacemaking would not be written unless I volunteered to write it myself. I thought this was completely impractical, and decided not to be a Don Quixote tilting at windmills. Then I recalled the bravery and commitment of a friend who was a co-founder of Greenpeace in 1969, when fourteen young men and women held meetings in a church basement in Vancouver, Canada, and decided to risk their lives to stop a U.S. underground nuclear test in Alaska. They had no money and no organization, but they held concerts to earn money and continued to mount campaigns against nuclear testing, whale and seal pup killing, and environmental degradation. They won worldwide support of the media and the public. Over two and one half million volunteers have since joined Greenpeace, today a worldwide organization respected by all nations, large corporations, and the public. Their story is a highlight of this book.

Greenpeace proved that the impossible can be made possible, and that an individual and a few friends could start a Peacemakers group and win supporters to make a peace movement grow. This became my dream, the same age-old dream that started with one person and a group of friends forming volunteer groups to work for peace. It was the dream of Henri Dunant, in 1901 the first Nobel Peace Laureate, who founded the Red Cross in 1863 and devoted the rest of his life to charity and to the building of the Red Cross. I felt it was important to write about the lives and work of the 110 Nobel Peace Laureates of every creed and color, from thirty-two nations, including ten women, eighty men, and seventeen peacemaking organizations. They are leaders who, by their lives, have encouraged volunteers to form thousands of new peacemaking organizations over the past 100 years. Reading about the lives of persons such as Albert Schweitzer, President Woodrow Wilson, Linus Pauling, Martin Luther

King Jr., Nelson Mandela, and Aung San Suu Kyi, shows today's generation that grass roots peacemaking is the only way to stop the barbarity of war.

This book confirms that there are three indispensable requirements for the growth of world peace. The first is the link between peace and democracy. *There is no peace without stable democracy, and no stable democracy without peace.* The second requirement is the link between peace and a fair and progressive social free enterprise system. This is the only system that can provide the resources necessary to bring to the destitute masses a full share in the future fruits of peace, freedom, and human rights. The third requirement is based on the fact that, as almost all of the monumental peace and war problems today are international, affecting all peoples and across all boundaries, an international approach by co-operating states is the *only* effective way of dealing with international problems. States will finally learn that the only road to peace is by way of the United Nations.

Many of the most intractable problems of war and peace today are assessed: collective security, or continuing wars; causes and cures of terrorism; threats of runaway populations, and nuclear weaponry; protection of the environment; sovereignty versus humanitarian intervention; globalization gains and costs; Muslim and Western relations; proliferation and use of weapons of mass destruction; abuses of human rights; extreme poverty and despair of much of the world population.

The time has come to help the grass roots learn more about problems of world peace, develop leaders and activist volunteers of many new small peacemaker groups, win more media and public opinion support for peacemaking, and develop political strength to put pressure on state governments and big business.

Chapter 15 explores the two main compelling *imperatives* that should govern the shape of foreign and defense policy of U.S. and world governments in the 21st century:

- *The Moral Imperative*: stop killing
- *The Multilateral Imperative*: collective decision making and collective security.

The last chapter is a response to the anticipated question of prospective new peacemaker volunteers—"I now understand the many threats to peace—I want to help—What can I do now?

It is hoped that this book will plant the seeds to grow many small grass roots groups of peacemakers working to create a peaceful world for present and future generations.

(Please note: masculine nouns and pronouns apply equally to women and men; all dollars are in U.S. $, unless stated otherwise; and when the names of Peace Laureates are followed by a date in brackets, this shows the date of award of the Peace Prize.)

P.S. The name of the 2003 Nobel Peace Prize winner—Shirin Ebadi—was announced after this book was closed for publication.

"In war, resolution; in defeat, defiance; in victory, magnanimity; in peace, goodwill."

Sir Winston Churchill,
Prime Minister, U.K.
Epigraph after the First World War.

"[The] post-Cold War international system [is] characterized by the presence of many dangerous, troubled, failed, and murderous states . . . . Military intervention is ethically justified when domestic turmoil threatens regional or international security and when massive violations of human rights occur."

Stanley Hoffmann, 1998
Professor
Harvard University, U.S.

"Military cemeteries in every corner of the world are silent testimony to the failure of national leaders to sanctify human life by the one radical solution—peace."

Yitzhak Rabin (1994)
Prime Minister of Israel

Chapter 1

HUMANITY AT THE CROSSROADS

The twentieth century saw the most slaughter of any century in history. Never before have there been such killings: nine million in the First World War; thirty million civilians killed by totalitarian governments between the wars; another twenty million in the Second World War; countless millions in China and Korea; roughly one million in Vietnam and S.E. Asia; eight hundred thousand hacked to death by machetes in Rwanda in just one hundred days; about five hundred thousand killed in the former Yugoslavia. The deadly toll goes on and on. In the past one hundred years there have been over two hundred wars, during which about 160 million were killed in armed conflict, more than ever before in human history. Add the many millions maimed for life, the despair and destitution of the families left without adult support, and the tragic losses of war have destroyed the lives of countless millions.

It is a mind-numbing exercise to spin the globe and discover how many wars, not only between states but also within states, have been witnessed by today's generation. Remember the drug wars in Columbia, the killing of native peoples in Guatemala, the civil wars in Chile and El Salvador. Cross the Atlantic and think of the suffering due to wars in Bosnia, Serbia, Kosovo, Iraq, Chechnya, and Afghanistan. Or cross the Pacific and recall the fighting in the Philippines, Sri Lanka, and East Timor. Spin the globe again and remember the almost forgotten wars of Nigeria, Rwanda, Burundi, Democratic Republic of the Congo, Liberia, and Sierra Leone; move a little north and you sink into the despair surrounding Sudan, Somalia, Ethiopia, Israel, Palestine, and Lebanon.

There is no peace in the many regions under the repressive control of dictators, as in Myanmar (formerly Burma), North Korea, and Zimbabwe. There is no peace in many countries where minorities are oppressed, where freedom fighters are warring to create a new state based on the right of peoples to self-determination, where terrorists are fighting for a wide number of causes, indiscriminately killing soldiers and civilians. Many terrorist organizations identify openly with armed violence and the killing of innocent civilians worldwide.

After the two World Wars, there have been bloody military conflicts in many countries; international armed interventions by India, Pakistan, Great Britain, France, Egypt, Israel, Jordan, Syria, Russia, China, and North Korea; major invasions by Russia, Iraq, France, Great Britain, and the United States of America. It is certain that wars will continue as long as the sovereignty of states is considered inviolable and states refuse to support collective international peacemaking to settle conflicts by non-violent means. The sovereign state presents a Catch 22 situation: the omnipresent threat of war justifies the military power of states to protect their citizens; the presence of state military powers in turn sets the stage for a continuing threat of war.

Wars of many different kinds have been fought since the beginning of history. During the past two centuries the major wars in Europe were waged between states and by revolutions within states. Napoleon conquered most of Western Europe until defeated at Waterloo in 1815 by the alliance of Great Britain and Prussia. The Treaty of Vienna in 1815 was crafted largely by Prince Metternich, foreign minister of the Austrian empire, mainly to reward the victors and to try to stabilize the states of Europe based largely on the principle of the *balance of power*, now proven a failed strategy to achieve stable long-term peace among nations. The Prussian general von Clausewitz and Prince Bismarck created modern Germany by military power, under the destructive linkage that "war is a continuation of politics by other means." The modus operandi was that the interests of the major powers could be best served not by frequent wars, but by alliances that would maintain peace through political settlements that satisfied each nation's pride and military power, but with no alliance so powerful that it would be tempted to launch a major war on its neighbors. There were no major wars between states in Europe after 1815 until the Franco-Prussian war of 1871-72, which left a powerful Germany with an overwhelming military strength. This led to complete instability in Europe after 1900, with the major powers devising a web of treaties and alliances—Germany, Austria, and Italy confronting Great Britain, France, and Russia, with a number of unstable minor powers attached to each major alliance by a series of open and secret guarantees pledged together like a house of cards. One outlet for the power-hungry rulers of Europe had been building colonial empires. But here also there was no international co-operation and peace was frequently broken. In the Far East major wars erupted between Japan, Russia, and China.

The American Civil War (1861-1865) was a different kind of war; one of attrition, with mass destruction and more powerful weapons used by "citizen soldiers" of both the north and south. Both sides were locked into a corner, allowing for no agreement on a cease-fire. The Civil War was the bloodiest in U.S. history. More Americans were killed than in all the later wars of the U.S. put together, including both World Wars, Korea, and Vietnam. War is emotional as well as physical, and the deep-seated scars of this devastating war are still closing over, 138 years later. In many respects war is a lingering disease of the spirit for many generations. History recorded once again the truth of the words of U.S. Union Forces General Sherman—"War is Hell."

The rapid build-up of a gigantic arms race in the first decade of the 1900s shattered hopes for peace in Europe. Standing armies were increased, vast munitions and other war material were stockpiled, and Great Britain and Germany rushed into a competition to build the most powerful navies. A few years before 1914, a British cabinet minister stated a familiar doctrine of folly at a great public meeting: *'"There is just one way in which we may have peace and be secure; and that is to be so much stronger than any potential enemy that he will not dare attack us. This I submit is a self-evident proposition.' Whereupon a thousand or so hard-headed businessmen cheered to the echo. The proposition they were cheering was that two nations likely to quarrel would keep the peace and be secure when each was stronger than the other.*[1] Norman Angell (1933) (All quotations of Laureates are from *The Words of Peace* and *The Nobel Peace Prize and the Laureates* by Irwin Abrams,[2] a leading historian of the Nobel Peace Prize, or from documents received from the Library of the Norwegian Nobel Institute.)

It should have been obvious that such an assertion defies logic and morality, and that more arms will not bring more peace. History shows that this is one of the great follies in the annals of war, which is still espoused by generals and politicians all over the world. The potential enemy has found ways since early history to foil the defenses of a rival by building a more efficient war machine; instability and rivalry led inevitably to war.

The First World War, 1914-1918, engulfed millions of combatants to a point of mutual exhaustion of men and resources, leaving a weakened and ravaged Europe, and Russia (called the Union of Soviet Socialist Republics after the revolution of 1917), ill-equipped to cope with post-war crises during the 1920s and 1930s. War, the Clausewitzian "continuation of politics," had gotten out of control. The horrors of trench warfare for four years left Europe mourning a lost generation and lacking the resources necessary to rebuild its shattered economies. U.S. President Wilson (1919) had proposed in January 1918 his famous "Fourteen Points" speech for a settlement based on "peace without victory." Wilson demanded an end to secret treaties and secret diplomacy and proposed many drastic changes in world affairs: open covenants openly arrived at; freedom of the seas alike in peace and in war; removal of barriers and inequalities in international trade; reduction of armaments by all powers; colonial readjustments; evacuation of occupied territory; all "peoples" have a universal right of national self-determination; a redrawing of European boundaries along national lines; and, most important, an international political organization to prevent war—a League of Nations.[3] President Wilson told his people that it was " . . . a war to make the world safe for democracy . . . a war for freedom and justice and self government amongst all the nations of the world . . . the German people themselves included." His reconciliation peace plan was unfortunately ignored in the Treaty of Versailles (1919) which stated the terms of settlement of the First World War. The victors insisted on making Germany pay for the war. They imposed unilateral disarmament of Germany, punishing territorial losses, and draconian monetary reparations demands. Wilson insisted, however, that the creation of a League of Nations should be a part of the peace treaties. Unfortunately for the cause of peace, the U.S. refused to join the League of Nations, due mainly to political rivalry, popular aversion to foreign commitments, and reluctance to restrict national sovereignty. It is tragic to note that only one of Wilson's "Fourteen Points" has been achieved as yet, and that is the international organization, now called the United Nations (UN).

The Treaty of Versailles sowed the seeds of future war. Attempts at reconciliation and peacemaking were made with the Locarno Treaties of 1925, which marked the highest point of international good will between the two World Wars. Germany signed a treaty with France and Belgium which guaranteed their respective frontiers unconditionally. In 1928, Foreign Minister Briand (1926) of France, and F. B. Kellogg (1929), U.S. Secretary of State, sponsored the Kellogg-Briand Pact, whereby sixty-five nations condemned recourse to war to settle international disputes, and affirmed their will to renounce war as an instrument of national policy. The economic collapse of Germany in 1927, the world depression of 1929 to the mid-thirties, massive unemployment, and worldwide growth of communism was followed by the public and the political leaders of the Great Powers failing to act when Mussolini, Hitler, and Stalin openly discarded all treaties. The League of Nations had no power to decide on counter measures to oppose breaches of treaties, and no resources to take effective action, lacking support from France and Great Britain. In 1937, Germany and Italy withdrew from the now rapidly failing League. As the war clouds gathered, Hitler invaded Austria and Czechoslovakia despite his agreements with Great Britain and France that he would not do this. History taught once again that appeasement of aggressors merely encourages their further aggressions, and that enduring peace cannot be secured on the principle of appeasement.

The Second World War began with Hitler's invasion of Poland.

France and Great Britain declared war on Germany on September 3, 1939. This war was entirely different from previous wars. Hitler quickly conquered most of western Europe by using brilliant new strategies of "blitzkrieg"—lightning strikes of mass attack by armored corps against static infantry groups, softened up by overwhelming air attacks of fighters and close-contact medium bombers, along with heavy bombers destroying allied towns, roads, railways, and supply depots. In April 1940, Germany invaded Norway and Denmark, followed by Holland, Luxembourg, and Belgium, by-passing the out-dated defensive Maginot Line of France. The British army was evacuated from the beaches of Dunkirk, and a few weeks later France signed an armistice and Great Britain stood alone.

The highlights of the fighter planes' Battle of Britain, the heavy bombing of London and other large cities, the submarine sinkings of Britain's lifeline of ships, the British offensive in North Africa, and Germany's control of almost all of Europe except Italy, Portugal, Spain, Switzerland, and Sweden are familiar history. It was a miracle that Great Britain and the free world survived, due in large part to inexplicable follies of Germany's invasion of the Union of Soviet Socialist Republics, and Japan's attack on the U.S. at Pearl Harbor on December 7, 1941, bringing the enormous military power of the U.S. into the war. A world controlled by Germany and Japan would have been an unmitigated disaster, devastating the future of the free world. Germany surrendered unconditionally to Great Britain, the U.S., France, and the U.S.S.R. on May 8, 1945.

The dropping, in August 1945, of nuclear bombs on Hiroshima and Nagasaki signalled that the war with Japan was over, but the world's problems of war and peace were just beginning. Wars continued in China, Korea, South East Asia, India, and the Middle East. The continued occupation by the U.S.S.R. of countries invaded by the Red Army marked the beginning of the Cold War in 1945 between the two remaining superpowers, the U.S. and the U.S.S.R. The United Nations had been created in 1945, saddled by the hope that the U.S. and U.S.S.R. would agree sufficiently to rebuild a stable world based on UN principles. The UN was hampered from the beginning due to the permanent members of the Security Council—the U.S., U.S.S.R.,

Great Britain, France, and China—having a power of veto over major decisions. The UN was designed to maintain international peace and security, and encourage co-operation in solving international social, economic, and cultural problems. (See Appendix D for the 2001 Nobel Peace Prize presentation ceremony speech of Gunnar Berge, Chairman of the Norwegian Nobel Committee, and the lecture of Kofi Annan, United Nations Secretary-General.) Under its constitution the UN had no powers or resources apart from those assigned to it by member-nations, and therefore no powers of independent action. International instability increased due to numerous wars of freedom from colonial powers, usually with the support of competing great powers. The North Atlantic Treaty Organization (NATO) was established by the U.S., Canada, and ten European nations, and was successful in opposing further advances in Western Europe by the U.S.S.R. after the Second World War. (Nine European states—Albania, Bulgaria, Estonia, Latvia, Lithuania, Macedonia, Romania, Slovakia, and Slovenia applied to join NATO in 2002, and discussions have been held on the issue of Turkey and Russia joining in the future.)

Warfare had been transformed during the Second World War into total wars of military forces and civilians alike, with massive destruction by air bombing, no static "front lines" as war was waged everywhere, and the use of nuclear bombs and long-range missiles. During the forty-five years of the Cold War from 1946 to 1991, the world was filled with arms as the major industrial states competed to arm themselves and to export weapons to keep state armed forces, guerrilla warfare, and terrorism fully supplied. Soon new weapons such as hand-held "Stinger" anti-aircraft missiles, helicopter gun ships, and cruise missiles were added to meet growing worldwide demand. The ultimate or final weapon, the nuclear bomb, was stockpiled during the Cold War by all the nuclear powers. In 1957, the U.S.S.R., to the world's astonishment, launched *Sputnik*, the first satellite to orbit in outer space. In 1958, the U.S.S.R. developed the first intercontinental ballistic missile (ICBM). Nuclear submarines, long-range bombers, and ICBMs could deliver nuclear bombs with destructive effect ten thousand times greater than the nuclear bombs dropped on Japan. Scientists, including Peace Laureate Linus Pauling (1962), fought an uphill battle to persuade the nuclear powers to reduce nuclear arms. He estimated in 1963 that the world stockpile of nuclear bombs was about 320,000 megatons (one million tons). *"If there were to take place tomorrow a 6-megaton war, equivalent to the Second World War in the total power of all explosives used, and another such war the following day and so on, day after day, for 146 years, the present stockpile would be exhausted—but in fact, this stockpile might be used in one single day, the day of the Third World War."* Linus Pauling (1962)

The Peace Prize lecture of Joseph Rotblat (1995), nuclear physicist and President of the Pugwash Conference on Science and World Affairs, called for the gradual mutual reduction of all nuclear weapons in ten years. He recalled the horror of the Cuban missile crisis of October 1962, *". . . when a decision of one man, Nikita Krushchev, Chairman of the U.S.S.R., could trigger a world war . . . which, unlike previous ones, destroys all of civilization . . . . Here then is the problem . . . stark and dreadful, and inescapable: shall we put an end to the human race: or shall mankind renounce war?"*

In 1972, U.S. President Richard Nixon and U.S.S.R. Chairman Leonid Brezhnev reaffirmed the goal of "peaceful coexistence" and signed the Strategic Arms Limitation Treaty (SALT I). (See Appendix J, summarizing the main treaties on nuclear and strategic ballistic missiles disarmament.) Each nation agreed to reduce its antimissile defence system to make it possible to work toward equality in offensive weapons. They also agreed to hold stipulated weapons to a fixed ceiling for five years. The Helsinki Accords of 1975 were a high point of the détente of the 1970s. The balance of power was still a "balance of terror" of mutually assured destruction, as more powerful nuclear weapons and delivery systems carrying up to ten nuclear warheads, each independently guided, were tested. The U.S. developed cruise missiles, the U.S.S.R. supersonic bombers. SALT II was signed in 1979. It placed further limits on offensive missiles. Although not ratified, it was adhered to by both nations throughout the 1980s. In 1987, U.S. President Ronald Reagan and U.S.S.R. Chairman Mikhail Gorbachev (1990) agreed to remove nuclear missiles in Europe. By 1990 the two superpowers each still had about 25,000 nuclear weapons.

In 1991, U.S. President George H. Bush and U.S.S.R. Chairman Mikhail Gorbachev signed a Strategic Arms Reduction Treaty (START I) pledging each nation to scale down by about a third its arsenal of long-range nuclear missiles, signalling the end of the Cold War. After years of procrastination, the Russian government ratified both the 1993 START II Treaty and the Comprehensive Test Ban Treaty of 1996. Negotiations have begun on a START III Treaty to make further cuts on the two nations' strategic nuclear arsenals. At the periodic five year review in 2001 of the 1970 Nuclear Non-Proliferation Treaty (NPT), the avowed nuclear weapon states—the U.S., U.K., France, Russia, and China—renewed their "unequivocal undertaking" to reduce and eventually eliminate their nuclear weapons. A number of states, represented as having nuclear weapons, have not signed the treaty—India, Pakistan, North Korea, and Israel. At the review conference, UN Secretary-General Kofi Annan warned that "the multilateral disarmament machinery had 'started to rust' because of an apparent lack of political will to use it." Progress has been slow as the Russians remained concerned that the U.S. "Star Wars" program would undermine the Anti-Ballistic Missile (ABM) Treaty of 1972, which they regard as the foundation for all nuclear arms control.

During President Reagan's terms, competition with the U.S.S.R. increased due to U.S. proposals for defensive missile interceptors of incoming ICBMs. The proposal for a National Missile Defense (NMD), reactivated in 2002 by President George W. Bush, has been criticized as the beginning of the militarization of space, and the destabilization of international relations. This defense proposal is bound to stir up enmity toward the U.S. In June 2001, the U.S. Army's Tactical High Energy Laser destroyed a test Katyusha Rocket in flight. The U.S. is continuing its development and tests of the destruction of incoming ICBMs, using a chemical laser weapon.[4]

Chemical and biological weapons of mass destruction were developed and stockpiled during the Cold War. In the 1980s, Iraq killed thousands of its citizens by poison gas, breaking the Geneva Protocol of 1925 against the use of chemical warfare, and confirming the failure of states to restrict the barbarity of chemical warfare. The research and production of chemical and biological weapons is relatively cheap and easy to hide, and in some cases, such as the 2001 incidents of mailing anthrax disease spores in the U.S., easy to deliver or to use to terrorize and blackmail. With these weapons a new and diabolical front has been opened up—attacks by unknown terrorists to kill and wreak havoc, not only on military operations, but also randomly and by stealth on any civilian population anywhere. Warfare and terrorism have been brought into the home front of any nation, and the best measures of defense cannot guarantee the safety of anyone.

Looking now at the *internal wars* of states, there have been about thirty-five major guerrilla wars since the end of the Second World War, with all but three outside Europe and North America. Some internal armed conflicts were triggered by revolutions, a common denominator of which was the persistent social and political instability of the less developed world (also called the Third World, or underdeveloped world). Leaders of guerrilla-type operations to overthrow colonial powers were supported in many cases by the competing powers U.S. and Russia (which replaced the name U.S.S.R. after its dissolution in the early 1990s), or suppressed by military coups as in Brazil and Indonesia in the early 1960s and Chile in 1970. The less developed world represents about five billion people, or almost eighty percent of the world's population, living in extreme poverty. Realistically, this is a global volcano waiting to erupt. Fidel Castro's revolution in Cuba in 1959 inspired "freedom fighters" throughout Latin America, largely drawn not from peasants but from students and the middle classes, and gradually spreading from back-country regions to "urban guerrillas" and terrorist groups. The student rebellions of the 1960s in both the more developed and less developed regions were often infiltrated by small clandestine "red brigades" or communist terrorists. The darkest era of terror, counter-terror, and torture in the history of the West marked the 1970s. Revisionist communist regimes continued the wave of revolution, mainly in South East Asia and Africa. As the U.S. had aligned itself with the conservative forces in most of the less developed regions, it was usually on the losing side of these revolutions. Due to repressive measures by despotic regimes, the social and political instability and the despair of the masses of poor, which generated the wave of revolutions, a growing world crisis developed. Small group violence increased in many regions. International terrorist incidents, such as the attempt to blow up the World Trade Center in New York (1992), increased continuously from 125 in 1968 to 831 in 1987 (UN World Social Situation, 1989). During the last decades of the twentieth century political assassinations increased. The sustained uprising of the Palestine *intifada* began in 1987, demonstrating that the period of Palestinian passive resistance had changed to street masses and to violent resistance. It was the readiness of the masses to control the streets that decided matters, as shown in the revolution that overthrew the Shah of Iran. Lenin's maxim applied—that "voting with citizens' feet could be more effective than voting in elections."

Armed violence in recent decades has become increasingly the indiscriminate slaughter of civilians—men, women, and children. The horror of mass graves in the former Yugoslavia and mutilated bodies in Africa is referred to as ethnic cleansing, a euphemism for ethnic butchery. Historians and psychologists will be able to identify the breeding grounds of these obscene acts which deny any vestige of humanity or morality. How does modern society produce such monsters, the leaders and the followers of mass murder under the bloodied banners of race or creed? The capture and arming of twelve-year-olds encouraged by ethnic war lords to rape and kill, and the holding of generations of youths in refugee camps, produces future generations of lawless, revengeful killers.

The September 11, 2001, destruction of the World Trade Center in New York, part of the Pentagon, and an airliner over Pennsylvania, causing about 3,000 deaths, brings into sharp focus the questions of relationships between the East and the West, between Christianity and Islam, between international terrorism and peace. Islamic "fundamentalism" is the fastest growing brand of theocracy in the world. Current reports on the world's main religions list two billion Christians and slightly over one billion Muslims, respectively thirty-three per cent and seventeen per cent of almost six billion worldwide adherents of all religions.[5] Osama bin Laden, the leader of the terrorist group al-Qaeda, boasted of his leadership of the September 11 killings.

He accused the U.S. of waging war against Islam, proclaimed a version of Islam that is hostile to other religions, and that it is the duty of devout Muslims to kill non-Muslims. He lumped all countries of Judeo-Christian society together as enemies. Virtually every Muslim government has rejected this terrorist interpretation of Islam. History shows many examples of Christians and Muslims learning to live in peace. For example, the Turkish people have developed good relations with the U.S. and western Europe. The peoples of most Muslim states are generally not believed to be hostile to western society, and appear inclined to emulate the West in many technological, political, economic, and social matters. The terrorists will continue to try to win the hearts and minds of Muslims antagonistic to the West and to their own rulers alike, for largely economic and political reasons. A clash between the West and Islam would be a major disaster for both peoples and for world peace. There is an urgent need for the leaders and the people of both heritages to ensure that the call to arms of Muslims hating the West and of Muslim terrorists does not succeed. The warning signals of anti-western and anti-Christian terrorist groups and of street masses capable of terrorist killings and general armed hostilities against the West and against the present governments of Islamic states are getting louder. Both western governments and Islamic governments can do much to reduce the basic causes of these hostilities. The war against terrorism and the invasion in 2003 of Iraq by the U.S. and coalition forces have widened the gap between the Muslim world and the West. A major effort must now be made by both communities to find the road to reconciliation and peace.

Attention will now be turned to assess the future prospects for war or peace facing mankind. As expected, there are many different points of view, varying from those of deep despair to those of faith in the ability of mankind to change course when the need to do so is strong enough to enlist the will, intelligence, and resources of the people. One of the most thoughtful and forward-looking books on the future challenges to mankind is *An Inquiry Into The Human Prospect* by Robert Heilbroner, 1974. (The many quotations in this Chapter from Professor Heilbroner are identified by page number in the Notes.)

He identified and assessed relevant data and concepts from philosophy, sociology, science, economics, and politics in his search for the essence of the future prospects facing mankind. His book received wide attention from the thinking public, media, and academics, based on it touching a raw public nerve, a *civilizational malaise* due to concern that the world is changing not for the better but for the worse, drifting toward a depressingly different and unforeseeable future. Heilbroner asks " . . . whether we can imagine a future other than a continuation of the darkness, cruelty, and disorder of the past; worse, whether we do not foresee in the human prospect a deterioration of things, even an impending catastrophe of fearful dimensions."[6] Most western industrial societies are worried about the barrage of deeply-rooted trends that have shaken confidence in the future of mankind: dysfunctional families; anti-social juvenile disorders and frequent violence and killings; abuse of women, children, the handicapped, and minorities; decay of inner cities; shocking crimes of youth and adults; rising suicide rates, especially among teenagers; fear for personal safety; drug-related problems and crimes; dire poverty amidst conspicuous affluence; financial scandals and dishonesty of the powerful; failures of social, political, economic, and ethical traditions and principles; failure of the present middle-aged generation to pass its values along to its children; the youth rebellions of the 1960s and 1970s; the growing disparity of the standards of living of the rich and the poor. The quality of life is steadily deteriorating. The list of shocking occurrences of the denial of justice, equality, and fraternity among peoples is endless.

In the early 1970s the world was shaken by a series of disturbing unforeseen events which ended the relative optimism of the 1960s: the Arab-Israeli war; the Arab oil embargo, an unprecedented action by the Arab world against the industrialized West; the detonation of an atomic bomb by India; a drought in the sub-Saharan area that claimed the lives of six million people. Heilbroner judged that comparable dangers were likely to continue despite efforts to adapt or to change the course of threats that were out of society's control. The pre-eminent danger stemmed from the inescapable demographic trends of the next thirty years and beyond for several generations. (See Appendix F.) The population was increasing at unmanageable rates, heading toward an inevitable *population explosion.* There are many views that the less developed regions' population of 4.9 billion in 2000 is not sustainable, a very serious population problem.

As Sam Goldwyn is alleged to have said, "Forecasting is very difficult, especially with respect to the future." The latest UN revision in 1999 of population trends presents a recent forecast. Comparing the year 2000 with a forecast for 2030, the world population will grow about two billion, from 6.1 billion to 8.1 billion. The more developed regions will increase only slightly to 1.2 billion. *But the less developed regions will increase by about two billion, from 4.9 billion to 6.9 billion.* All of the world's two billion increase would be mainly in the urban areas of the less developed world. The impact on the lives of children born after the year 2000 is tragic—to force the urban population of 1.9 billion of the less developed regions in the year 2000 to live in unbearable poverty and degradation, with 3.9 billion people in year 2030, would create unthinkable problems. *The use of the world's resources would not be sustainable.* The rural population of the less developed world would be static, so the urban regions would need massive imports of food. The population of the urban areas of the less developed world is forecast to double every thirty years, showing on paper an impossible increase of this population of 3.9 billion in 2030 to an unsustainable population of 7.8 billion by 2060. Children born today may live more than sixty years, and the resources and environment of the world will not be able to sustain them. The urban areas of the less developed world will be growing and overcrowded breeding grounds of even more poverty, despair, and violence than these urban slums are today. The demographic outlook for the urban areas of the less developed world is unsustainable and must be changed by a drastic drop in population growth, either voluntary or involuntary.

Heilbroner assesses the possibility of these horrific population growth rates remaining unchecked, depending on two main variables. The first is the possibility of the poverty-stricken less developed regions developing effective and stringent birth control programs. Despite government efforts, this has had no success in India, Egypt, or Latin America. Only China tried to achieve a zero growth rate by the year 2000, but indications are that this was not achieved. The Malthusian checks of famine and disease could be offset by a large increase in food production, in the use of "miracle seeds" as developed by Peace Laureate Norman Borlaug (1970).

His "green revolution" showed many less developed regions how to increase yields of wheat and rice up to fifty percent in two years. Sustaining high yields will require massive use of fertilizers, but at increased costs and on such a scale as to surpass the ecological tolerance of the soil to chemical additives.[7] The torrent of human growth imposes intolerable social strains on the less developed regions, as well as hideous costs on their individual citizens. "Of the world's population of 6 billion in year 2000, 2.5 billion people lack access to even the most minimal of toilet facilities . . . . Some 160,000 people are moving to cities from the countryside every day . . . . At least 600 million people in Africa, Asia, and Latin America now live in squatter settlements without any sanitation whatever, and governments are unable to cope."[8] The needs of about seven billion people in less developed regions in 2030 for food, fuel, fertile land, water, infrastructure, and the other requirements of life cannot be met on a sustainable basis. Efforts to make serious progress toward reducing the population of the less developed world before 2030 would require major social, political, and economic changes. During a visit by the author and his family in the 1970s to a primitive Zambian village, it was found that the boys were not in school, but were out looking after a few cattle; the women did all the domestic work, finding wood for fuel, tending crops, and carrying infants with the help of three-year-old girls; and the men, looking worn out at thirty to forty years, were all sitting in a hut, drunk on local brew alcohol by noon, and incapable of doing any work. This social pattern will obviously break down unless it is changed drastically.

In most poverty-stricken areas of the less developed world a family of many children is needed to support non-functional parents who are unable to support themselves. Many children are the poor family's only "pension fund" and are often abused as a source of cheap labor. There will be inadequate birth control until the wealthy nations send massive funds and development projects to raise the standard of living of the poor in the less developed regions.

The necessity of curbing the population explosion has been advocated for several generations, but the political will to do it is lacking, except in communist China. To do it elsewhere could possibly require the rise of "iron" police-state governments with strong military support. Governments of less developed regions could be forced to take advantage of the changing technology of war, whereby a war of terror can be well-financed and carried out anywhere in the world with a minimum of cost and resources. If conditions in the less developed regions remain as today, there will always be a continuing supply of terrorists who were raised in squalid refugee camps or have never worked, and have the support of their people. The inevitable outcome of overcrowded populations of less developed countries living in utter poverty is a "steadily worsening social disorder, further stunting of physical and mental capabilities, political apathy intermingled with riots and pillaging when crops fail. Such societies would probably be ruled by dictatorial governments serving the interests of a small economic and military upper class and presiding over the rotting countryside with mixed resignation, indifference, and despair."[9]

The second major danger is the proliferation of terrorists and "rogue states" capable of developing nuclear weapons with their potential of total destruction. Nuclear capability has spread to Israel, India, Pakistan, North Korea, and probably other countries. North Korea exports arms to pay for nuclear weapons and the technology and necessary components, or can accumulate the by-products of nuclear power plants. It has been suggested that poor nations can use their nuclear weapons "as an instrument of blackmail to force the developed world to undertake a massive transfer of wealth to the poverty-stricken world."[10] Even if such blackmail could be contained by military force, the expense of eliminating guerrilla and terrorist groups, or of being the world's policeman, would bankrupt even the most wealthy nation. During the 1960s and 1970s, the U.S. was the world's largest net foreign creditor nation. In 1982, the U.S. became a net foreign debtor nation, with net foreign debt of 1.1 percent of

Gross Domestic Product (GDP). As of 1999, the net foreign debt was over two trillion dollars, 22.6 percent of the GDP,[11] and is still increasing, as of June, 2003.

A third all-encompassing danger facing mankind, after population growth and war, is that "ultimately there is an absolute limit to the ability of the earth to support or tolerate the processes of industrial activity, and there is reason to believe that we are now moving toward that limit very rapidly."[12] "In the developed world, industrial production has been growing at a rate of about seven percent a year, an exponential growth of doubling every ten years . . . In another fifty years, the demand for resources will have doubled five times, requiring resource extraction thirty-two times larger than today's. If we look ahead over the ten doublings of a century, the amount of annual resource requirements will have increased by over a thousand times."[13] Recycling, reduced consumption, and technological change can increase some resources or reduce the demand, but the odds of reducing the demands of an expanded industrial capacity would be too low to be contemplated. If a significant reduction would reduce the demand on the environment from a ten-fold increase to a five-fold increase over today's demand, the world would still be faced with an unalterable law of physics. "There remains one barrier that confronts us with all the force of an ultimatum from nature . . . all industrial production . . . requires the use of energy, and all energy . . . is inextricably involved with the emission of heat."[14]

"The limit on industrial growth therefore depends in the end on the tolerance of the ecosphere for the absorption of heat. Here we must distinguish between the amount of heat that enters the atmosphere from the sun or from the earth, and the amount of heat we *add* to that natural and unalterable flow of energy by man-made heat-producing activities, such as industrial combustion or nuclear power. Today the amount of heat added to the natural flow of solar and planetary power is estimated at about 1/15,000 of the latter—an insignificant amount."[15] The emission of man-made heat is, however, growing exponentially, as both a cause and consequence of industrial growth. This leads us to face the incompatibility of a fixed "receptacle," however large, and an exponentially growing body, however initially small. According to the calculations of Robert Ayres and Allen Kneese, of *Resources for the Future*,[16] we therefore confront the following danger:

"Present emission of energy is about 1/15,000 of the absorbed solar flux (i.e. heat from the sun and earth). But if the present rate of growth continued for 250 years emissions would reach 100 percent of the absorbed solar flux. The resulting increase in the earth's temperature would be about fifty degrees C—a condition totally unsuitable for human habitation."[17]

Heilbroner considers next that if the average rate of yearly increase in energy use would be limited to four percent, the average yearly increase since the Second World War, energy use would double every eighteen years. "This would allow us to proceed along our present course for about 150 years before the atmosphere would begin to warm up appreciably, let us say by about three degrees. At this point, however, the enormous multiplicative effects of further exponential growth would suddenly descend upon us. For beyond that threshold, extinction beckons if exponential growth continues for only another generation or two. Growth would therefore have to come to an immediate halt. Indeed, once we approached the threshold of a 'noticeable' change in climate, even the *maintenance* of a given industrial level of activity might pour man-made heat into the atmosphere, necessitating a deliberate cutting back in the energy use . . . . In point of fact, serious climatic problems may be encountered well before that dangerous threshold. Noticeable fluctuations are anticipated by climatologists when global man-made heat emissions reach only one percent of the solar flux, *little more than a century from now.*"[18]

These estimates make no allowance for massive industrialization in the underdeveloped regions, where per capita energy use is now only about one-tenth of its use in the Western world. As the less-developed regions become more industrialized and the population within these areas doubles or quadruples over the next one hundred years, the threshold of *noticeable* change in climate will arrive in less than 150 years. Increases in the efficiency of power generation or utilization, new technologies using solar, wind, geo-thermal, fuel cells, and future safe and efficient atomic fission will reduce industrial heat emissions, as would a shift away from material production to the production of "services." "Every sign, however, points in the same direction: industrial growth must surely slacken and likely come to a halt, in all probability long before the climatic danger zone is reached."[19]

A main underlying cause of society's failure to cope with the threats of population explosion, war, and potential environmental collapse is the rapid advance of science and technology without a corresponding growth in the moral and ethical ties that bind together the brotherhood of man. We have not coped with the dangerous tendencies of industrial civilization. In the face of these growing dangers we have not developed adequate measures of social control. Heilbroner studied the socio-economic capabilities of mankind to respond to these dangers, and concluded that the dangers are derived from *social* and *ethical* problems originating in human behavior and therefore capable of ameliorization by changes in human behavior, providing mankind develops the will to do so. "We are entering a period in which rapid population growth, the presence of obliterative weapons, environmental deterioration and dwindling resources will bring international tension to dangerous levels for an extended period. There seems no reason for these levels of danger to subside unless population equilibrium is achieved and some rough measure of equity reached in the distribution of wealth among nations, either by great increases in the output of the underdeveloped world or by massive redistribution of wealth from the richer to the poorer lands."[20]

" . . . external challenges of the human prospect, . . . can be seen as an extended and gnawing crisis induced by the advent of a command over natural processes and forces that far exceeds the reach of our present mechanisms of social control . . . . It goes without saying that this unequal balance between power and social control enters into, or provides the underlying basis for, . . . mankind's 'civilizational malaise.'"[21]

The next question is to examine what response mankind can muster against these critical challenges, and against the dangerous tendencies of industrial civilization itself. The threats of population explosion and war will have to be dealt with, well or poorly, sooner or later, by the ability of mankind to live as a universal brotherhood, with nations treating one another as they would like to be treated, and by the understanding by all peoples of the obscenity of war and of their heart-felt desire for peace. This leaves the challenge of mankind's capabilities in dealing with the environmental limitations that are emerging inexorably as the most uncompromising challenge faced by mankind. Heilbroner's analysis leads to the conclusions that the present orientation of society must change. Industrial production cannot continue to grow, and must eventually be curtailed. Excessive consumption in the industrialized world must be reduced. Post-industrial society of the future will be as different from today's industrial society as the latter from pre-industrial society. Such massive changes will test the political and psychological adaptabilities of the human capacity for responses that will enable future generations to survive.

Heilbroner examines the likely timetable mankind has to reduce population growth, to adapt to the use of dwindling resources, and to achieve a redistribution of wealth from richer to poorer nations. These are all compelling mandates that will increase international tensions to dangerous levels. The present objectives of governments to alleviate these dangers by the *increase* of industrial production in the richer *and* poorer nations presents the risk of entering the danger zone of climatic change in three or four generations. In the decades ahead, the powerful nations will delay the impacts of declining material output per head by the traditional use and abuse of national power. Recurrent crises of wars such as the Gulf War of 1991 and the destruction of the World Trade Center in New York on September 11, 2001, the impact of the economic recession of 2001-2002, and the many continuing wars within less developed countries, mark the end of the post-Cold War period and the beginning of a radically new world in which society will have to cope with massive change. The twenty years after 1973 are described by Eric Hobsbaum in *The Age of Extremes*[22] as "a world which lost its bearings and slid into instability and crisis." Changes in this period were minor compared with the dangers facing the new world of the next fifty years.

The capacity of human nature to cope with massive recurrent social, economic, and political change is not known. As evidence, however, no developing country has faced the problem of severely limiting its industrial development. No capitalist nation has faced the alterations it must undergo to develop a viable stationary and stable social, economic, and political structure. There seems no hope for rapid changes in the human character traits that would have to adjust to bring about a peaceful and organized change of lifestyles. A drift toward a strong exercise of political power appears necessary to administer major changes in both production and consumption. *No substantial voluntary diminution of industrial growth, or a planned reorientation of society, is imaginable today.*[23]

It is useful to summarize the main premises on which Heilbroner's argument in *The Human Prospect* are based:

- Population is expanding at unmanageable rates, in many parts of the less developed regions;
- Capability of waging nuclear war is moving into the hands of the less developed world, radically altering the balance of power between rich and poor nations;
- The process of industrial growth will become increasingly difficult to sustain because of resource limitations, and increasingly dangerous because of pollution problems, including the ultimate fatal pollution of an overheated atmosphere, unless industrial growth is curtailed;
- There is at present a widespread malaise or pessimism about the future, caused in part by the industrial basis on which our civilization is based—material advance has been unable to satisfy the human spirit. A society dominated by the machine process is finally insufficient to retain people's loyalty;
- Continued global industrialization is a process of gravest perils for mankind;
- If the grinding poverty of the less developed world is not addressed, it will be forced to consider both nuclear and economic blackmail—such as Middle East oil—as countervailing weapons;
- Efforts to stop the population explosion might require the rise of strong authoritarian "military" governments as the only kinds of regimes capable of establishing and enforcing major viable social and economic change. A drift toward authoritarian

measures may be the only means by which a suicidal struggle of
one class against another can be avoided;

- "Wars of redistribution" could become a new, powerful force
shaping the future in many parts of the world.

Heilbroner concludes that sustained and convulsive change is
the inescapable lot of human society for a very long time to come. He
reluctantly senses that a major and protracted crisis, slated to deepen
and intensify rather than to lessen and disappear, is a premonition
shared by many. Heilbroner feels that the reluctance of humans to
recognize impending dangers and to have the capacity to accept many
radical social and economic changes will necessitate a degree of harsh
authority, depending on the extent of willing self-discipline. This is where
faith in democracy and in the public exercise of intelligence, goodwill,
and self-restraint is a necessary social ingredient. But there will not be any
easy subordination of the private interest to the public interest.

If there is any doubt remaining about the marked increase in
current wars and of the underlying conditions which created them,
the recent locations of violence by army units/guerrilla/terrorist/
military coups in the Britannica Book of the year 2002 should settle
the question; Guinea, Eritrea, Liberia, Ethiopia, Sierra Leone, Israel,
Palestine, Yugoslavia (Serbia, Kosovo, Herzegovina), Macedonia,
Albania, Kurd regions of Turkey and Iraq, Sudan, Chechnya Republic,
Islamic fighting in Kyrgyzstan—Tajikistan—Uzbekistan, Afghanistan,
Iraq, Sri Lanka, Philippines, Ecuador, Columbia, Democratic
Republic of Congo, Rwanda, Uganda, Burundi, and Somalia.[24]

Mankind is truly at the crossroads of war or peace. The last century
saw the worst horrors of war in history. The evidence of social, moral,
and political decline toward armed violence, and of man's inhumanity
to man, is prevalent and irrefutable. Today's generation is faced with
the prospect that the odds are very poor for our children,
grandchildren, and great—grandchildren (many will live to see year
2100) to have healthy, happy, meaningful, and peaceful lives. Past
history is replete with the lessons of failures to achieve peace.

The ultimate question is whether the present generation will
make massive sacrifices *now* in order to provide a good and sustainable

life for future generations. It is well understood that the degree of sacrifice will become increasingly onerous as each year of overuse of the world's resources continues, and that the most difficult generation to start making a drastic change in "lifestyles" is today's generation. Rational reasoning would reject giving the rights of humanity and the welfare of future generations preference over today's way of life. By far the largest percent of people would opt to enjoy life to the fullest now possible. But there is still a powerful instinct inside all mankind to pass along to future generations the heritage that our forefathers gave to us. Each generation is aware of the eternal mandate that we are each responsible for future generations, and that this survivalist ethic has brought us to where we are today. This ethic will come to the fore again when the threats to mankind increase and become compelling. Our consciences will not allow us to be the executioners of future generations. The future of our children, grandchildren, and great-grandchildren is more important to us than anything else in this world. We will make whatever sacrifices are necessary for future generations to survive, even as previous generations have done.

A logical start to understanding the failing process that has held humanity in a vice of continuing wars and poverty is to look at persons who have devoted their lives to working for peace over the last hundred years—the Nobel Peace Laureates, called the "Champions of Peace." The ten women, eighty men, and seventeen institutions who were selected by the Norwegian Nobel Committee for the Nobel Peace Prize as the person or persons "who shall have done the most or the best work for fraternity between nations" were outstanding in their work for peace, and achieved many successes in their peacemaking.

The inspiration that moved Alfred Nobel to create the Nobel Peace Prize, the devotion to peacemaking that has been shown in the work of the Norwegian Nobel Committee, and the record of their outstanding achievement of honoring leading world peacemakers over the past one hundred years is presented in Chapter 2—Story of the Nobel Peace Prize.

"In a dark time, the eye begins to see."

Theodore Roethke
Educator and poet

*"In brutal strife your sword and shield shall be belief in life
and human dignity."*

Nordahl Grieg
Norwegian poet

Chapter 2

STORY OF THE
NOBEL PEACE PRIZE

The world takes notice each October that the Norwegian Nobel Committee has awarded the Nobel Peace Prize to the person or organization who during the preceding year has made the greatest contribution to world peace. (See Appendix A for an extract from Alfred Nobel's will.) The 2001 Peace Prize was approximately $1,000,000 U.S., divided equally between two recipients—Mr. Kofi Annan, Secretary-General of the United Nations, and the United Nations organization. The 2002 Peace Prize was awarded to the former President of the U.S., Mr. Jimmy Carter.

The first Peace Prize was awarded in 1901. The roster of 110 Peace Laureates is shown in Appendix B. Most of the Peace Laureates are names recognized worldwide. The roster also lists names of persons known mainly in their own country for their commitment to lifelong work for peace "in the trenches," out of the glare of world publicity. The Nobel Peace Prizes are among the most prestigious and most valuable in the world. A summary of the main categories of Peace Laureates is shown in Appendix C, Tables 1 to 4, by Irwin Abrams, from his book *The Nobel Peace Prize and the Laureates.*[1]

Categories Number of awards

* Statesmen and political leaders   37
* Organizers of volunteer peace movements   31
* Humanitarian workers   23

- Human rights activists   15
- International jurists   4
                                   Total   *110*

A brief outline of the life of each Peace Laureate is shown in Chapter 3. It is an honor role of great men and women who have devoted their lives to the cause of world peace. Peace Laureates include many famous peacemakers of the twentieth century: U.S. President Wilson (1919), Fridtjof Nansen (1922), Albert Schweitzer (1952), Linus Pauling (1962), Martin Luther King Jr. (1964), Willy Brandt (1971), The Fourteenth Dalai Lama (1989), Mikhail Gorbachev (1990), and Nelson Mandela (1993), to list a few to show the caliber of the Nobel "Champions of Peace."[2] They include outstanding philosophers, statesmen, scientists, jurists, religious leaders, doctors, social workers, human rights activists, and leaders in many walks of life. In many cases there were two awards for the one year, each Laureate receiving one-half of the prize amount.

Alfred Nobel, born in Sweden in 1833, was an engineer and entrepreneur who amassed a large fortune in a worldwide industrial empire based mainly on inventions of increasingly powerful explosives and other industrial products. Nobel dynamite was used worldwide in armaments, mining, blasting, public works, and a wide variety of construction projects. At the time of his death in 1896, he held about 355 patents, in many countries. His life was dedicated to solving complicated technical problems by analyzing them, deciding what should be done, and then putting all his energies into solving them. A close friend described him as, "A thinker, a poet, and a man given to superb flights of mind . . . passionately in love with the far horizons of human thought . . . understanding everything and hoping for nothing."

It is a paradox that the inventor of powerful explosives left a magnificent legacy for peace. He was convinced that more destructive armaments would lead inevitably to more cataclysmic wars which would destroy civilization unless mankind learned to live in peace. He wrote, "If the world is not peaceful . . . (within thirty years) it would go directly back to barbarism"—a prescient forecast of the barbaric First World

War. He was inspired by his belief in the community of man, had studied the problems of war and peace, and had met many leaders of peace societies. After reading the anti-war novel of a friend, Baroness von Suttner (1905), *Lay Down Your Arms*, Nobel decided that the world needed activist peacemaking leaders, and that he would provide generous funding to enable them to work full-time in the cause of peace. The initial value of each prize was the equivalent of about $41,800, twenty-five times the annual income of a Swedish university professor at that time.

Nobel bequeathed the bulk of his fortune to create a fund for five equal prizes annually to those who . . ."shall have conferred the greatest benefit on mankind." The fund received about $8.6 million in 1901 dollars, a record endowment at that time. The prizes were for the most important discovery or invention in physics, chemistry, medicine, literature of an idealistic tendency, and a prize for "the person who shall have done the most or the best work for fraternity among nations, for the abolition or reduction of standing armies and for the holding and promotion of peace congresses"—called the Peace Prize. In 1968 a sixth prize, the Bank of Sweden Prize in Economic Sciences in Memory of Alfred Nobel, was added, it being equal to that of the other prizes.

The concept of a Peace Prize became more important as the twentieth century of bloodbaths of two World Wars demonstrated the inability of mankind to find a path to peace. Wars had become more destructive, involving not just armies, but whole populations. The advancements of science produced the ultimate weapon, the thermonuclear bomb. As Dr. Tore Browaldh, deputy chairman of the Nobel Foundation, said in 1982, in the *Atomic Age, "The unthinkable has been made possible: to transform Spaceship Earth into a nova, an exploding star, by means of new world war. Today the Nobel Peace Prize stands as the symbol of the struggle to prevent the extinction of man as a species."*

The statutes governing the Nobel Foundation and the Norwegian Nobel Committee have been amended from time to time to ensure that the awards reflect social and political trends since the late 1890s. The process of awarding the Peace Prize is unique in ensuring the complete independence of the Norwegian Nobel Committee, subject to the wisdom of the Norwegian Storting, or Parliament, to honor the wishes of Alfred Nobel "for peace and the fraternity of peoples." To assist this, members of Parliament are not eligible for appointment to the Norwegian Nobel Committee. The tendency of many political powers to dictate to subsidiary public bodies subject to their control, to meet their political motives, has been avoided to a major degree, a rare and long-sighted achievement.

The Norwegian Nobel Committee of five is chosen by the Norwegian Parliament. Members are eligible for re-election at the end of a six-year term. It has been the custom for members to be re-elected until they decide to step down. This has made for extraordinary continuity and excellent governance by long-serving Chairmen and members. The Committee has been composed of some of the most prominent figures in Norwegian public life. Its main function is to select the Laureates for the Peace Prize. An added function is the establishment of the Norwegian Nobel Institute "to follow the development of international relations . . . to work for mutual knowledge and respect, for peaceful intercourse, justice, and fellowship between nations." A first-class library assists staff and visitors. Head Librarian, Anne C. Kjelling, not only administers a highly specialized collection of international records, but also is an unparalleled source of information about the Peace Prize and is an extremely helpful consultant to scholars near and far. In 1992, a research program was instituted with a director of research, and annual research programs are attended by scholars and visiting professors. A series of lectures each spring brings distinguished scholars and public figures to the Institute. Seminars and conferences on current topics of peace and international relations are also sponsored.

Ninety Peace Prizes have been awarded to individuals and twenty to organizations. Appendix C gives information on the various main categories of Peace Prize winners:[3]

Table 1—Prize Winners by Category

Table 2—Prize Winners by Country

Table 3—Awards to Institutions and Associations

Table 4—Women Laureates

The Nobel Peace Prize selection procedure begins each autumn with thousands of circulars sent to distinguished persons, including members of national governments, jurists, university professors, peace organizations, and former winners of the Peace Prize. By the deadline of February 1, several hundred bona fide nominations will have been received. Letters come from many individuals nominating themselves, which is not permitted. An annotated list of over 150 valid nominations is discussed at the first meeting of the Norwegian Nobel Committee in February, which selects fifteen to twenty to be reviewed for further consideration. The members of the Committee, plus any specialists desired, share the work of carefully investigating each candidate for presentation of detailed "advisers' reports" at the next meeting in late summer. After extensive discussions at one or two meetings, the winner is announced in October. The formal award ceremony takes place on December 10, the anniversary of Nobel's death. The task of winnowing out the hundreds of nominations to select one or two persons or organizations each year is surely a most formidable duty. Readers will enjoy reviewing the long list of each year's dedicated peacemakers, and will realize that it would be very hard to find a more creditable performance of any comparable selection each year of worldwide interest.

There were nine years of world war when no prize was awarded, and twenty years when the award was reserved or given the following year. The Peace Prize is awarded to any man or woman of any nationality, creed, or race who has shown evidence of Nobel's thinking about humanity in its broadest sense. While Nobel thought in terms of encouraging individuals, the Committee has given twenty awards to organizations and institutions, achieving the best of both worlds. Most of the institution Laureates were founded and supported by individual peacemakers of civil society, and were not founded by governments. Nobel would have been happy with an award to either an individual peacemaker or an organized group of many committed peacemakers. Nobel said he wanted to make life easier for "spiritual dreamers" whose work for peace could be regarded as impractical, or not worthy of financial support. He wanted to foster ongoing work for peace, rather than to honor past achievement. Most of the Laureates have been encouraged to continue to work for peace, with a new worldwide audience and with new uses for the prize money that enhanced their future work as peacemakers.

It is of interest to follow the significant enlargement by Peace Laureates of the concept of peace, from an "absence of war" to including all the important factors of peacemaking that remove the conditions that are the breeding grounds of denial of human rights, conflict, violence, war, poverty, and sub-standard living conditions. Significant examples of this wider comprehensive concept of peacemaking stressed in the work of the peace Laureates are as follows:

- International systems such as arbitration to resolve conflicts before resorting to violence and arms;
- Establish systems based on international law;
- International support for peoples who are oppressed, hungry, without clean water and sanitation, medical facilities, shelter, safety, education, jobs—all the political, social, and economic benefits of modern society;
- International support for human rights, justice, and equality of opportunity to lead a good life;
- International support for safety, and for protection from terrorism, ethnic cleansing, and genocide.

In brief, peace can grow only where there is massive support for the humanity of all peoples. For example, when a minority is oppressed, there is no peace.

In the book *The Nobel Peace Prize and the Laureates* by Irwin Abrams[1], an assessment is given of the decisions of the Norwegian Nobel Committee—were they faithful to the intentions of Alfred Nobel? Some key trends are listed as follows:

- From 1901 to 1918 the emphasis was on statesmen and the organized international peace movement;
- From 1919-1939 the main groups were the same, with the addition of a new emphasis on statesmen and political leaders;
- From 1940-1959 humanitarians were the largest group;

- From 1960-1987 awards were mainly to statesmen and the organized international peace movement, with a new emphasis on human rights activists;
- From 1988-2002 the emphasis again was on statesmen and political leaders, and on human rights.

The Norwegian Nobel Committee has continued to broaden its scope by searching for all developments that had a potential for advancing world peace.

Chapter 3 presents brief summaries of the lives and extracts from the presentation lectures of the Nobel Peace Laureates, a renowned group of peacemakers, both as individuals and as volunteers who founded and supported peace associations and institutions. The Peace Laureate's work was supported at all times by the main traditional grass roots bodies of peacemakers; religious adherents, humanitarian organizations, charitable societies, and the many millions of volunteers active in non-governmental organizations (NGOs), working for the causes of peace and humanitarian help for all humanity. In turn these organizations were undergirded by a civil society which was slowly learning to believe in and live with the responsibility of the individual to work for peace and in mutual support of the brotherhood of mankind.

Individual duty is the basis for our *civil society*. This is a relatively new term which describes a vigorous citizenry engaged in the culture and politics of a free society. The term includes all the traditional volunteer organizations and societies working in humanitarian, peace, charitable, and direct social service activities that are not provided by government. There are over 80,000 registered charitable organizations in Canada alone. To this is added many volunteer workers not in charitable organizations but who work on an individual basis for a multitude of social aid causes, such as service clubs for men and women, rehabilitation organizations, and religious charities. Civil society includes activist groups of volunteers who develop large international organizations which have attracted enough public support to influence decisions of government with respect to their particular mission. They are organized and operate free of any form of control of government or the UN. These non-governmental organizations are the "front line activists" of civil society in dealing with state governments or the UN. Examples are the Red Cross, Amnesty International, Oxfam, International Physicians for the Prevention of Nuclear War, International Campaign to Ban Landmines, and Doctors Without Borders. Some NGOs aim to develop programs which would involve government support, such as the International Campaign to Ban Landmines, and some have decided to be completely independent of government, such as Amnesty International and Doctors Without Borders.

The only obligation that comes with the Nobel Peace Prize is the requirement that, whenever possible, the prize winner deliver a public lecture in Oslo within six months of receiving it. The award ceremony includes a speech by the Chairman of the Norwegian Nobel Committee and a lecture by the prize winner. The audience includes the King and Queen of Norway, the diplomatic corps, and Norway's leading cultural and intellectual citizens.

A verbatim record of the Nobel lectures by the Peace Laureates and of the presentation speeches by the Chairman of the Norwegian Nobel Committee is available to the public. Biographical information is also available from a number of sources. The Swedish Nobel Foundation, Stockholm, website *www.nobel.se* has the speeches, biographies, and lectures for each award ceremony of all the Nobel Peace Laureates. This is useful information for those who have Internet access, removing the need to go to the printed volumes. English language volumes are available from the following:

- Nobel Lectures : Peace : 1901-1970. Frederick W. Haberman, ed., Amsterdam: Elsevier, 1972. 3 volumes;
- Nobel Lectures : Peace : 1971-1995. Irwin Abrams, ed., Singapore: World Scientific, 1997-1999. 3 volumes.

The 1998-2002 lectures are available on the website of the Nobel Institute Library, Oslo, *www.nobel.no.* One can also check the Norwegian Nobel Institute library catalog from the above site: click on Library, then on Search for the library's database. The library does not sell books. Volumes can be bought from bookstores, or ordered from publishers.

The biographical notes in Chapter 3 of the Nobel Peace Laureates are necessarily brief. The quotations shown were chosen to give readers a quick look at the essence of the thinking expressed during each Laureate's lecture at their Peace Prize presentation ceremony in Oslo, Norway. The main sources of biographical data in Chapter 3 are material received from the Head Librarian of the Norwegian Nobel Institute, Anne C. Kjelling and from the website *www.nobel.no.*

"Today in the nuclear age, peace has a most urgent meaning. But survival is not the only goal. Again and again in its selections, the Norwegian Nobel Committee has emphasized the positive meaning of peace, pointing to the foundation on which a true peace must rest, and has set before us an array of inspiring human beings, who sustain in the rest of us what they themselves had in such abundance, what Martin Luther King, Jr., called 'an audacious faith' in humankind."

Irwin Abrams
The Nobel Peace Prize and the Laureates

Chapter 3

LIVES OF THE
NOBEL PEACE LAUREATES
1901

HENRI DUNANT (1828-1910), Switzerland: *Founded the International Red Cross in 1863; active in the newly-formed Young Men's Christian Association (YMCA); lifetime work for peace in evangelical and humanitarian missions.*

Dunant was a ceaseless worker against slavery, neglect of the wounded in war, neglect of the poor and homeless, treatment of prisoners of war, and the lack of public welfare. He lived the last eighteen years of his life in poverty, having bequeathed all of the Nobel Prize money to provide hospices for the homeless in his village. Dunant showed that one man could awaken the conscience of the world and bring governments to agreement on higher levels of conduct on humanitarian issues. World Red Cross Day is celebrated every year on Dunant's birthday, May 8.

"Could not the means be found in time of peace to organize relief societies whose aim would be to provide care for the wounded in time of war by volunteers of zeal and devotion, properly qualified for such work?" Henri Dunant

1901

FRÉDÉRIC PASSY (1822-1912), France: *Co-founder of the Interparliamentary Union in Geneva, Switzerland in 1889; leader of the pre-*

1914 peace movement; organizer of peace societies in most European nations and of international congresses.

Passy was a member of the French Chamber of Deputies and supported arbitration to end the Franco-Prussian war of 1870-71. He was active as a peacemaker until age ninety, busy with writing on peace problems and lecture tours. He worked with the British statesman R. Cremer (1903) in establishing the Interparliamentary Union, based on meetings at regular intervals of interested members of parliament of all countries, where international issues and exploring ways of improving collaboration between nations via their parliamentary institutions were discussed. The Interparliamentary Union is still active, with politicians of more than one hundred countries attending two conferences each year to discuss international issues. Headquarters are in Geneva.

"Though no one, it is true, wants to attack, and everybody protests his love of peace and his determination to maintain it, yet the whole world feels that it only requires some unforeseen incident, some unpreventable accident, for the sparks to fall in a flash . . . on those heaps of inflammable material which are being foolishly piled up in the fields and on the highways and blow all Europe sky-high." Frédéric Passy

(There are many thousands of active peace societies worldwide which are often unknown by the general public. The Yearbook of International Organizations lists the addresses of over 700 in a section on peace.)

1902

ÉLIE DUCOMMUN (1833-1906), Switzerland: *Veteran peace advocate, editor, legislator, railroad executive; first honorary secretary of the Permanent International Peace Bureau (awarded the Peace Prize in 1910.) The Peace Bureau is still active, with headquarters in Geneva.*

Ducommun virtually *was* the Peace Bureau, keeping contact with over two hundred peace societies worldwide. He wrote many articles and pamphlets on peace and the futility of war—refuting the popular idea that the next war would be of short duration, and predicting with frightening accuracy the horrors of four years of trench battles of attrition in Belgium and France in the First World War.

"One question often asked of pacifists is: Granted that war is an evil, what can you find to put in its place when an amicable solution becomes impossible? The treaties of arbitration concluded in the past few years provide an answer to this question . . . . The Convention for the Pacific Settlement of International Disputes signed at The Hague in 1899* by twenty-six nations offers a solution to international conflicts by a method unknown in the ancient world, in the Middle Ages, or even in modern history—a method of settling quarrels between nations without bloodshed." Élie Ducommun

(*This was soon established as the Permanent Court of Arbitration.)

1902

ALBERT GOBAT (1843-1914), Switzerland: *Lawyer, legislator, first secretary-general of the Interparliamentary Bureau and of the International Peace Bureau.*

Gobat was an active supporter of the Hague Convention for the Settlement of International Disputes. Among his many books was *The Nightmare of Europe* (1911), a clear warning of the catastrophe to happen in 1914. Like Ducommun, Gobat was a firm believer in arbitration and had great hopes that The Hague Convention represented the first step towards world peace.

"If we examine The Hague Convention carefully, we see that it considers the offer of good services a duty of every nation. In other words, such offers should be made whenever a dispute becomes critical and threatens to explode into war . . . . At the beginning of the war between Russia and Japan, the president of the United States persisted in offering his good services to the Russians and Japanese. Neither party chose to condemn the offer as an unfriendly act. Exhausted by a terrible war, both accepted, and peace was concluded . . . . U.S. President Roosevelt (1906) was the first head of state to apply the rules of The Hague Convention concerning the preservation of general peace." Albert Gobat

1903

WILLIAM RANDAL CREMER (1828-1908), Great Britain: *Labor leader in the early peace movement in Great Britain; founder of the International*

Arbitration League; long time member of the House of Commons; co-founder with Passy of the Interparliamentary Union. He was a dedicated activist for social justice and world peace.

Cremer was a shipyard worker at age twelve. He was knighted at age seventy-nine in recognition of his lifetime of work for international peace. In 1887, he carried an appeal from the House of Commons to the Congress and President of the United States to conclude a treaty with Britain stipulating that any unsettled dispute between the two should be referred to arbitration. It was approved by President McKinley and a majority vote in the Senate, but not of sufficient majority to secure its ratification. It was not until 1904 that the United States finally ratified arbitration with a number of European states.

"It may be that for a long time some nations will continue to fight each other, but the example of those nations who prefer arbitration to war, law courts to the battlefield, must sooner or later influence the belligerent powers and make war as unpopular as pugilism is now." William Randal Cremer

1904

INSTITUTE OF INTERNATIONAL LAW: *Founded in Ghent, Belgium, in 1873; it was initially a private association of politicians and international jurists, organized by Dr. Rolin-Jacquemyns, editor of the International Law Review.*

In 1879, an Institute resolution appealed to the European powers to declare the Suez Canal zone neutral and place it under international protection—a treaty to this effect was signed in 1885.

The Institute's work was to develop international public law for peaceful ties between nations, and international private law to minimize or eliminate differences existing in the laws of different countries.

"If our work has had some success, it is undoubtedly because of our efforts to 'calculate the limits of the possible,' as one great statesman put it; because of our patience in refusing to advocate premature solutions; and because of our belief in the necessity of developing gradually and progressively as our statutes bid us . . . The goal, the undisputed and inviolable region of law in international relations,

is most certainly still a long way off." Georg Francis Hager, President of The Institute of International Law

1905

BERTHA VON SUTTNER (1843-1914), Austria: *Inspired Alfred Nobel to endow the Peace Prize; a leading advocate of pacifism; author of a widely read anti-war book "Lay Down Your Arms"; first woman political journalist; editor of a leading peace journal.*

Baroness von Suttner warned of the dangers of militarizing China and of the airplane as a weapon of war. She warned again and again that "Europe is one" and that uniting it was the only way to prevent the world disaster (the First World War), which was imminent.

"One of the eternal truths is that happiness is created and developed in peace, and one of the eternal rights is the individual's right to live. The strongest of all instincts, that of self-preservation, is an assertion of this right.

"Europe is one, and uniting it is the only way to prevent the world disaster that is imminent. If the Triple Alliance included every state instead of only three, then peace would be assured for centuries." Bertha von Suttner

1906

THEODORE ROOSEVELT (1858-1919), United States: *President of the United States.*

Roosevelt was the architect of the peace treaty between Russia and Japan, 1905. He supported the concept that a "balance of power" between leading states would maintain peace. He established a permanent industrial peace commission in Washington to promote peace in the industrial world. Roosevelt made a strong call for naval disarmament by international agreement. He supported calls for international arbitration, giving The Hague Court its first case.

"I cannot help thinking that the Constitution of the United States offers certain valuable analogies to what should be striven for in order to secure, through The Hague Courts and conferences, a species of world federation for international peace and justice." Theodore Roosevelt

1907

LOUIS RENAULT (1843-1918), France: *Leader of the French peace movement, liberal internationalist, expert on international law; counsellor to the French Ministry of Foreign Affairs.*

Renault served as France's representative at many international meetings. He was editor of a large pacifist newspaper; active at The Hague Peace Conference in 1907, and in supporting international arbitration as a member of the Permanent Court of Arbitration at The Hague. Like so many of the Laureates, Renault clearly realized that, for all their work, war remained a distinct possibility.

"Anything that contributes to extending the domain of law in international relations contributes to peace. Since the possibility of a future war cannot be ignored, it is a far-sighted policy that takes into account difficulties created by war in the relations between belligerents and neutrals; and it is a humanitarian policy that strives to reduce the evils of war in the relations between the belligerents themselves and to safeguard as far as possible the interests of noncombatants and the sick and wounded. Whatever may be said by those who scoff at . . . peace conferences, wars will not become rarer by becoming more barbarous." Louis Renault

1907

ERNESTO TEODORA MONETA (1833-1918), Italy: *Editor of one of the most influential newspapers in Italy; publisher of a leading pacifist magazine; chief Italian representative on the Commission of the International Peace Bureau established in 1891.*

Moneta sponsored disarmament, the establishment of a league of nations, and the settlement of all international disputes by arbitration. He saw no basic incompatibility between a nation's right to fight for freedom and national unity, and the work of promoting international peace.

"Reasonable ideas which find their sanction in the conscience of the righteous do not die; they are consequently realities and active forces, but they are so only to the extent that those who profess them know how to turn them to account. It depends on us, then, and on our judgment and steadfastness, whether or not the

idea of peace will root itself ever more firmly in public awareness until it grows into the living and active conscience of a whole people. " Ernesto Moneta

1908

KLAS PONTUS ARNOLDSON (1844-1916), Sweden: *Sweden's leading peace activist. Inspired by his Christian upbringing, he served the peace cause as a member of parliament, organizer, and influential orator and publicist.*

Arnoldson was one of the founders of the Swedish Peace and Arbitration Association. He worked for the peaceful dissolution of the Swedish-Norwegian Union in 1905. He sought a guarantee for the permanent neutrality of the Nordic nations, and proposed a world referendum on peace, to be signed by every adult man and woman.

"No interests, however great, are higher than those common to the whole of mankind . . . . You are all of one blood. Love one another. People can. Nations can. All this is eminently possible because love is as natural as national hatred is the most unnatural of all human feelings. "

Arnoldson's suggested referendum on peace—*"If other nations will abolish their armed forces and be content with a joint police force for the whole world, then I, the undersigned, wish my nation to do the same. "* Klas Arnoldson

1908

FREDRIK BAJER (1837-1922), Denmark: *Scandinavia's foremost peace advocate; journalist, pacifist, and leader of the popular and parliamentary peace forces in Denmark.*

Bajer was one of the early politicians to work for the emancipation of women. He was co-founder of the Danish Peace Society and first president of the International Peace Bureau in Berne. He founded the Danish Interparliamentary Group and was active in international peace congresses.

"There are in most states one or two ministers of war. I would not wish on any account to abolish them; as long as the status of international law is no better than it is at present, we cannot very well do without them. But I feel convinced, and I venture even to prophesy in this regard, that the time will come when there will also be a minister of peace in the cabinet. " Fredrik Bajer

1909

AUGUSTE BEERNAERT (1829-1912), Belgium: *Statesman and international jurist. Prime Minister, Honorary President of the International League of Catholic Pacifists.*

Beernaert developed proposals for the restriction of armaments at the first Hague Conference. He was an active member of the Permanent Court of Arbitration, the International Law Association, and President of the Council of the Interparliamentary Union. He sought, unsuccessfully, to end child labor in the mines.

1909

PAUL HENRI d'ESTOURNELLES de CONSTANT (1852-1924), France: *Foremost international leader in Europe before the First World War; diplomat, senator, representative at the first Hague Conference.*

D'Estournelles de Constant was largely responsible for arbitration treaties between France and several other countries. He advocated the formation of a European Union, a Franco-German reconciliation, and a Franco-British entente.

"War drives the republics into dictatorship, and the monarchies into the grip of revolution . . . . The Americans are businessmen, and they prefer well-organized and stable conditions to the armed peace which presents a constant menace to World Peace." Paul Henri d'Estournelles de Constant

1910

PERMANENT INTERNATIONAL PEACE BUREAU: *Founded in Berne, Switzerland, in 1891. Fredrik Bajer (1908) of Denmark was the first president. It was basically an office to collect and disseminate information on the activities of Peace Societies and to promote the concept of peaceful settlement of international disputes.*

The outbreak of war in 1914 ended the Peace Societies' work temporarily, but the International Peace Bureau continued after the war. It is now located in Geneva and active in organizing peace seminars and facilitating communication between government and non-governmental organizations.

1911

TOBIAS ASSER (1838-1913), Netherlands: *International jurist, counsellor to the Dutch Foreign Office, minister of state.*

Asser was the Dutch delegate to two peace conferences at The Hague, and the arbiter in the Bering Straits dispute between Russia and the U.S. He persuaded the Dutch government to hold four conferences at The Hague on international private law. He was one of the founders of the Institute of International Law, and co-founder of the Permanent Court of Arbitration, The Hague. He devoted his life mainly to teaching, scholarship, and politics.

"Asser's view on the subject of private international law was that the most practical method would be for nations at international conferences to agree as far as possible on common solutions to legal conflicts. In this way, the legislation in the various countries could gradually be brought to conform; and this, in practice, is how it has worked out." Tony Gray, *Champions of Peace.*[1]

1911

ALFRED HERMANN FRIED (1864-1921), Austria: *Founder of the German Peace Society; publisher of a leading peace journal; idealist and dedicated peace activist.*

In 1914 Fried left Germany to avoid death for high treason, and continued his work in Geneva as an editor of peace magazines. He organized a press campaign against the Versailles Treaty of 1919, which he believed sowed the seeds of a future war.

"There is an utter lack of interest by the general public in matters of fundamental importance. The events of an international bicycle race are . . . eagerly swallowed up by the reader, just as the least significant comedian . . . is better known to the public than the people who make world history." Alfred Fried

1912

ELIHU ROOT (1845-1937), United States: *Statesman, jurist, secretary of war, secretary of state, U.S. senator; president, Carnegie Endowment for International Peace, and American Society of International Law.*

Root was responsible for organizing affairs in Cuba and the Philippines after the Spanish-American war, and for bringing about a better understanding between the countries of North and South America by founding the Pan-American Bureau in 1908. He was an energetic champion for an unconditional arbitration treaty between the United States and Great Britain. In 1908-09, he concluded twenty-three arbitration treaties with various Latin American and European countries, and with Japan. He was a leading supporter of the League of Nations, and was a member of the League's commission of jurists who framed the statute for the Permanent Court of International Justice. The failure of the U.S. to join the World Court in 1921 was a great disappointment for Root. The "Good Neighbor" policy he inaugurated is one of the brighter elements of American foreign policy. Root sponsored a post-war treaty to restrict the use of submarines and poison gas in warfare, but this was not supported by the leading powers.

"The attractive idea that we can now have a parliament of men with authority to control the conduct of nations by legislation or an international police force with power to enforce national conformity to rules of right conduct is a counsel of perfection. The world is not ready for any such thing, and it cannot be made ready except by the practical surrender of the independence of nations, which lies at the basis of the present social organization of the civilized world . . . . Human nature must come much nearer perfection than it is now, or will be in many generations, to exclude from such control prejudice, selfishness, ambition and injustice. An attempt to prevent war in this way would breed war, for it would destroy local self-government and drive nations to war for liberty.

"Under the present organization of civilization in independent nationalities . . . questions of vital interest cannot be submitted to arbitration because that would be an abdication of independence and the placing of government (to a considerable degree) in the hands of others." Elihu Root

1913

HENRI LA FONTAINE (1854-1943), Belgium: *International lawyer, politician and delegate to the Paris Peace Conference in 1919 and to the League of Nations Assembly in 1920; leader of the popular peace movement in Europe;*

president of the International Peace Bureau in Berne for thirty-six years; first socialist Peace Laureate.

La Fontaine was a leader of the Interparliamentary Union. He proposed a set of principles for international organization—not for a world state, which he realized would come only in a distant future, but for some sort of society of nations with international courts and provision for military sanctions.

"The people are not awake . . . . I foresee the renewal of . . . the secret bargaining behind closed doors. People will be as before, sheep sent to the slaughterhouses . . . . International institutions ought to be, as the national ones are in democratic countries, established by the peoples for the peoples." Henri La Fontaine

1914-1916 No Peace Prize awarded

1917

THE INTERNATIONAL COMMITTEE OF THE RED CROSS: *Founded in Geneva, Switzerland in 1863 by fourteen countries.*

Henri Dunant (1901), the first advocate of Red Cross societies, drafted the first Red Cross Convention, drawn up at Geneva in 1864. This committed governments to caring for the wounded in time of war, whether friend or foe. Later, new conventions were adopted to protect victims of warfare at sea, the care of prisoners of war, the care of civilians in wartime, the relief of human suffering in time of peace as well as war, and the proclamation of the neutrality and inviolability of ambulances and hospitals.

The first four national Red Cross societies were formed in 1864. By 1914, thirty-seven national societies were established. Many humanitarian issues were fought for, including the right of medical personnel and seriously wounded to be repatriated or interned in Switzerland, and the neutrality of hospital ships. Many millions of Armenians fleeing Turkish massacre in 1916 were given support.

"The work of the Red Cross in peace and in war . . . provides an endless fascination. In peace, it is the strong support of beneficent service, and in emergencies a wave and pillar of succor for the distressed. In war, it is a liaison,

a medium of practical help to the wounded and the prisoner, a symbol that beyond the knives and guns, the larks and the angels are watching."

John MacAulay, Red Cross Societies

"We must draw close in body and in spirit in order to merit the name by which the magnificent symbol of the Red Cross calls us, the name Man, the name Christian." Edouard Chapuisat, International Committee Red Cross

1918 No Peace Prize awarded

1919

WOODROW WILSON (1856-1924), United States: *President of Princeton University; wartime and peacemaking president of the U.S., 1913-1921; primary force in establishment of the League of Nations.*

The U.S. declared war on Germany in April, 1917. The First World War ended on November 11, 1918, after worldwide slaughter of men and destruction of resources. Wilson's famous principles for post-war reconciliation—his "Fourteen Points"[2]—were presented to the Paris Peace Conference of 1919 as the "only possible program of the world peace." Wilson lost control of the Senate in November, 1918. The U.S. Senate did not ratify the creation of the League of Nations, and Wilson's influence on peace negotiations was greatly weakened.

The Treaty of Versailles, June 1919, based largely on revenge and crippling reparations demands, emasculated Wilson's proposals and planted the seeds of Hitler's rise to power. The Treaty provided for the creation of the League of Nations. The refusal of the U.S. to join the League of Nations set the stage for the failure of the League. The world still awaits the fulfillment of Wilson's dreams—the First World War was to be "the war to end all wars."

Wilson had championed a clause in the Treaty giving all peoples the right to self-determination. This concept has been twisted many times to serve political ambitions, not public welfare. It has become a major cause of armed conflicts for many minority ethnic peoples against a nation state and against one another.

Wilson's words were an affirmation of his life-long faith: *"There is one thing that the American people always rise to . . . and that is the truth of justice and of liberty and of peace. We have accepted that truth and we are going to be led by it, and it is going to lead us, and through us the world, out into pastures of quietness and peace . . . whatever has been accomplished in the past is petty compared to the glory and promise of the future.* "Woodrow Wilson

1920

LÉON BOURGEOIS (1851-1925), France: *Spiritual father of the League of Nations; lawyer, senator, chairman of the Commission of Arbitration at the first Hague Conference (1899); member of the Permanent Court of Arbitration, The Hague.*

Bourgeois was a leader in the groundwork for the League of Nations. He was convinced that international justice could be enforced only by sanctions, whether diplomatic, economic, or military. He stressed the necessity for civilized nations to join together for the defense of law and order and the maintenance of peace. The League of Nations became a reality in June, 1919.

Bourgeois proposed a Commission of Mutual Intellectual Co-operation which was adopted by the League . . . an early version of the later UN Educational, Scientific, and Cultural Organization (UNESCO).

"The success of any international league would have to be based on the sovereignty of each nation. It would not be a 'superstate' imposing its will on member states or an organization that would involve a state in military operations to which it had not given its consent. It must be a community of thought and feeling . . . among the associated states . . . that shares a common understanding of the principles of international order. To help create this community of understanding there must be intellectual co-operation. " Léon Bourgeois

1921

KARL HJALMAR BRANTING (1860-1925), Sweden: *Premier for the third time in 1921; "father" of socialism in Sweden; closely involved in achieving the peaceful dissolution of the union between Sweden and Norway in 1905.*

Branting led the successful movement to bring Sweden into the League of Nations. He criticized severely the Treaty of Versailles for its punitive provisions against Germany. He advocated that the League of Nations should go all-out for total disarmament, in contrast to Laureate Bourgeois who believed that the League should only have the power to impose military sanctions if necessary.

Branting pinned his hopes on the League, but recognized that the League had a daunting task.

"To create an organization which is in position to protect peace in this world of conflicting interests and egotistic wills is a frighteningly difficult task. But the difficulties must not hold us back . . . whatever the obstacles may be, we must go forward: If the nations do not try to annihilate war, then war will annihilate them." Karl Branting

(This was said in 1921—twenty-four years before Hiroshima.)

1921

CHRISTIAN LANGE (1869-1938), Norway: *Internationalist scholar and executive; secretary-general of the Interparliamentary Union (1909-1933), which he kept alive during the First World War and moved to permanent offices in Geneva in 1921; member of the Norwegian delegation to the League of Nations.*

Lange believed strongly in the unity of mankind and was an outspoken advocate for disarmament. He organized the Norwegian Nobel Institute and dreamed that one day the Institute would be the first world centre for peace research. Lange joined the Bureau of the Interparliamentary Union, with major emphasis on support of the League of Nations. He was a guiding spirit of the Union for almost twenty-five years.

Lange was a leading expert on internationalism through his work at the Nobel Institute and the Interparliamentary Union. He saw no conflict of internationalism with nationalism, only with one-sided nationalism. He saw the territorial state as becoming obsolete by the increasing development of international interdependence technically, economically, and intellectually.

"If the territorial state is to continue as the last word in the development of society, then war is inevitable. For the state, by its nature, claims sovereignty, the right to an unlimited development of power, determined only by self-interest. It is by nature anarchistic . . . . Therefore all hope for a better future for mankind rests on the promotion of a higher form of development for world civilization, an all-

embracing human community . . . . The sovereign state has in our times become a lethal danger to human civilization because technical developments enable it to employ an infinite number of means of destruction." Christian Lange

1922

FRIDTJOF NANSEN (1861-1930), Norway: *Scientist and arctic explorer, he worked for the repatriation of prisoners of war and refugees. He was the League of Nation's First High Commissioner for Refugees, 1921-1930.*

After the First World War, Nansen organized a massive relief program, assisted by President Hoover and the Quakers, for up to twenty million people. In 1922, Nansen arranged for the repatriation of over one million Greeks living in Turkey and over 500,000 Turks living in Greece, and for aid for millions facing famine in the U.S.S.R. The identification card for displaced persons gained universal validity as the "Nansen Passport." The Nansen International Office for Refugees, created in 1930, saved the Armenian people from extinction in Turkey, by resettling over 40,000 Armenians.

Nansen was a realist who saw that "the land lies in ruins everywhere, and the foundations of earth's communities are crumbling . . . politics and new political programs are no longer of service to the world . . . the diplomats have brought mankind more harm than good . . . we can no longer look to traditional leadership for any hope of salvation." Nansen's answer was to organize massive help himself, wherever it was needed.

"The only avenue to salvation lies in co-operation between all nations . . . the only road to this goal lies through the League of Nations . . . . Christmas is approaching . . . the message to mankind is: Peace on earth. Never has suffering and bewildered mankind awaited the Prince of Peace with greater longing." Fridtjof Nansen

1923, 1924—No Peace Prize awarded

1925

CHARLES GATES DAWES (1865-1951), United States: *Vice-President under President Coolidge; financier, Chairman of the League of*

Nations commission to investigate German capacity to pay excessive war reparations; ambassador to Great Britain (1929-1932).

The Dawes Plan (1924) provided for a reorganization of Germany's finances with loans from the victors, and restored the economy of Europe by postponing the collapse of the German economy. It marked the beginning of a policy of reconciliation and paved the way for the Locarno Pacts, which guaranteed Germany's western frontier, and for Germany to join the League of Nations.

Dawes served as the United States delegate to the London Five-Power Naval Conference of 1930, at which a pact agreeing on navy size limits was signed by the United States, Great Britain, France, Italy, and Japan.

Referring to the Dawes Plan: *"It was the endeavour of the experts to found their plan upon the principles of justice, fairness, and mutual interest."* Charles G. Dawes

"It [the Dawes Plan] marked the beginning of the policy of reconciliation and peace which led to the Locarno agreements. This was the first dawning of the day after a long darkness." Fridtjof Nansen

1925

AUSTEN CHAMBERLAIN (1863-1937), Great Britain: *Statesman, co-architect of the Locarno Agreements of 1925.*

The main signatories to the Locarno Agreements—Germany, Belgium, France, and Great Britain—agreed not to make war on one another unless the Treaty of Versailles was violated. This and the later Kellogg-Briand pact of 1928 "gave the League of Nations a twist out of its right path," as nothing changed the relationship of European states, based on the balance of political, economic, and military power.

The two Agreements were considered to be a new approach to the prevention of war among major powers in Europe, but in essence the concept of quadrilateral agreements pledging not to go to war against one another marginalized the responsibility for peace for the League of Nations and made no progress in removing the underlying causes of future conflict.

1926

GUSTAV STRESEMANN (1878-1929), Germany: *Politician and statesman; founder of the German People's party; worked to achieve Germany's admission to the League of Nations in 1926; advocated a German policy of reconciliation and peace as foreign minister from 1923-1929.*

Prospects for peace had no chance against the crushing burdens of the Versailles Treaty, relentless post-war inflation, the onset of a long and severe world depression, the rise to power of Hitler, and the growing destabilization of excessive rearmament expenditures throughout Europe.

"Is the recent development of the German people such as to justify the award being given for a policy aimed at peace? One may well say that the question is answered by the very existence of the German policy of reconciliation and peace, for this policy would have been impossible had it not been in accord with the deepest desire of the German people, the desire for peaceful international co-operation in justice and freedom." Gustav Stresemann

1926

ARISTIDE BRIAND (1862-1932), France: *Lawyer, journalist, and statesman; ten times premier of France during years of French government instability; foreign minister, a co-founder with F. B. Kellogg, U.S. Secretary of State, of the 1928 Kellogg-Briand Pact, signed by sixty-four states, including all the major powers.*

A main aim of the founders of these pacts was that war should be abolished. No process for arriving at the abolition of war, and enforcement to secure such abolition, was proposed. No distinction was made between wars of aggression and defensive wars. The big powers believed that disarmament would never be achieved until war as an institution had been abolished, and made no plans for securing the reduction of armaments.

Briand's last major proposal was a comprehensive plan for a European Union, proposed at the League of Nations in 1930, but largely ignored.

1927

FERDINAND BUISSON (1841-1932), France: *Lifelong champion of human rights and peace; progressive educator and statesman; after the Dreyfus trial, founded the League of the Rights of Man, in France.*

At age eighty-three Buisson toured Germany, speaking on the need for reconciliation between France and Germany. He prophesied that there would be no defense against chemical and germ warfare from the air, "making resistance totally impossible."

He attacked the punitive terms of the Treaty of Versailles, and criticized the League of Nations as a power-sharing of victors. Nevertheless, he stated that the League must be supported and transformed into a true instrument of international solidarity by the pressure of public opinion.

"A force exists which is far greater than France, far greater than Germany, far greater than any nation, and that is mankind. But above mankind itself stands justice, which finds its most perfect expression in human brotherhood.

"Before there could be the disarmament of nations there had to be the disarmament of hatred." Ferdinand Buisson

1927

LUDWIG QUIDDE (1858-1941), Germany: *Historian, journalist, veteran peace leader, politician, delegate at World Peace Congress in 1901; president of the German Peace Society.*

Quidde was jailed twice for anti-militarist speeches. When Hitler came to power he fled to Geneva. He felt the arms race was a potential cause of war, but that disarmament only began to answer the peace question.

Quidde's life exemplifies a great love of justice. He was a fearless worker for peace in a country which had been taken over by totalitarian militarism, state aggrandizement, and monstrous cruelties.

"The endless arms race—this in itself is a potential cause of war. Influential military men want to demonstrate that their profession has some use. Many people who are disturbed by the terrible growth of armaments become accustomed

and resigned to the belief that war is inevitable. They say 'Better a terrible end than an endless terror.' That is the greatest cause of war . . . . " Ludwig Quidde

1928 No Peace Prize awarded

1929

FRANK KELLOGG (1865-1937), United States: *Ambassador to Great Britain; co-sponsor of the Kellogg-Briand Pact, 1928; Secretary of State, 1925-1929; lawyer and senator.*

Kellogg voted against the ratification of the Treaty of Versailles. He served as a judge of the Permanent Court of International Justice at The Hague. Referring to the numerous predictions of war in Europe, he said "Western civilization would not survive another conflict [such as the First World War], but would disappear in the universal chaos."

The Kellogg-Briand Pact denounced war as an instrument of national policy. But war was underway between Russia and China, followed by Japan's invasion of China, and later by Italy's invasion of Ethiopia. The Kellogg-Briand Pact did not provide for any joint action against an aggressor, consultation with other members in case of a violation, or sanctions against a violator. It was an exercise in futility in the guise of peacemaking.

1930

NATHAN SÖDERBLOM (1866-1931), Sweden: *Theologian, scholar, Lutheran archbishop; champion of world peace through church unity.*

Soderblom laid the foundations for a renewed ecumenical movement and a legal and judicial system to settle disputes without war. He was the first leader of a religious faith to receive the Peace Prize. He was active in organizing international conferences of religious leaders, and in delivering lectures to widen the understanding of the role of religion in building peace.

"If peace is to become a reality . . . it must be founded in the hearts of the people. The church must fully participate in efforts to remove the causes of war,

whether these are of a social, economic, or political nature. Nations and communities, like individuals, must act according to ethical principles, basing their hopes for coexistence on the principles of truth, justice, and love. " Nathan Söderblom

1931

JANE ADDAMS (1860-1935), United States: *Leader of the American settlement house movement, social reformer, worker for women's suffrage and many pioneer welfare laws to assist women in poor industrial areas; head of the Women's Peace Party; co-founder of the Women's International League for Peace and Freedom, The Hague.*

Addams founded Hull House in a Chicago slum, established to give mainly immigrant students an opportunity to live and work in a poor industrial area and contribute to its life and the help of the most needy. Addams rose to national and international prominence at a time when most professions were closed to women. She was reviled in the press when she publicly opposed the U.S. entry into the First World War in 1917. She worked as an assistant to Herbert Hoover in providing relief supplies of food and medical support to the women and children of enemy nations.

". . . living in an industrial quarter . . . is interesting and makes the human appeal . . . [with] the conviction . . . that the things which make men alike are finer and better than the things which keep them apart, and that these basic likenesses . . . easily transcend the less essential differences of race, language, creed and tradition. " Jane Addams

1931

NICHOLAS MURRAY BUTLER (1862-1947), United States: *Author of a large number of books, reports, speeches; President of Columbia University in New York; largely responsible for Carnegie's Endowment for International Peace; president of the American branch of Conciliation Internationale.*

Butler was a leader in rallying public support in America for the Kellogg-Briand pact. He was chairman of conferences on international arbitration. He served in many senior capacities in the work of the Carnegie Endowment for International Peace for over thirty-five years.

"The great hope is of a world that has learned the supreme lesson that civilization has to teach—that might does not make right and that war between nations is now as much out of date as the torture chamber and the scalping knife." Nicholas Murray Butler

1932 No Peace Prize awarded

1933

NORMAN ANGELL (1872-1967), Great Britain: *Economist, author, politician, newspaper editor, active member of the League of Nations Union, well-known worker and prodigious writer for world peace.*

Angell's highly successful book *The Great Illusion* became a peace classic. He argued that European nations were moving toward war, not understanding "that it is an economic impossibility for one nation to sieze or destroy the wealth of another, or for one nation to enrich itself by subjugating another . . . ."

"Defense must be a collective function or it cannot exist effectively at all. The obstacles to peace are in the hearts and minds of men." Norman Angell

1934

ARTHUR HENDERSON (1863-1935), Great Britain: *Labor leader, parliamentarian, foreign secretary; delegate to the League of Nations; dedicated service to the cause of peace and disarmament, both in and out of office. He held office continuously in the Ironfounders' Union, and was a leader in organizing the new Labor party.*

Henderson prodded the League of Nations to hold a world Disarmament Conference in 1932, and presided over its opening sessions. The failure of this conference foreshadowed the Second World War.

"The very nations that are chiefly responsible for the Disarmament Conference are also the nations that have begun the new arms race . . . . There can be no real disarmament except on the basis of the collective peace system of the League of

Nations. The establishment of a world commonwealth is . . . the only alternative to a relapse into a world war." Arthur Henderson

1935

CARL VON OSSIETZKY (1889-1938), Germany: *Soldier turned pacifist; co-founder of a peace movement with the slogan "No More War"; secretary of the German Peace Society.*

Ossietzky published numerous articles attacking the Reichswehr for condoning paramilitary organizations and secret rearmament in violation of the Treaty of Versailles, for which he was convicted of treason and imprisoned.

When the Peace Prize was awarded to Ossietzky, he was in a concentration camp, ill with tuberculosis. The German government refused to release him, demanded that he reject the prize, and refused him a passport. He died in 1938, still under strict surveillance in a Nazi sanatorium.

"The unforgettable figure of this brave and pure-minded journalist could grow with time into that of a fighter for humanity and martyr of almost legendary proportions." Thomas Mann

1936

CARLOS SAAVEDRA LAMAS (1878-1959), Argentina: *Statesman; president of the eighth Pan-American Conference; professor of international and labor law.*

Lamas succeeded as mediator in ending the Chaco War between Paraguay and Bolivia (1932-1935), and became president of the Assembly of the League of Nations in 1936. He was the first South American to win the Nobel Peace Prize.

As foreign minister, Lamas proposed the Declaration of August 1932, whereby eleven Latin American states pledged to refuse any territorial change in the hemisphere brought about by force. This Anti-War Pact was encouraged by the League of Nations.

"We are living in the aftermath of a great war. The fabric which civilization has been weaving in its efforts of centuries, once broken is difficult to reconstruct.

Under its broken web there appears to be a native barbarism, . . . a cruelty which in centers of the oldest civilization emerges from the immense depths to which they have fallen, destroying the most beautiful entity in their intoxication of destruction.

"Wars of aggression, war which does not imply defense of one's country, is a collective crime." Carlos Lamas

1937

LORD ROBERT CECIL (1864-1958), Great Britain: *Co-founder of the League of Nations; lawyer, parliamentarian, cabinet minister, delegate to the League; president, League of Nations Union; co-president, International Peace Campaign.*

Woodrow Wilson, Jan Smuts (Prime Minister of South Africa), and Lord Cecil gave the necessary leadership to ensure that the covenant of the League of Nations was a part of the Treaty of Versailles. Cecil followed through with leadership of League of Nation affairs throughout the 1920's. Cecil had wanted Germany to be in the League from the beginning, but was denied this. He succeeded in laying the basis for a World Court, despite Wilson's resistance.

Cecil challenged the League to go on from strength to strength, to avoid respectable mediocrity and "useless complication with the diplomatic machinery of the world."

"We have seen the forcible reoccupation of the Rhineland provinces, the intervention of aggressor nations in Spain, and the absorption of Austria by Germany . . . after these defeats of the League, compared with six or seven years ago, . . . the contrast is terrible.

"The armament interests . . . became active in their efforts to destroy the [League] . . . . I have no doubt that they have contributed to the difficulties of the League." Lord Robert Cecil

1938

NANSEN INTERNATIONAL OFFICE FOR REFUGEES: *Authorized by the League of Nations in 1930 and founded in Geneva in 1931.*

The Nansen Office was a successor of the High Commission for Refugees, the first international agency dealing with refugees and established by the League under the direction of Fridtjof Nansen, the Peace Laureate of 1922.

Nansen is an outstanding example of one man achieving humanitarian aims by endless hard work and a determined practical approach. The "Nansen Passport" and relocation support saved millions of lives. During and after the First World War there were tens of millions of refugees—mainly from the U.S.S.R. and throughout the Middle East after the collapse of the Turkish Empire. Nansen's work continued until his death in 1930. However, the need for the protection of refugees was still so great that the League created the Nansen International Office for Refugees.

"Nansen was a champion of a cause new to politics, the cause of brotherly love, and he performed wonders, first for prisoners of war and then for political refugees.

"The refugee problem has, all in all, become the greatest problem of our time. It can be solved, but only by the energetic co-operation with the League of Nations by governments aware of their responsibility to mankind." Michael Hansson, president, Nansen Organization, 1938.

1939-1943 No Peace Prize awarded

1944

THE INTERNATIONAL COMMITTEE OF THE RED CROSS (ICRC): *Previously awarded the prize in 1917.*

During the Second World War, the Red Cross contacted and saved countless numbers of prisoners of war and civilians. It had in its service large numbers of ships to carry mail and relief supplies to internment and refugee camps in most war zones.

By October 1946, the Red Cross had on file thirty-nine million names of refugees, with 45,000 more names coming in daily. The agency now had a staff of several thousand, mainly volunteers. National societies had been organized to provide relief and to assist other countries needing help.

"The Red Cross achieved results which measured up to all of its hopes; but it also realizes that what it had been given to do was . . . of little significance when

compared to the sum total of suffering it encountered in the course of its work. It strove to alleviate what misery it could; it tried to raise its flag above the ruins of the world to show that human hope should never falter." Edouard Chapuisat, Peace Prize lecture, 1944.

1945

CORDELL HULL (1871-1955), United States: *Secretary of State 1933-1944; described by U.S. President Franklin Roosevelt as the "father of the United Nations."*

Hull laid the foundations for the "good neighbor" policy among the twenty-one American nations, achieved reciprocal trade agreements with many countries, and was a senior adviser to the United Nations Conference in San Francisco in 1945.

Hull's major work during the Second World War was the preparation of a blueprint for an international organization dedicated to the maintenance of peace with sufficient legislative, economic, and military power behind it.

Hull had a severe stroke after tireless work for his last twelve years in the creation of the U.N. He is buried in the crypt beneath the National Cathedral in Washington, D.C.—"reserved for those who have given service of an outstanding nature to God and mankind."

"I am firmly convinced that, with all its imperfections, the United Nations Organization offers the peace-loving nations of the world, now, a fully workable mechanism which will give them peace, if they want peace . . . . Alfred Nobel, were he alive today, would, I am sure, have joined me in the unshakable faith that this crucial test will be met: that the searing lessons of this latest war and the promise of the United Nations Organization will be the cornerstones of a new edifice of enduring peace and the guideposts of a new era of human progress." Cordell Hull

1946

EMILY GREENE BALCH (1867-1961), United States: *Social reformer, writer of numerous pacifist books, active in leagues for women's rights and peace; a delegate to the nine congresses held between the two wars; secretary-general of the International Women's League, Geneva.*

Balch was active in many League of Nations projects including disarmament, the internationalization of aviation, drug control, and strengthening the role of the League. After the Second World War she was a strong supporter of the UN.

"The future shape of the new organization will not depend on what the documents appear to state, but on what the members make of it. Practice in co-operation is what will give the United Nations its character. Plans have not been set up for a utopia, but for Europe, Russia, America, and all other countries with their conflicting interests and ideas. And it is precisely because the proposals we have before us are fairly modest that they may perhaps be realized . . . . International unity is not in itself a solution. Unless this international unity has a moral quality, accepts the discipline of moral standards and possesses the quality of humanity, it will not be the unity we are interested in." Emily Greene Balch

1946

JOHN RALEIGH MOTT (1865-1955), United States: *Secretary of the Young Men's Christian Association, travelled among students of American and Canadian universities; world ecumenical leader and evangelist.*

Mott founded several worldwide organizations which have united millions of young people in work for the Christian ideals of peace and good will between nations. He organized teams in both World Wars to aid combatants and prisoners of war, and wrote sixteen books on evangelism and a world mission for peace and tolerance to strengthen the universal support for the ideals on which peace necessarily depends.

In 1914, he presided over the first U.S. congress for black and white Christians from both the north and south states. "If we are Christians," Mott said, "we must be able to live side by side as true friends, in equality, justice and mutual respect."

"The most trustworthy leader is one who adopts and applies guiding principles. He trusts them like the North Star. He follows his principles no matter how many oppose him and no matter how few go with him. This has been the real secret of the wonderful leadership of Mahatma Gandhi. In the midst of most bewildering conditions he has followed, cost what it might, the guiding principles

of non-violence, religious unity, removal of untouchability, and economic independence." John Raleigh Mott

1947

FRIENDS SERVICE COUNCIL (FSC), founded in 1927, Great Britain; AMERICAN FRIENDS SERVICE COMMITTEE (AFSC), founded in 1917, United States: *The two largest Quaker organizations engaged in relief and reconstruction during and after major twentieth century wars and peacetime disasters.*

Quakers are best known for their humanitarian work since the sect was formed in the seventeenth century (see Chapter 9 for an assessment of the role of Quakers in peacemaking today). In the early nineteenth century they helped found the first peace societies.

In their Nobel lectures, the Quaker representatives stressed the religious basis of Quaker work for humanity and peace. The Peace Prize was the first for advocates of non-violence, and they used the occasion to explain absolute Christian pacifism . . ."that way of life which holds each individual to be a child of God and therefore of supreme value."

"We believe that war is a habit, a curious habit, a somewhat accidental habit that men have adopted, although in other areas they have found different means for pursuing similar ends . . . . We recognize that there are times when resistance appears at first to be a real virtue, and then only those most deeply rooted in religious pacifism can resist by other than physical means. We have learned that in the end only the spirit can conquer evil and we believe that in many recent situations those who have unwillingly employed force have learned this lesson at the last . . . .

"Today there are millions of men in nearly every great nation who have taken part in war and they still believe that that war, or their part in it, was justified. As long as they hold that view, they seem to me to be a risk against world peace. Those people who have once believed that war is justified can readily be persuaded that it will be justified again . . . . So perhaps in a world like this there is room for a few thousand persons like Quakers who take the opposite view, who begin with the assumption that war is not and has not been and will not be justified on either practical or moral grounds . . . . Of course, Friends have found it

*necessary to think through their position on this as on many awkward questions.
For example, they have had to think whether this view is disloyalty to the state,
and they have had to learn to distinguish loyalty to the policy of a government
in power from loyalty to the true interests of a nation . . . .*

"*We have learned that few wars are justified by their results and that victory
in war sometimes in itself makes real peace difficult.*" Henry J. Cadbury,
chairman, American Friends Service Committee

(Margaret Backhouse gave the acceptance lecture for the Friends
Service Committee, Great Britain.)

1948 No Peace Prize awarded

1949

JOHN BOYD ORR (1880-1971), Great Britain: *A scientist who was
the nutrition expert for British food policy in the Second World War; co-founder
and head of the Food and Agriculture Organization (FAO) of the UN; president
of the National Peace Council of more than fifty British peace organizations
and of the World Union of Peace Organizations.*

After the Second World War, Boyd Orr set up an International
Emergency Food Council which was responsible for averting famine
in many threatened countries. He suggested a World Food Board to
stabilize food prices in world markets, to create reserves of food to
meet local shortages, and to raise capital to finance the sale of surplus
food. Great Britain and the U.S. did not support these proposals. The
world today is still faced with starvation and malnutrition in developing
countries, and surplus crops in other countries. Food supply and
economics remains a major problem affecting world peace. Boyd Orr
preached his policy of a world peace based on world plenty.

"*It is of no use trying to build the new world from the top down, with political
ideas of spheres of influence and so on. We have to build it from the bottom
upwards, and provide first the primary necessities of life for the people who have
never had them . . . . Agreements between nations not to go to war have never
lasted, and will never be enough to maintain peace. The nations must construct
peace through daily co-operation, with a positive goal in view, a goal which is*

seen to be mutually advantageous. Only this can remove the principal causes of war.

"Permanent peace cannot be attained merely by efforts to prevent war. We will be on the road to world unity and peace when nations begin to co-operate on a world scale to apply science to develop the resources of the earth for the benefit of all . . . . The difficulty is to get a real beginning. Why should we not consider some concrete measure like the elimination of preventable disease through the World Health Organization or doubling the world food supply to meet all human needs through the joint work of the other agencies, with all nations contributing through the World Bank, in proportion to their wealth, to provide the necessary funds? In working together for a concrete world plan for the benefit of all countries, the present misunderstandings which divide nations would gradually become meaningless . . . .*

"The new powers which science has let loose cannot be bottled up again. They must be used for constructive ends or they will break loose in another world war which will destroy our European civilization . . . . For Europe at least, peace is inevitable. It can either be the peace of the grave, the peace of the dead empires of the past, which lost their creative spirit and failed to adjust themselves to new conditions, or a new dynamic peace applying science in a great leap forward in the evolution of human society to a new age in which hunger, poverty, and preventable diseases will be eliminated from the earth—an age in which the people in every country will rise to a far higher level of intellectual and cultural well-being, an age in which 'iron curtains' will disappear and people, though intensely patriotic for their own country, will be able to travel freely as world citizens. That is the hope science sets before us."* John Boyd Orr, Lord Boyd Orr of Brechin

1950

RALPH JOHNSON BUNCHE (1904-1971), United States: *The first black Nobel Peace Laureate. An expert in colonial affairs in the State Department, he was a member of the U.S. delegation to the UN conferences in London in 1945 and 1946 and one of the representatives to the 1946 ILO conference in Paris. In 1946, he was also appointed director of the Trusteeship Department of the UN Secretariat. He was Count Bernadotte's collaborator in the UN Truce Commission to the Palestine conflict of 1948, and after Bernadotte's assassination became his successor and was able to achieve an armistice.*

Bunche directed UN intervention in several world crises. He recognized that in order to achieve peace the UN would have to be prepared to use "military strength of sufficient dimensions to make certain it can meet aggressively military force with international military force speedily and conclusively."

Bunche believed that the suppressed masses of the less developed regions of the world are entitled to enjoy a full share in the future fruits of peace, freedom, and security. He stressed a problem which was increasingly to occupy the attention both of the UN and of the Nobel Committee: the importance to future world peace of conditions in the emerging less developed regions.

"... *Europe, and the Western world generally, must become fully aware that the massive and restive millions of Asia and Africa are henceforth a new and highly significant factor in all peace calculations. The hitherto suppressed masses are rapidly awakening and are demanding, and are entitled to enjoy, a full share in the future fruits of peace, freedom, and security.*" Ralph Johnson Bunche

1951

LÉON JOUHAUX (1879-1954), France: *An international labor leader who believed that peace could be achieved through unity in the international labor movement. He spent his life working for that ideal through the International Federation of Trade Unions, the International Labor Organization (ILO) which he was instrumental in founding, the League of Nations, the United Nations, and the European Movement, of which he was made president in 1949.*

After the fall of France in 1940, Jouhaux joined the Resistance. He was captured and held in Buchenwald prison until it was liberated in May 1945.

Jouhaux believed that co-operation reaching across national frontiers and the removal of social and economic inequalities both within nations and between nations represented the most important means of combating war. But he had an even broader objective: to

mould a social environment capable of breeding a new sort of man
who would create a society in which war would no longer be possible.

   *"The final and essential goal, the only valid goal, is to extend the well-being
of the worker, to give him a more equitable share of the products of collective work,
to make Europe a social democracy, and to ensure the peace desired by men of
every race and tongue by proving that the democracies can bring about social
justice through the rational organization of production without sacrificing the
liberty and the dignity of the individual . . . ."* Léon Jouhaux

1952

ALBERT SCHWEITZER (1875-1965), France: *Philosopher, musician,
medical doctor and missionary, pastor and founder of a hospital at Lambaréné,
a small village deep in the jungle in West Africa.*

   Schweitzer lived in Africa for fifty-two years, until he was ninety,
leaving only to give concerts and lectures and publish several books
to finance the expansion of his hospital. He used the Peace Prize to
add a leprosarium at Lambaréné.

   Schweitzer's Nobel award lecture presents his philosophy that
unless the progress of civilization is based on some universal ethical
principle, it will not advance civilization but will contribute to its
dissolution. Schweitzer believed that this latter state of affairs had
been reached in western civilization at the end of the nineteenth
century. He maintained that the one redeeming principle to create
harmony between the actions and thoughts of civilized man was
"respect for life."

   Schweitzer's lecture, a unique document in the search for peace,
is presented in full in Appendix E. Schweitzer had always avoided
making political statements, but after receiving the Peace Prize, he
said, "I should do something to earn it." He became an active
peacemaker, making many public statements against nuclear testing
and for a renunciation of nuclear weapons.

   Schweitzer's enduring principle for peace has been an inspiration
for countless peacemakers. He wrote, "The League of Nations and
the UN, being only legal institutions, are unable to create a prevailing

spirit directed toward peace, and have failed to achieve peace." He was certain that the human spirit is capable of creating in our time a new ethical mentality, saying, "Only when an ideal of peace is born in the minds of the peoples will the institutions set up to maintain this peace effectively fulfill the function expected of them."

In his Nobel award lecture, Schweitzer stated that *". . . all that we have ever possessed of true civilization, and indeed all that we still possess, can be traced to a manifestation of an ethical spirit based on respect for life.*

"Is the spirit capable of achieving what we in our distress must expect of it?" he asked, and replied: *". . . The height to which the spirit can ascend was revealed in the seventeenth and eighteenth centuries. It led those peoples of Europe who possessed it out of the Middle Ages, putting an end to superstition, witch hunts, torture, and a multitude of other forms of cruelty or traditional folly. It replaced the old with the new in an evolutionary way that never ceases to astonish those who observe it.*

"The idea that the reign of peace must come one day has been given expression by a number of peoples who have attained a certain level of civilization . . . . People have labelled it a utopia. But the situation today is that it must become reality in one way or another, otherwise mankind will perish . . . . The only originality I claim is . . . the intellectual certainty that the human spirit is capable of creating in our time a new mentality, an ethical mentality. Inspired by this certainty, I too proclaim this truth in the hope that my testimony may help to prevent its rejection as an admirable sentiment but a practical impossibility. Many a truth has lain unnoticed for a long time, ignored simply because no one perceived its potential for becoming reality." Albert Schweitzer

"He made a statistically small but spiritually vast contribution to the plight of his fellow man." Tony Gray—*Champions of Peace*[3]

1953

GEORGE CATLETT MARSHALL (1880-1959), United States: *Chief of Staff of the U.S. Army from 1939 to 1945, General Marshall built up and directed the largest army in world history. As Secretary of State he fought for two years for his Marshall Plan, a program of post-war economic and social aid to Europe.*

Marshall believed passionately that the only justifiable objective of war must be to make another war impossible. To the end of his life Marshall was haunted by the fact that of the first U.S. division of 27,000 men sent to France in 1917, 25,000 became casualties.

Marshall's thinking behind the Marshall plan was—"We must present democracy as a force holding within itself the seeds of unlimited progress by the human race." He stressed "the most important thing in the world today in my opinion is a spiritual regeneration which would re-establish a feeling of good faith among men generally."

"There has been considerable comment over the awarding of the Nobel Peace Prize to a soldier. I am afraid this does not seem as remarkable to me as it quite evidently appears to others. I know a great deal of the horrors and tragedies of war. Today, as chairman of the American Battle Monuments Commission, it is my duty to supervise the construction and maintenance of military cemeteries in many countries overseas . . . . The cost of war in human lives is constantly spread before me, written neatly in many ledgers whose columns are gravestones. I am deeply moved to find some means or method of avoiding another calamity of war." George C. Marshall

1954

OFFICE OF THE UNITED NATIONS HIGH COMMISSIONER FOR REFUGEES (UNHCR*): Established by the UN General Assembly in 1951, its aim is to promote international legal regulations for the benefit of refugees and to ensure that they are treated in accordance with such regulations, in particular as regards the right to work, social security, and the freedom to travel.*

Since the 1922 award to Fridtjof Nansen, the Norwegian Nobel Committee has continued to recognize work for refugees in its awards. In 1938, the Nansen office for refugees in Geneva received the prize again. A UN organization carried on refugee support in the Second World War and maintained it continuously since then, operating as the UNHCR after 1951.

The third award of 1954 was followed by a fourth in 1981, bearing witness to the increasing number of refugees resulting from the continuing "total wars" of destruction, genocide, and ethnic butchery (euphemistically called "ethnic cleansing") of combatants and civilians, and to the acceptance of the need for justice and humanitarian aid for all refugees.

The objectives of the UNHCR are to promote international regulations for the benefit of refugees, to find nations willing to accept them, and to ensure that all refugees are treated in accordance with these regulations. These rights are deemed necessary to heal the wounds of war and to promote the human rights and brotherhood of mankind.

After the Nazis came to power in Germany the flood of refugees became so great a new agency of the League, the Office of the High Commissioner for Refugees, was opened in 1938 in London. The great need of assistance for refugees increased again during and after the Second World War. The United Nations High Commissioner for Refugees began activities in 1951 to provide legal and political protection for the world's refugees.

A report of September 8, 2001 in *The Economist* shows that the country with the most refugees is Pakistan with over two million; then Iran (1.9 million); Germany (.9 million) and Tanzania (.7 million), and concludes—"Rich countries should recognize their relative good fortune, set generous quotas for needed immigrants and then set about the admittedly difficult task of rejecting others . . . of distinguishing between immigrants seeking a better life and those with a well-founded fear of persecution."—the acid test for automatic admission as a refugeee set by a UN convention in 1951.

The refugee question became a greater part of the national security problem after the deaths and destruction in the U.S. on September 11, 2001, carried out by al-Qaeda terrorists who had entered and lived in the U.S. secretly and illegally.

The *Encyclopaedia Britannica 2001*, reported that the total of refugees on record was slightly over 22.3 million in 1999. Many more have fled war and ethnic butchery since then. About fifty-two percent were women; forty-one percent were children under eighteen years old. More than 1.6 million refugees returned to their homes in 1999.

There are refugees and displaced persons who have not been able to return to their homes and have been forced to live in squalid camps since the 1940s. A whole generation has grown up in environments of hatred and violence. Many situations defy all efforts to solve the intractable problems creating these self-perpetuating situations whereby violence breeds more violence. The time for peacemaking is long overdue, and the inseparable realities that there can be no peace without security, and no security without peace, must be faced to achieve peace.

"There can be no real peace in this world as long as hundreds of thousands of men, women and children, through no fault of their own, but only because they sacrificed all they possessed for the sake of what they believed, still remain in camps and live in misery, and in the greatest uncertainty of their future. Eventually, if we wait too long, the uprooted are bound to become easy prey for political adventurers, from whom the world has suffered too much already." Dr. Gerrit Jan van Heuven Goedhart, UN High Commissioner for Refugees

1955-1956 No Peace Prizes awarded

1957

LESTER BOWLES PEARSON (1897-1972), Canada: *Statesman, diplomat, Canada's foreign minister from 1948 to 1957, and Prime Minister from 1963 to 1968; attended major international conferences in the thirties and forties, including the establishment of the UN in 1945 in San Francisco. He headed the Canadian delegation to the UN from 1946 to 1956 and was largely responsible for creating the UN emergency peacekeeping force used successfully during the Suez crisis in 1956.*

Pearson headed the Canadian delegation to join the North Atlantic Treaty Organization (NATO) in 1949. He was a strong supporter of the UN, helping to establish the UN Relief and Rehabilitation Administration (UNRRA) and the Food and Agriculture Organization (FAO). During the Korean war he opposed the bombing of China and advocated a ceasefire and negotiations to end the conflict.

"The stark and inescapable fact is that today we cannot defend our society by war since total war is total destruction, and if war is used as an instrument of policy, eventually we will have total war. Therefore, the best defence of peace is not power, but the removal of the causes of war, and international agreements which will put peace on a stronger foundation than the terror of destruction."
Lester Bowles Pearson

1958

FATHER DOMINIQUE PIRE (1910-1969), Belgium: *Dominican priest, chaplain to the Belgian Resistance movement in the Second World War; cited for his efforts to help refugees return to their homelands. He used the Peace Prize to found seven small European villages for the resettlement of refugees and to provide homes for the elderly.*

Father Pire was a fearless worker in the escape system for allied airmen hiding to avoid capture in the Second World War. After the war he set up camps for elderly refugees—"They have been sitting on their luggage and waiting twelve or fourteen years for a train that never comes."

In 1950 he formed the society L'Aide aux Personnes Deplacées (Aid to Displaced Persons), an international organization to repatriate refugees.

"Let us be wary of mass solutions . . . . We must love our neighbors as ourselves . . . . There is perhaps no surer road to peace than the one that starts from little islands and oases constantly growing in number and being continually joined together until eventually they ring the world.

"For us who have so little influence on . . . the UN and elsewhere, Aid to Displaced Persons . . . is as effective a means as any of working for peace . . . . Whereas the man in the street despairs of having a say in major political questions, he has every say and every opportunity to put his words into practice on the displaced persons problem.

"I believe that the world is making progress spiritually, slowly no doubt but still making progress. We proceed, as it were, at the rate of three steps forward and two steps back. The important thing is to take that third extra step. In this lies man's only chance . . . ." Father Dominique Pire (Georges Charles Clement Ghislain Pire)

1959

PHILIP NOEL-BAKER (1889-1982), Great Britain: *Cabinet minister and statesman; peacemaker during a lifetime of service, first for the League of Nations and then for the UN; assisted Nansen (1922) in prisoner-of-war and refugee work.*

Noel-Baker commanded Quaker ambulance units in both France and Italy in the First World War. He helped to draft the UN Charter, and supported regulation of arms trafficking, nuclear arms control, economic aid for refugees, the Nansen "passport," and abolition of poison gas and biological warfare.

Noel-Baker took the arms race as the subject for his Nobel lecture, citing frightening facts: "In 1914 the nations had over five million men in their standing peacetime armies; in 1960 they had over sixteen million. In 1954 the thermo-nuclear hydrogen bomb had more than a thousand times the power of the Hiroshima nuclear bomb.

"Defeatism about the future is a crime . . . . We must destroy the old bridges behind us which lead back to the old policy and the old system, both of which are such utter failures . . . . In the age when the atom has been split, the moon encircled, diseases conquered, is disarmament so difficult a matter that it must remain a distant dream? To answer 'Yes' is to despair of the future of mankind."

Referring to the absolute necessity of disarmament—*"Against a great evil, a small remedy does not produce a small result; it produces no result at all.*

"The most dangerous thing in the world is to try to leap a chasm in two jumps. There is a great chasm, a great gulf, between the armed world of today and the disarmed world which we must have on some near tomorrow." Philip Noel-Baker

1960

ALBERT JOHN LUTULI (1898-1967), South Africa: *Teacher, Zulu chieftain, and president-general of the African National Congress, leader of ten million black people in a non-violent campaign for human rights in South Africa.*

Lutuli was harassed under the apartheid laws, forbidden to attend public gatherings, charged with treason, and was jailed twice. He was awarded the Peace Prize for service to the cause of peace and brotherhood between men and "for the recognition and preservation of the rights of man and the establishment of a truly free world for a free people."

"As a Christian and a patriot, I could not look on while systematic attempts were made . . . to debase the God-factor in man or to set a limit beyond which the human being in his black form might not serve his Creator to the best of his ability. To remain neutral in a situation where the laws of the land virtually criticized God for having created men of color was the sort of thing I could not, as a Christian, tolerate." Albert John Lutuli

1961

DAG HAMMARSKJÖLD (1905-1961), Sweden: *Statesman, finance and foreign ministries and UN Affairs; Secretary-General of the UN from 1953 until his death in a plane crash on a UN mission in the Congo. His "quiet diplomacy" led to settlements of the Suez crisis in 1956, and to ceasefires in the Lebanon and Jordan conflicts.*

In 1960 the UN sent a peacekeeping force to the Congo, engulfed in civil war, where everything went tragically wrong. Premier Khrushchev of the U.S.S.R. demanded Hammerskjöld's resignation, but he battled on despite heavy personal attacks in the UN. Hammarskjöld made it clear that he was responsible to all the nations of the UN, large and small, and would carry on as long as he had their confidence.

Hammarskjöld looked forward to the fulfilment of the charter of the UN as a guide for the future development of the nation state into an organized international community.

Referring to the structure of the UN— *"Either it could be a conference machinery for sovereign states, with the Secretariat reflecting their competing interests in its staff members, or it could become an organic body, moving beyond national sovereignties, with member states faithfully carrying out their obligations and with a truly international Secretariat, whose staff would not be subjected to pressures from their own national governments. In this conception the Secretary-General would be above the conflicts, free to act for the safeguarding of peace even in the absence of specific directions from the Security Council and the Assembly."* Dag Hammarskjöld

1962

LINUS PAULING (1901-1994), United States: *Winner of the Nobel prizes for Peace and Chemistry; a ceaseless campaigner against the development and spread of nuclear weapons. He drew up an appeal, signed by ten thousand scientists from forty-nine countries, against nuclear tests in the atmosphere and was largely responsible for the partial Nuclear Test Ban Treaty, signed in 1963.*

The U.S. tested its first hydrogen bomb in November 1952. The U.S.S.R. exploded a nuclear bomb in 1953. Pauling led an appeal against nuclear weapons in the Mainau Declaration of 1955, signed by fifty-two Nobel laureates, most of them scientists. In the same year, his passport was withheld by the U.S. Passport Office. In 1958 the U.S.S.R., Great Britain, and the U.S. stopped conducting nuclear tests. Twenty-five years after receiving the Peace Prize, Pauling was still an active peacemaker.

"In extreme danger no nation will deny itself the use of any weapon that scientific technology can produce. All nations must come to the decision to renounce force as a final resort of policy. If they are not prepared to do this, they will cease to exist."

"Now we are forced to eliminate from the world forever this vestige of prehistoric barbarism, this curse to the human race . . . we are privileged to be alive . . . to see the future, the great future of peace, justice, morality, and human well-being . . . of the abolition of war and its replacement by world law . . . of the better use of the earth's resources, of the discoveries of scientists, and of the efforts of mankind, [free] from hunger, disease, illiteracy, and fear, and that we shall in the course of time be enabled to build a world characterized by economic, political, and social justice for all human beings and a culture worthy of man's intelligence." Linus Pauling

1963

INTERNATIONAL COMMITTEE OF THE RED CROSS (ICRC), Geneva: *Founded in 1863 to serve as a link between national societies operating on the original Red Cross principles, and granting recognition to new members; awarded the Peace Prize in 1917 and 1944.*

LEAGUE OF RED CROSS SOCIETIES, Geneva: *The League was a reorganization to represent the federation of separate national societies in 1928.*

In 1961, the Red Cross reaffirmed its basic principle of promoting "a lasting peace amongst all peoples," and has always been ready to take on unprecedented humanitarian initiatives in the cause of peacemaking and humanity.

The twentieth International Conference in 1965 adopted seven fundamental principles:

- HUMANITY: "Its purpose is to protect life and health and to ensure respect for the human being. It promotes mutual understanding, friendship, co-operation, and lasting peace amongst all peoples."
- IMPARTIALITY: "It makes no discrimination as to nationality, race, religious beliefs, class, or political opinions."
- NEUTRALITY: "The Movement may not take sides in hostilities or engage at any time in controversies of a political, racial, religious, or ideological nature."
- INDEPENDENCE: "The National Societies . . . must always maintain their autonomy, so that they may be able at all times to act in accordance with the principles of the Movement."
- VOLUNTARY SERVICE.
- UNITY: "There may be only one . . . Society in any one country."
- UNIVERSALITY: "The Movement, in which all Societies have equal status and responsibility, is worldwide."

An update on the activities of the Red Cross in 2001 is shown in Chapter 9.

"Whatever new challenge may come its way, the Red Cross can stand on its long and distinguished record of demonstrating in the most trying circumstances the bonds of our common humanity." Irwin Abrams—*The Nobel Peace Prize and the Laureates*[1]

1964

MARTIN LUTHER KING, JR. (1929-1968), United States: *Baptist pastor, leader of the first great non-violent protest of black peoples in the U.S.; leader of the National Association for the Advancement of Colored People (NAACP).*

King was deeply influenced by the life and work of Mahatma Gandhi, who he said "was probably the first person in history to lift the love ethic of Jesus above mere interaction between individuals to a powerful and effective social force . . . I found in the non-violent resistance philosophy of Gandhi . . . the only morally and practically sound method open to oppressed people in their struggle for freedom."

For eleven years King campaigned tirelessly for rights for black people, led the peaceful march of 250,000 people on Washington, and was largely responsible for the Civil Rights Bill signed by President Johnson in 1964. He was arrested more than twenty times and was assaulted at least four times.

At his Oslo Peace Prize presentation he was described as "the first person in the western world to have shown us that a struggle can be waged without violence." King explained his philosophy—"Non-violence has meant that my people in the agonizing struggles of recent years have taken suffering upon themselves instead of inflicting it on others . . . . Our actions must be guided by the deepest principles of the Christian faith . . . . If you will protest courageously, and yet with dignity and Christian love, you will live a great people . . . the movement seeks no victory over anyone. It seeks to liberate American society and to share in the self-liberation of all the people."

In April 1968, a day before a peaceful protest march in support of striking garbage workers in Memphis, Tennessee, King was killed by a sniper. The U.S. celebrates Martin Luther King Jr. Day as a national holiday each year on his birthday, the twenty-first of January.

King's voice was truly heard around the world. In Vancouver, Canada, a letter in 2001 to the editor of the *Vancouver Sun*, read as follows:

Protester stands up for truth

Congratulations to Zenon Dolnyckyj
for his courage in going to Tiananmen
Square to appeal for the Falun Gong.
(Chinese police beat me, says Canadian,

Nov. 22.) This spiritual movement is
welcomed in more than 50 countries
and only China tortures and murders
its own citizen practitioners. This is
not just a China issue.

Killing innocent, kind people who
live by truth, compassion and tolerance
is not only utterly devoid of conscience,
it is a persecution against the basic right
of human beings to exist and against the
right to believe.

As Martin Luther King said: "Any place
without justice is a threat to all places with
justice.... He who is silent in the face of evil
is as guilty as the one perpetrating the evil."
Bravo, Zenon. This would be a far more
benevolent world if more people cared as
deeply as you.

HEIDI BALABAN
Vancouver

King fought against "the greatest evils, racial injustice, poverty,
and war." He had "an audacious faith in humankind." He protested
against the Viet Nam war, showing great courage.

*"The most pressing problem confronting humanity today is the poverty of the
spirit which stands in glaring contrast to our scientific and technological
abundance. This was apparent in the three evils that had grown out of man's
'ethical infantilism'—racial injustice, poverty, and war . . . so we must fix our
vision not merely upon the negative expulsion of war, but upon the positive
affirmation of peace . . . . In short, we must shift the arms race into a 'peace'
race.*

*"We as Peace People . . . believe in taking down the barriers, but we also
believe in the most energetic reconciliation among peoples by getting to know each
other physically, philosophically, and spiritually . . . . The only force which can*

break down those barriers is the force of love, the force of truth, soul-force." Martin Luther King, Jr.

1965

UNITED NATIONS CHILDREN'S FUND (UNICEF): *UNICEF was established by the UN in 1946.*

After the Second World War there were twenty million children in Europe in urgent need of care. In the winter of 1947-48, UNICEF gave six million children and mothers in fourteen countries at least one meal a day, as well as clothing and medical supplies.

In 1950 the UN directed UNICEF to use its resources mainly in less developed countries.

In 1959 the UN adopted a Declaration of the Rights of the Child, which stressed children's rights to parental protection, health, adequate food, shelter, and education.

In the 1960s, as many states in Africa and Asia broke away from colonial rule, the plight of children was desperate, and UNICEF took on the job of providing aid on a large scale. In the 1980s there were many emergencies, such as famine in Africa. Despite UNICEF income increasing to over $400 million, many millions of children died each year due to lack of funds, when there was no shortage of funds for nuclear submarines and fighter planes.

The work of UNICEF was so important that a plan was evolved requiring all countries receiving aid to match the UNICEF contribution with local products, personnel, and support services. UNICEF is financed by grants from governments, private individuals, and thirty-seven organizations worldwide. UNICEF supports children's aid programs in 162 countries.

In this age of billions being spent on armaments, UNICEF must turn down many worthy projects due to lack of funding. Mrs. Lionaes, Chairman of the Norwegian Nobel Committee, said, "It is an agonizing predicament to know that millions of children will die each year who might have lived if the needed funds could be provided."

A 2001 report of UNICEF states:

"There have been serious setbacks, slippage, and in some cases real retrogression, some of it serious enough to threaten earlier gains. The stark challenges that face us today are that:

- More than ten million children die each year from preventable causes;
- 150 million still suffer from malnutrition;
- 100 million children are still not in school—most of them girls; the resources that were promised at the Summit have yet to materialize and there has been inadequate investment in social services; lives of millions continue to be devastated by hazardous labor, by the sale and trafficking of women and children, the militarization and prostitution of children, and by general abuse, exploitation, and violence."

"The welfare of today's children is inseparably linked with the peace of tomorrow's world. The longer the world tolerates the slow war of attrition which poverty and ignorance now wage against over 800 million children in the developing countries, the more likely it becomes that our hope for lasting peace will be the ultimate casualty." Henry Labouisse, Executive-Director, UNICEF

"The world has fallen short of achieving most of the goals of the recent World Summit for Children, not because they were too ambitious or were technically beyond reach." Kofi Annan, UN Secretary-General

1966, 1967 No Peace Prizes awarded

1968

RENÉ-SAMUEL CASSIN (1887-1976), France: *International jurist, humanitarian, and architect with Eleanor Roosevelt of the UN Charter of Human Rights; President of the Court of Arbitration at The Hague and of the European Court of Human Rights.*

Cassin was awarded the prize for his "respect for human worth, irrespective of nationality, sex, or social position . . . and for his contribution to the protection of humanity and the rights of man, as set out in the UN's Universal Declaration of Human Rights in 1948.

This declaration was a major document of an ethical sort. The UN Charter did not define human rights, and it took two years to formulate a declaration which everyone could accept. The countries which voted for the Declaration did not commit themselves, but declared themselves 'in agreement' that all people should have the right to life, liberty, and security of person; that everyone is entitled to freedom of conscience, of religion, of expression, and of assembly; that everyone is entitled to work, to equal compensation for equal work, to reasonable working hours, and to free education."

A salient characteristic of the Declaration is its universality: it applies to all human beings without discrimination; it also applies to all territories, whatever their economic or political position. The recognition of the inalienable human rights of all mankind was now an essential part of the struggle for peace.

"We are witnessing today the violation of the right to live. Murders and massacres are perpetrated with impunity. The exploitation of women, mass hunger, widespread racial discrimination—all these evils are too prevalent to be overlooked." René-Samuel Cassin

1969

INTERNATIONAL LABOR ORGANIZATION (ILO), Geneva: *Established in 1919 by the Versailles Treaty, which contained principles which are regarded as the Magna Carta of the labor movement.*

The ILO serves over 150 member states. The main program areas are: improvement of working conditions and industrial relations among governments, employers, and employees; and the promotion of world employment and the advancement of human rights in social and labor fields. The ILO has a staff of 2,000 in Geneva, and over 900 experts on technical co-operation, standard-setting, and vocational training—in over forty countries.

The Director-General of the ILO, David Morse, stressed in his acceptance lecture the importance of social justice as a basic foundation for a secure world peace. He offered a new challenge—to make industrialized societies more human, with more opportunities for all people to lead fuller and richer lives in a spiritual as well as a material sense.

The ILO has added a vast new dimension of technical co-operation with the less developed countries, and international machinery to monitor the conventions and agreements registered with the ILO. The observations of the ILO supervisory bodies have resulted in several thousand changes in national laws and practices to bring them into conformity with ratified conventions.

*"The ultimate objective of the ILO is the elimination of poverty, hardship, and privation which weigh so heavily upon the dispossessed peoples of the earth, to raise their standards of living, to improve their living and working conditions, and to secure to them fundamental human rights, to the end that they may take their place in society as free, dignified, and self-governing people. "*David Morse, Director-General, ILO

"The ILO's main task will be to ensure that this new world is based on social justice; . . . to fulfill the command preserved beneath the corner stone in ILO headquarters in Geneva "Si vis pacem, cole justitiam *(If you desire peace, cultivate justice).*

"Just as peace is indivisible, so also is justice. " Mrs. Aase Lionaes, Chairman, Norwegian Nobel Committee

1970

NORMAN ERNEST BORLAUG (1914—), United States: *Agricultural scientist, geneticist, plant pathologist, and father of the "green revolution. "*

Borlaug developed high-yield disease-resistant dwarf wheat, rice, cereals and maize adapted for use in less developed regions. The Norwegian Nobel Committee appreciated that developing more efficient food crops would make a big contribution to increased food supply, and to the growth of world peace.

The new seeds and farming methods were a great success in Central America and many Asian and African countries, where over seventy percent of the population are farmers, mostly at the subsistence level.

The "green revolution" generated new hope for the future. In many regions grain yields doubled and importing areas became self-sufficient.

"Never before in the history of agriculture has a transplantation of new varieties coupled with an entirely new technology been used on such a massive scale, and with such great success."

However, Borlaug warned that the world population explosion would have to be controlled in order for mankind to benefit from the "green revolution."

"Most people still fail to comprehend the magnitude and menace of the 'Population Monster' . . . by the time of Christ, the world population had probably reached 250 million . . . now, it has grown to 3.5 billion . . . . If it continues to increase at the present estimated rate of two percent a year, the world population will reach 6.5 billion by the year 2000 . . . . Where will it all end?"
Norman Borlaug

(By the year 2000 the world population was 6.1 billion!)

1971

WILLY BRANDT (1913-1992), Germany: *As mayor of Berlin, minister of foreign affairs in West Germany's coalition government, and then Chancellor of West Germany (1969-1974), he was largely responsible for initiating Ostpolitik, a more active policy of détente in relation to the Soviet Union, East Germany, and the Eastern European countries generally.*

Brandt sought military and economic co-operation with Germany's former wartime enemies, stating—"The day will arrive when the inevitable hate of wartime will be forgotten. It must then become a reality, this Europe in which we can all live as Europeans."

He stressed the importance of a pan-European federation, "A good German cannot be a nationalist . . . he knows that he cannot be other than a good European." He saw that the solving of the great problems of Europe demanded peace as a prerequisite.

"My country is no longer a great power and can never be one again, but we are an economic and scientific power . . . prepared to work together with other nations.

"We know that we can play a great role as peacemakers . . . . Peace is far more than the mere absence of war . . . a lasting and just peace would mean equal chances of development for all the peoples of the world.

"Peace, like freedom, is no original state which existed from the start; we shall have to make it, in the truest sense of the word.

"A durable and equitable peace system requires equal development opportunities for all nations." Willy Brandt

1972 No Peace Prize awarded

1973

LE DUC THO (1911-1990), Vietnam: *Founded the Vietminh, the provisional government of North Vietnam; refused to accept the prize, saying, "For centuries Vietnam has been one: the Vietnamese people from north to south aspire with all their heart not only to a peaceful settlement of the Vietnam problem, but also to the reunification of their country."*

1973

HENRY A. KISSINGER (1923—), United States: *Political scientist, statesman; Harvard University professor; National Security adviser; Secretary of State (1973-1977).*

Kissinger was instrumental in negotiating a cease-fire in Vietnam in January 1973, after discussions had gone on for nearly two years. The fighting continued until the U.S. forces pulled out of Vietnam in 1975, leaving the country to be reunified under Le Duc Tho.

President Nixon announced the cease-fire agreement as "peace with honor." Unfortunately, there followed no peace and no honor.

"America's goal was a stable world, not as an end in itself but as a bridge to the realization of man's noble aspirations of tranquility and community." Henry A. Kissinger

1974

EISAKU SATO (1901-1975), Japan: *Civil servant, Premier from 1964-1972; he worked for the peaceful use of nuclear energy. Japan had agreed in its new constitution not to develop nuclear weapons and to be a pacifist nation.*

Sato believed that the renunciation of war, as stated in the 1947 Japanese constitution, must be the basis of Japan's policy. He travelled throughout Asia to improve trade relations, increase aid to developing countries, and generally encourage greater co-operation. In 1961 he concluded a treaty with the United States securing the return to Japan of Okinawa, and the promise that nuclear arms would not be maintained on American bases on Okinawa and local islands.

In his acceptance lecture Sato emphasized that peace is grown at the grass roots, tied to the daily life of each individual and each family.

Sato expressed three principles on the peaceful use of nuclear energy— *"First, we need to create international safety standards; next, an international agreement on the exchange and allocation of nuclear fuels, to avoid an unbridled race for the acquisition of nuclear fuels; and third, there must be international co-operation in research and development work on nuclear fusion, because the rapid development of a system for the effective use of thermonuclear energy seems to be beyond the capacity of a single nation, no matter how great its resources may be."*

"If the attainment of peace is the ultimate objective of all statesmen, it is, at the same time, something very ordinary, closely tied to the daily life of each individual. In familiar terms, it is the condition that allows each individual and his family to pursue, without fear, the purpose of their lives. It is only in such circumstances that each individual will be able to devote himself, without the loss of hope for the future of mankind, to the education of his children, in an attempt to leave upon the history of mankind the imprint of his own creative and constructive achievements in the arts, culture, religion, and other activities fulfilling social aspirations. This is the peace which is essential for all individuals, peoples, nations, and thus for the whole of humanity." Eisaku Sato

1974

SEÁN MacBRIDE (1904-1988), Ireland: *Journalist, lawyer, and statesman, he was one of the foreign ministers responsible for piloting the European Convention on Human Rights through the Council of Europe in 1973. He served for many years as president of the International Board of Amnesty International.*

MacBride supported the establishment of a Human Rights Court, maintaining that no state can claim absolute sovereignty where basic human rights are concerned.

Suggesting that the use of nuclear weapons should be completely outlawed, he dismissed delays and arguments over inspection, and advocated: "Why not begin quite simply by outlawing the use, manufacture, sale, transfer, and stockpiling of all nuclear weapons and components thereof?" MacBride believed in the peacemaking power of ordinary people and public opinion.

"If disarmament can be achieved it will be due to the untiring, selfless work of the non-governmental sector. The signpost just ahead of us is 'Oblivion.' Can the march on this road be stopped? Yes, if public opinion uses the power it now has." Seán MacBride

1975

ANDREI SAKHAROV (1921-1989), U.S.S.R.: *Nuclear physicist who worked on the development of nuclear arms. In 1968 he issued a manifesto appealing for worldwide co-operation in the control of nuclear power. In an attempt to institute constructive reforms for the protection of human rights within the framework of law, he and two other scientists founded the Committee for Human Rights in the Soviet Union in 1970.*

The chief aims of the Human Rights Committee were: the abolition of secret trials, a free press, prison reform, amnesty for political prisoners, the abolition of the death penalty, open frontiers, and a ban on the use of psychiatric institutes for political ends. Many of these ideas were incorporated in the Agreement on Security and Co-operation in Europe, signed by thirty-five nations in Helsinki in 1975. (The U.S.S.R. government would not allow Sakharov to leave Russia to accept the Nobel Peace Prize. His wife, Elena, was out of Russia, and went to Oslo and read his lecture.)

"In struggling to protect human rights we must, I am convinced, first and foremost act as protectors of the innocent victims of regimes installed in various countries, without demanding the destruction or total condemnation of these regimes. We need reform, not revolution. We need a pliant, pluralistic, tolerant community, which selectively and tentatively can bring about a free, undogmatic

use of the experiences of all social systems. What is détente? What is rapprochement? We are concerned not with words, but with a willingness to create a better and more friendly society, a better world order . . . ." Andrei Sakharov

1976

MAIREAD CORRIGAN (1944—), Ireland: *Co-founder with Betty Williams of the Community of the Peace People. Corrigan worked with Catholic organizations as a volunteer and helped to establish clubs for physically handicapped children. She was devoutly religious, and as a youth leader went to church conferences in Thailand and to the Soviet Union to make a film on the life of religious people in the U.S.S.R.*

1976

BETTY WILLIAMS (1943—), Ireland: *Co-founder of the Community of the Peace People. She had joined a movement started in 1972 by a Protestant clergyman to try to end the violence in Northern Ireland.*

The senseless street killing in 1976 of three children sparked a wave of revulsion against the violence that had engulfed Northern Ireland for so long. Mairead Corrigan sobbed on a television program the next day—"Only one percent of the people want this slaughter," and condemned those who encouraged young people to join paramilitary groups. Corrigan joined Williams to lead a march of thirty-five thousand from a Catholic to a Protestant area of Belfast, which captured the sympathy of the world and was given wide publicity. The quickly-organized Peace People led marches in Northern Ireland and Great Britain.

The two Peace Laureates called on women everywhere to encourage men to have the courage to say no to war, and to break down the barriers between people.

"The voice of women has a special role and a special soul-force for a non-violent world. We believe that women have a leading role to play in this great struggle." Betty Williams

"The message of the Peace People is just as relevant today . . . that non-

violence is the only way forward for the human family, and it has not failed, it has just not been tried with enough determination by enough people. "Mairead Corrigan (December, 1977)

1977

AMNESTY INTERNATIONAL: *Worldwide organization established in 1961 by Peter Benenson, a British lawyer, to protect the human rights of prisoners of conscience and appeal on their behalf for amnesty.*

Amnesty International is independent of all governments and is neutral in its relation to political groups, ideologies, religion, and ethnic origin. It works for the release of women and men who have been arrested and held in prison without due process of law, provided they themselves have not used force or urged others to resort to violence.

Amnesty has been guided by the principle that work for human rights and work for world peace are inseparable. Where there is injustice, there is the seed of conflict, and where human rights are violated, there is no peace. The UN Universal Declaration of Human Rights, 1948, affirms that "recognition of the inherent dignity and of equal and inalienable rights of all members of the human family is the foundation of freedom, justice, and peace in the world."

The Amnesty program has been carried out mainly by small groups of volunteers in worldwide non-governmental organizations. The heart of the program is based on letter-writing groups working for peace and human rights for all prisoners of conscience. In 2001, Amnesty International had over 1,874 volunteer groups in 140 countries and territories, with over one million members and subscribers.

"The main principles of Amnesty with respect to human rights are summarized as follows: . . . human rights are ends, rather than means, . . . indivisible, . . . concrete and specific, . . . and universal. Human rights will not be protected if left solely to the governments."

Mümtaz Soysal, Ankara, Turkey, Amnesty International Vice-Chairman

1978

MOHAMED ANWAR el-SADAT (1918-1981), Egypt: *President, Arab Republic of Egypt.*

1978

MENACHEM BEGIN (1913-1992), Israel: *Prime Minister of Israel.*

The Nobel award recognized their contribution to the two framework agreements on peace in the Middle East and between Egypt and Israel, signed at Camp David in 1978, after four wars between the two countries since the state of Israel was established in 1948. The President of the U.S., Jimmy Carter, played a key role in clearing the way for peace.

Sadat and Begin lived in a century of global wars and major revolutions, of racial hatreds and foreign domination. Both had suffered in combat and prisons and faced violent opposition in their homeland, but they supported the miracle of peace. They shook hands to confirm "the greatest of all victories—conciliation and lasting peace based on respect for human rights and human dignity."

(Anwar Sadat was killed by Egyptians in 1981 during a military march-past in Cairo.)

"Peace is the smile of a child . . . the love of a family . . . the advancement of man, the victory of a just cause, the triumph of truth. Peace is all of these, and more and more . . . the hour has struck to rise and fight—for the dignity of man, for survival, for liberty, for every value of the human image a man has been endowed with by his Creator, for every known inalienable right he stands for and lives for . . . work for peace because there is no mission in life more sacred."
Menachem Begin

"Any life lost in war is the life of a human being, irrespective of whether it is an Arab or an Israeli.

"The wife who becomes widowed is a human being, entitled to live in a happy family, Arab or Israeli.

"Innocent children, deprived of paternal care and sympathy, are all our children, whether they live on Arab or Israeli soil, and we owe them the biggest responsibility of providing them with a happy present and bright future.

- *For the sake of all this, for the sake of protecting the lives of all our sons and brothers;*
- *For our societies to produce in security and confidence;*
- *For the development of man, his well-being and his right to share in an honorable life;*
- *For our responsibility toward the coming generations.* "Mohamed Anwar el-Sadat

1979

MOTHER TERESA (1910-1997), India: *Founder and head of a Roman Catholic order, Missionaries of Charity.*

Mother Teresa had over fifty relief projects in India, working among slum-dwellers, children's homes, homes for the dying, clinics, and a leper colony. The Order has spread to do relief work for the poorest of the poor in Africa, Asia, Latin America, Italy, Great Britain, Ireland, and the U.S.

Mother Teresa carried her Christian love and faith in all her work— love for all mankind, for the poor and needy, sick and dying, all creeds and color. "We have a home for the dying in Calcutta, where we have picked up more than 36,000 people from the streets, of whom more than 18,000 have died a beautiful death."

"If we could only remember that God loves me, and I have an opportunity to love others as he loves me, not in big things, but in small things with great love, then our countries will become nests of love.

"It is not how much we do, but how much love we put into it. The moment we have given it to God, it becomes infinite.

"In these twenty years of work among the people, I have come more and more to realize that it is being unwanted that is the worst disease that any human being can ever experience . . . the worst disease is the feeling of being uncared for and deserted by everybody.

". . . I think that . . . we don't need bombs and guns, to destroy, to bring peace—just get together, love one another, bring that peace, that joy, that strength of presence of each other in the home. And we will be able to overcome all the evil that is in the world." Mother Teresa

1980

ADOLFO PÉREZ ESQUIVEL (1931—), Argentina: *Teacher and sculptor, devout Christian; Secretary-general of Service for Peace and Justice (the Latin-American non-violent human rights organization); a champion for social and political liberty, human rights, non-violence between nations, and improving the lives of native peasants.*

A military junta took power in Argentina in 1976 and increased a cruel campaign of imprisonment, torture, and killing of alleged left-wing elements. Esquivel founded two human rights organizations to support victims of oppression and injustice. He was tortured and imprisoned for fourteen months. During this time he was proposed for the Peace Prize. Amnesty International, religious leaders, the U.S. government, and peace leaders worldwide secured his release in 1978.

In his acceptance lecture of the Peace Prize Esquivel had words of reproach for the great powers: *"The rule . . . they have inflicted on the world permits the biggest crime of our time, the arms race.*

"My voice would like to have the strength of the voice of the humble and lowly. It is the voice that proclaims hope in God and humanity . . . . We act by means of evangelical non-violence, which we see as a force for liberation." Adolfo Pérez Esquivel

1981

OFFICE of the UNITED NATIONS HIGH COMMISSIONER for REFUGEES (UNHCR): *Established in 1951, when there were more than ten million refugees worldwide. This was the fourth Nobel Peace Prize for refugee aid.*

A primary function of the UNHCR is to provide refugees with legal protection. It fights against the evils of persecution, violation of human rights, armed conflicts, and ethnic butchery. The need for this work has steadily increased to provide aid for twenty-three million refugees worldwide. Total personnel is 5,200, including 4,200 working in 274 field offices in 120 countries. Most of the workers are volunteers. The budget of the worldwide organization was $934 million in 2001.

The protection of refugees is mandated in the Universal Declaration of Human Rights, Article 14—"Everyone has the right to seek and to enjoy in other countries asylum from persecution." The UNHCR has had to continuously expand its services to carry out new programs of voluntary repatriation, relocation, and rehabilitation. Violence and ethnic butchery in the former Yugoslavia, Africa, and Asia have greatly increased the need for refugee assistance for persons in jeopardy on account of their religion, nationality, political views, or membership of any group in a world in which people must flee from war and civil strife, abuses of human rights, and lack of legal protection.

"Peace is more than just absence of war. It is rather a state in which no people of any country, in fact no group of people of any kind live in fear and in need . . . . Today, more than twenty million refugees live in fear or in need. On our road towards a better future for mankind we certainly cannot ignore the presence of those millions for whom peace does not exist. Whenever we solve one single problem we have contributed to peace for the individual. Whenever we bring peace to the individual we are making our world a slightly better place in which to live.

"The UN Commission for Refugees is a bridge linking the world community conceived as a community of states and the world community conceived as a community of men and women." Poul Hartling, representing UN High Commissioner for Refugees

1982

ALVA REIMER MYRDAL (1902-1986), Sweden: *Sociologist and social reformer; author, diplomat, parliamentarian; Sweden's international disarmament negotiator.*

Alva Myrdal was active in leadership roles in the UN departments of Social Affairs and Social Sciences. She was Sweden's ambassador to India, followed by eleven years as a cabinet minister, when she took a leading role in Sweden's unilateral renunciation in 1968 of nuclear weapons and chemical and biological warfare. She denounced the leaders of the nuclear arms race as guilty of "a clearly irredeemable misconception: that the use of war and violence can lead to victory."

"The misconception that 'a victory is worth the price' has in the nuclear age become a total illusion . . . .

"The experts have as a rule arrived at the conclusion that the target for a sufficient deterrent would involve something like 400 missiles, capable of reaching from one continent to the other. Any developments over and above this have simply meant one more step in the direction of increased instability. It has been unnecessary, and at what a cost!

"I shall go on repeating, until the politicians get it into their heads, that 'when one has sufficient, one does not need more.'

"The nuclear rivalry [of the superpowers] not only faced the world with the threat of extinction but had helped produce the cult of violence that made our age one of barbarism. Everyday violence, in the streets and in the media, is to a large extent a result of a spread of arms." Alva Reimer Myrdal

1982

ALFONSO GARCÍA ROBLES (1911—), Mexico: *Diplomat, foreign minister chiefly responsible for the treaty banning nuclear weapons in Latin America; UN official, champion of disarmament in the UN.*

The Treaty of Tlatelolco (1967) took thirteen years of negotiations. It was the first of its kind in the world to ban nuclear weapons— "Nuclear weapons . . . constitute . . . an attack on the integrity of the human species and ultimately may even render the whole of the earth uninhabitable. Mankind is confronted with a choice: we must halt the arms race and proceed to disarmament or face annihilation."

Robles recognized the paramount need of mobilizing world public opinion if progress was to be made in disarmament, and as a UN official emphasized the UN program stressing the importance of nuclear free zones.

"The military denuclearization of Latin America . . . will constitute a measure which will spare their peoples from the squandering of their limited resources on nuclear armaments and will protect them against possible nuclear attacks on their territories, and will be . . . a powerful factor for general and complete disarmament." Preamble, Treaty of Tlatelolco (1967)

1983

LECH WALESA (1943—), Poland: *Leader of Solidarity, Polish trade union movement.*

In 1970, Walesa organized a strike and occupation of the Gdansk shipyard, leading up to the killing of fifty-five men by the oppressive military dictatorship of Poland. A wave of strikes followed in many regions. The Catholic Church and public opinion supported Solidarity. Martial law was declared and Walesa was interned for almost a year. The U.S. applied economic sanctions, and eventually martial law was lifted.

Oppression by the Kremlin-dominated military dictator Jaruzelski continued. Walesa did not go to Oslo to receive the Peace Prize, as he feared being denied re-entry to Poland. His acceptance lecture, presented by a union comrade, stressed—"We can effectively oppose violence only if we ourselves do not resort to it. Peace and justice go together . . . the two are like bread and salt for mankind."

After the fall of communist control, in 1990 Walesa was elected president of Poland and served for five years.

"We desire peace—and that is why we have never resorted to physical force. We crave for justice, . . . for freedom of convictions . . . . We are fighting for the right of the working people to association and the dignity of human labor. We respect the dignity and the rights of every man and of every nation. The path to a brighter future of the world leads through honest reconciliation of the conflicting interests and not through hatred and bloodshed . . . . To follow that path means to enhance the moral power of the all-embracing idea of human solidarity.

"The defense of our rights and dignity, as well as our efforts never to let ourselves be overcome by the feeling of hatred—this is the road we have chosen."
Lech Walesa

1984

ARCHBISHOP DESMOND TUTU (1931—), South Africa: *General Secretary, South African Council of Churches, Anglican archbishop of Capetown, leader in non-violent struggle for racial equality and human rights in a country of about four million whites and thirty-nine million blacks.*

Desmond Tutu was a leader of many religious followers of all races, united in opposition to the oppressive government policies of apartheid as inconsistent with the principles of Christianity. When the African National Congress (ANC) encouraged violence by blacks,

Tutu condemned this, but warned that "oppressed people will become desperate, and desperate people will use desperate methods."

Tutu was secretary-general of the South African Council of Churches (SACC), where about eighty percent of members are black, and they hold the top positions. He led the SACC in a non-violent struggle for the same aims of Chief Lutuli (1960)—a non-racial, truly democratic and just society.

In his award acceptance lecture Tutu said he had never learned to hate, and he told black South Africans, "Be nice to whites; they need you to rediscover their humanity."

"When there is no justice, there is no peace. When will we learn that human beings are of infinite value because they have been created in the image of God, and that it is blasphemy to treat them as if they were less than this and to do so ultimately recoils on those who do? In dehumanizing others, they are themselves dehumanized. We can be human only in fellowship, in community, in peace."
Archbishop Desmond Tutu

1985

INTERNATIONAL PHYSICIANS FOR THE PREVENTION OF NUCLEAR WAR (IPPNW): *Dr. Yevgeni Chazov of the Soviet Union and Dr. Bernard Lown of the U.S. received the award on behalf of their organization, founded in 1980.*

The IPPNW is a non-partisan global federation of national medical organizations in more than sixty countries, dedicated to research, education and advocacy relevant to the prevention of nuclear war. Total membership, mostly volunteers except for a small staff, is over 200,000. The 1961 budget was $1,600,000.

The IPPNW has its Central Office in Boston, and a European Office in London.

In 1985, Secretary Gorbachev said the U.S.S.R. would unilaterally refrain from nuclear testing, a position urged by IPPNW. Unfortunately, the U.S. did not support the stand of the U.S.S.R.

Dr. Lown's Nobel lecture stressed "that the production of nuclear arms keeps countless millions in poverty, lack of food, of health, and medical services . . . when science and technology have brought mankind to the prospects of an age of abundance."

The IPPNW are strong international activist doctors researching the consequences of nuclear wars and explaining the issues to governments, scientists, and the public.

"For the physician, whose role is to affirm life, optimism is a medical imperative. What humanity creates, humanity can and will control.

"A single modern submarine has eight times the total firepower of World War Two, sufficient to destroy every city in the Northern Hemisphere. Why then the stockpiling of 18,000 strategic weapons?

"In order to be effective, nuclear deterrence must operate perfectly and forever. So such expectations are not permissible for any human activities." Bernard Lown, Harvard University School of Public Health

"(What is the) rationale applied today when they speak about the research objectives of the space militarization programme, about its defensive significance? Cannot we discern it as an attempt to gradually accept the idea of weapons over our heads, in outer space? . . . . The 'space shield' will mean one step toward nuclear catastrophe, not only because it would create temptation to effect a first strike with impunity. Any defence will inevitably lead to the creation of the means to overcome it. Thus the spiral of the arms race—nuclear, conventional, laser, and other—will again soar steeply, undermining strategic stability.

"Any reasonable man finds it hard to believe that while hunger, diseases, social inequality, economic underdevelopment, and illiteracy are in existence, hundreds of billions of dollars are wasted to feed the insatiable monster—the arms race." Yevgeni Chazov, U.S.S.R. Cardiological Institute

1986

ELIE WIESEL (1928—), United States: *University professor, survivor of Buchenwald, author; a leading interpreter of the holocaust and a spiritual leader.*

Wiesel's main concerns are the question of what measures mankind can take to prevent another holocaust, and to maintain the fight for freedom and human dignity. He believes in God, humanity, and in the future, despite the horrors of the past.

He cries out "against injustice and suffering, victims of hunger, political persecution, prisoners in so many lands. Human rights are being violated on every continent. More people are oppressed than free."

"The world had been silent during the Holocaust, and that is why I swore never to be silent whenever and wherever human beings endure suffering and humiliation. As long as one dissident is in prison, our freedom will not be true. As long as one child is hungry, our lives will be filled with anguish and shame.

"None of us is in a position to eliminate war, but it is our obligation to denounce it and expose it in all its hideousness . . . . Mankind needs peace more than ever, for our entire planet, threatened by nuclear war, is in danger of total destruction. A destruction only man can provoke, only men can prevent.

"Mankind must remember that peace is not God's gift to his creatures, it is our gift to each other." Elie Wiesel

1987

OSCAR ARIAS SÁNCHEZ (1941—), Costa Rica: *Lawyer, author, statesman; President of Costa Rica (1986-1990); architect of the Central America Peace Plan.*

In 1986, Arias initiated negotiations with the Presidents of Guatemala, El Salvador, Honduras, and Nicaragua. All signed an agreement to commit to conciliation, agreement, and verification procedures to settle all conflicts between signatory states. Arias supports democracy as a decisive precondition for a long-lasting peace. In 1948, it was approved that Costa Rica would have no military force, a prohibition still honored today.

The governments of Costa Rica have traditionally given priority to education, health, and economic development, based on firmly-rooted democratic traditions.

The Arias peace plan was the product of the Central American presidents themselves, who wanted outside intervention to cease. The plan coupled democracy with peace—"democracy is a means, the end is always the human being."

"Peace is a never-ending process. It is an attitude, a way of life, a way of . . . resolving conflicts. We seek in Central America not peace alone . . . but peace and democracy, together, indivisible, an end to the shedding of human blood, which is inseparable from an end to the suppression of human rights.

"Peace consists, very largely, in the fact of desiring it with all one's soul. The inhabitants of my small country, Costa Rica, have realized those words by Erasmus. Mine is an unarmed people, whose children have never seen a fighter or a tank or a warship.

"My country is a country of teachers. It is therefore a country of peace . . . we closed the army camps, and our children go about with books under their arms, not with rifles on their shoulders. We believe in dialogue, in agreement, in reaching a consensus." Oscar Ariaz Sánchez

1988

UNITED NATIONS PEACEKEEPING FORCES: *Peacekeeping operations began in 1948 when unarmed observer groups monitored ceasefire agreements. A UN emergency peacekeeping force of lightly armed troops and unarmed observers was first used in the Suez crisis of 1956.*

Today the Blue Helmets are provided by UN member countries, as approved by the Security Council, and stationed in areas where a ceasefire has been established.

The original architects of an ongoing peacekeeping UN function were three Nobel Peace laureates, Ralph Bunche, Dag Hammarskjöld, and Lester Pearson. The plan makes the UN not just an administrative organization, but an active instrument in the achievement of peace, a focus for international law and human rights, and a forum for the development of inter-racial understanding. See Chapter 8 for a recent update on UN Peacekeeping Forces.

In 2001, the Peacekeeping group totalled 43,000 personnel in twenty operations. The annual budget was three billion dollars. (See Appendix H for a list of current UN Peacekeeping operations.)

"Peacekeeping uses soldiers as servants of peace rather than as instruments of war. It introduces in the military sphere the principle of non-violence . . . . Their presence is often the essential prerequisite for negotiating a settlement. They have, or should have, a direct connection with the process of peacemaking.

"Never before in history have military forces been employed internationally not *to wage war,* not *to establish domination, and* not *to serve the interests of any power . . . but rather to prevent conflict between peoples."* Javier Pérez de Cuéllar, representing the UN Peacekeeping Forces

1989

Fourteenth DALAI LAMA (TENZIN GYATSO) (1935—), Tibet: *Scholar and man of peace; Buddhist monk, religious and political leader of the Tibetan people; Head of State at sixteen. In 1959 he was forced into exile in India after the Chinese military occupation of Tibet. In 1987 he proposed a Five-Point Peace Plan based on a democratic Tibet and restoration of the fundamental rights of Tibetans, while accommodating China's own interests. (China has not responded as of 2003.)*

The Dalai Lama maintains contact with many world leaders in government and religion. He advocates peaceful solutions based on tolerance and mutual respect in order to preserve the historical and cultural heritage of the Tibetan people. He stresses the principles of absolute non-violent struggle and of simple human-to-human relationship, universal responsibility, love, compassion, and kindness.

"Basically, universal responsibility is feeling for other people's suffering just as we feel our own. We must recognize that all beings want the same thing that we want.

"Peace starts within each one of us. When we have inner peace, we can be at peace with those around us. When our community is in a state of peace, it can share that peace with neighboring communities, and so on. When we feel love and kindness toward others, it not only makes others feel loved and cared for, but it helps us also to develop inner peace and happiness."
The Dalai Lama

1990

MIKHAIL GORBACHEV (1931—), Soviet Union: *President of the Soviet Union, lawyer; he proposed communism break away from its past and develop new principles of perestroika and glasnost to achieve a renewal and transformation of his society, based on major changes in every department of life.*

Gorbachev's philosophy led to much greater openness in international relations, comprehensive agreements on disarmament, and co-operation between East and West. In his Nobel Prize acceptance lecture he said "Immanuel Kant prophesied that mankind would one day be faced with a dilemma: either to be joined in a true union of nations or to perish in a war of annihilation ending in the extinction of the human race. Now, as we move into the third millennium, the clock has struck the moment of truth."

Gorbachev stressed that many changes in the transformation of Soviet society had to be solved solely by constitutional means and a process of democracy and reforms. With *glasnost* Gorbachev gave freedom to the people as a whole to criticize and stir up the communist party. He also stated " . . . there is already a consensus in our society that we have to move toward a mixed market economy." Gorbachev proceeded with a process of *perestroika*, a moving away from the centralized command economy, but not to a complete market economy.

"Today, peace means the ascent from simple co-existence to co-operation and common creativity among countries and nations.

"Peace is movement towards globality and universality of civilization. Never before has the idea that peace is indivisible been so true as it is now.

"Peace is not unity in similarity but unity in diversity, in the comparison and conciliation of differences. And, ideally, peace means the absence of violence. It is an ethical value.

"Knowledge and trust are the foundations of a new world order . . . . We need maximum insurance to guarantee that decisions taken by members of the world community should not affect the security, sovereignty, and vital interests of its other members or damage the environment and the moral climate of the world.

"It is my profound conviction that the problems arising in the course of our transformations can be solved solely by constitutional means . . . within the confines of democracy and reforms . . . . This applies also to the problem of self-determination of nations . . . . We are looking for mechanisms to solve that problem within the framework of constitutional process; we recognize the peoples' legitimate choice, with the understanding that if a people really decides through a fair referendum, to withdraw from the Soviet Union, a certain agreed transition period will then be needed.

"A balance of interests rather than a balance of power, a search for compromise and concord rather than a search for advantages at other people's expense, and respect for equality rather than claims to leadership . . . these elements should be readily acceptable for reasonable people informed by the experience of the 20th century." Mikhail Gorbachev

1991

AUNG SAN SUU KYI (1945—), Myanmar (Burma): *Daughter of Aung San, a leader in Myanmar's struggle for liberation; devout Buddhist, graduate of Oxford, and visiting scholar at leading universities in Japan and India.*

Aung San Suu Kyi returned to Myanmar in 1962 during the second struggle against heavy oppression by the military regime and presented a program based on human rights, democracy, and non-violence at open rallies of many thousands throughout the country. In 1989, she was placed under house arrest. Despite this, a National League for Democracy, led by Suu Kyi, won the election by over eighty percent of the seats. The military then in effect annulled the election and increased their brutality and oppressive violations of human rights.

Suu Kyi was confined to house arrest again in 2003. She continues the fight for the right of all people to life and to respect, a fundamental prerequisite for peace. Her sons represented her at her Laureate lecture which made plain the plight of Myanmar. The military regime's oppression and misrule of forty years has brought the country untold suffering. The once prosperous "Golden Land" of Burma has been reduced to one of the world's poorest nations.

"Our quest is basically spiritual . . . the quintessential revolution is that of the spirit and spiritual aims of our Buddhist heritage . . . our struggle is for democracy . . . and the right of a people to live whole, meaningful lives as free and equal members of the world community.

"Where there is no justice there can be no secure peace." Aung San Suu Kyi

1992

RIGOBERTA MENCHÚ TUM (1959—), Guatemala: *Raised in a destitute peasant village; prominent in women's rights activities and social reform; a Quiché Indian whose family was tortured and killed and land confiscated; a founding member of a society in Guatemala to do missionary work to help poor Indian families; one of the first delegates to a UN group that works for human rights and the cause of indigenous peoples.*

In her book *A Strategy for Peace,* she describes the brutalizing effect of the use of violence—"Violence breeds violence and hate breeds hate. People who preserve their humanity in brutal and violent surroundings give us hope that there are ways out of the vicious cycle."

Rigoberta Tum spent many years in exile in Mexico, but on three occasions returned to Guatemala to plead the cause of the Indian peasants. Death threats have forced her to return into exile.

Rigoberta Tum has become widely known as a leading advocate of the human rights of Indians and of ethno-cultural reconciliation, not only in Guatemala, but also in the Western Hemisphere generally.

She has a fervent belief that "the most pressing task in my country is to achieve peace and social justice." In 1944, the Guatemalans achieved a period of democracy in a struggle for complete national freedom, but were soon defeated by an armed invasion and increased oppression. Among the most bitter results has been a forced exodus of a great percentage of the population.

"The case of the displaced and refugees in Guatemala is heartbreaking; some are condemned to live in exile . . . the great majority live in exile in their own country . . . condemned to poverty and hunger. There must be reorganization of land ownership . . . democracy and social justice . . . a solution to infant mortality, malnutrition, lack of education, wages insufficient to sustain life."
Rigoberta Menchú Tum

1993

NELSON R. MANDELA (1918—), South Africa: *Son of a tribal chief; lawyer; joined the African National Congress (ANC) in 1944; leader of resistance to apartheid; in 1960 elected President of the ANC; imprisoned for twenty-six years, 1964 to 1990; he was the symbol and leader of the fight for freedom and equality for black peoples; President of South Africa, 1994 to 1999.*

Nelson Mandela and Frederik Willem de Klerk gave the leadership that resulted in a fundamental change in South Africa, in ending the discrimination against black peoples and achieving freedom and equality for all without the feared bloodbath to avenge the oppression and inhumanity of the past.

"This must be a world of democracy and respect for human rights, a world freed from the horrors of poverty, hunger, deprivation, and ignorance, relieved of the threat and the scourge of civil wars and external aggression, and unburdened by the great tragedy of millions forced to become refugees.

"Let the striving of us all prove Martin Luther King Jr. to have been correct, when he said that humanity can no longer be tragically bound to the starless midnight of racism and war.

"The normal condition for human existence is democracy, justice, peace, non-racism, non-sexism, prosperity for everybody, a healthy environment, and equality of solidarity among the peoples.

"We commit the new South Africa to the relentless pursuit of the purposes defined in the World Declaration on the Survival, Protection and Development of Children." (Approved unanimously by the UN General Assembly in 1959, proclaiming ten fundamental rights of children.)

"A joyful peace will triumph, because of the common humanity that bonds both black and white into one human race . . . . Thus we shall live, because we will have created a society which recognises that all people are born equal, with each entitled in equal measure to life, liberty, prosperity, human rights, and good governance." Nelson Mandela

(South Africa is going through a complete transformation that has many problems, but the progress for peace is ongoing and must surely be one of the greatest accomplishments in the history of world peacemaking.)

1993

FREDERIK WILLEM de KLERK (1936—), South Africa: *Lawyer, statesman, leader of the National Party; served seventeen years in parliament; State President from 1989 to 1994; lifted the ban on the ANC and other anti-apartheid organizations, released Nelson Mandela, and negotiated with black leaders to build a new South Africa with equal rights, treatment, and opportunity in every sphere of endeavour—constitutional, social, and economic—for all peoples.*

In his first speech as President he called for a non-racist South Africa and for negotiations about the country's future. In co-operation with Mandela, apartheid was ended and a new constitution enacted affirming human rights and a democracy based on the principle of one person, one vote.

"*Peace does not simply mean the absence of conflict. There can be no peace without justice or consent. Neither does peace necessarily imply tranquility . . . new tensions build up and need to be defused. There can be no real peace without constant effort, planning, and hard work . . . . Peace is a frame of mind, in which people seek to resolve differences through negotiation and compromise, instead of threats, compulsion, and violence . . . . Peace is also a framework of rules, laws, agreements, and conventions . . . providing mechanisms for the peaceful resolution of inevitable clashes of interest between communities and nations . . . . Peace is lost where there is poverty and deprivation, ignorance, lack of education and information, repression, injustice, and exploitation, inter-group fear and envy . . . . Racial, class and religious intolerance and prejudice are the mortal enemies of peace.*

"*Hand in hand with economic development goes democracy, with representative institutions which invariably develop a framework for peace. It is highly significant that there has never been a war between genuine and universal democracies.*

"*. . . the single most important factor which became the driving force toward a totally new dispensation in South Africa, was a fundamental change of heart.*

"*The new era which is dawning in our country . . . will lift us out of the silent grief of our past and into a future . . . of opportunity and space for joy and beauty—for real and lasting peace.*

"*. . . this framework for peace will succeed if we can now establish the frame of mind . . . which is necessary for peace—the frame of mind which leads people to resolve differences through negotiation, compromise, and agreements, instead of compulsion and violence.*" Frederik de Klerk

1994

YASSER ARAFAT (1929—), Palestine
SHIMON PERES (1923—), Israel
YITZHAK RABIN (1923-1995), Israel

The award was given to the three men leading the efforts to create peace in the Middle East, the signing of the Oslo Accords of 1993, and their follow-up actions in a historic process through which peace and co-operation could replace war and hate.

YASSER ARAFAT

In 1974 he won a UN vote to grant the Palestine Liberation Organization (PLO) observer status at the UN and to formally acknowledge Palestinian's right to self-determination. His mission was to reclaim Palestine by political settlement, in contrast to the impossible aims of some Muslim states to destroy the State of Israel.

Yasser Arafat led the Palestinian quest for a just and lasting peace based on "land for peace" and compliance with international legitimacy and resolutions for Palestinian independence and sovereignty. The next steps would involve the transfer of power and Israeli withdrawal from the West Bank and the Settlements. In his lecture, he addressed many unsolved problems: Jerusalem, the spiritual haven for Muslims, Christians, and Jews; detainees, prisoners, refugees and terrorism.

"I assure you . . . that we shall discover ourselves in peace more than we have with war and confrontations, as I am sure that the Israelis in turn shall find themselves in peace more than they have found themselves in war." He ended with words from the Holy Koran: *"Then if they should be inclined to make peace, do thou incline towards it also, and put thy trust in Allah."* Yasser Arafat

SHIMON PERES

Peres worked twenty years at the Ministry of Defence; directed the Entebbe rescue operation; was prime minister when Israel withdrew from Lebanon; and was foreign minister in the coalition government of Yitzak Rabin, in charge of negotiations with the PLO.

In his acceptance lecture he said, ". . . we won all the wars forced upon us, but we did not win the greatest victory that we aspired to: release from the need to win victories . . . . Today, war is no longer a choice . . . dialogue is the only option for our world.

"We learned that victors do not necessarily win peace. It is no wonder that

war, as a means of conducting human affairs, is in its death throes and that the time has come to bury it. "

Peres stressed that the source of material wealth and power today is a consequence of intellectual potential through education. Armies of occupation are a thing of the past. He was a prophet regarding increasing terrorism.

"Classical diplomacy and strategy were aimed at identifying enemies and confronting them. Now they have to identify dangers, global or local, and tackle them before they become disasters." Shimon Peres

YITZHAK RABIN

Was in military service from 1940 to 1968, rising to Chief of Staff and Commander of the Israel Defense Force during the Six-Day War. After a term as ambassador to the U.S. he served in government; in 1962 Rabin was elected to lead a coalition government committed to carrying on peace negotiations which culminated in a Declaration of Principles known as the "Oslo Accords"; disengagement agreements were signed with Egypt and Syria.

In his acceptance lecture he stressed the Bible message of the Sanctity of Life.

"Leaders must enable their people to enjoy life; freedom of speech and of movement; food and shelter, and the most important of all: life itself. Military cemeteries in every corner of the world are silent testimony to the failure of national leaders to sanctify human life by the one radical solution—peace.

"I stand here as . . . the emissary of poets and of those who dreamed of an end to war . . . the emissary of sons of the Jewish people . . . the emissary of the children who drew their visions of peace . . . as the emissary of our neighbours who were our enemies . . . . I stand here mainly for the generations to come.

"I wish to thank our partners—the Egyptians, Jordanians, and the Chairman of the Palestinian Liberation Organization, Mr. Yasser Arafat— who have chosen the path of peace and are writing a new page in the annals of the Middle East." Yitzhak Rabin

(Rabin was assassinated by an Israeli extremist in 1995—a tragic blow to the cause of peace between Israel and Palestine.)

(Comments by Professor Francis Sejersted, Chairman of the Norwegian Nobel Committee, Oslo, December 10, 1994, with reference to the Oslo Accords, are summarized as follows:

The Oslo Accords concluded between Israel and the Palestine Liberation Organization (PLO) were revolutionary, affirming de facto *mutual recognition by the two parties. The accords opened up a possible way out of the vicious cycle of violence breeding violence, and towards peaceful co-existence. The Oslo Accords opened up opportunities for a normalization of relations with the entire world.*

The three Laureates took a great risk of showing their opposite numbers a trust that peace feelers were genuine. On that bet they staked their political lives. That takes great courage on both sides, and which has opened up opportunities for a new development towards fraternity in the Middle East.

Concession must be followed by concession. Our hope as the process continues is that neither side will be driven to breaking these "rules of the game.")

Any genuine settlement would have to revolve around the formula "land for peace," with Israel giving back the territory occupied since 1967. By the Oslo Accords of 1993, Israel recognized the PLO as representative of the Palestinian people and agreed to the first steps for Palestinian self-government in the occupied territories. The PLO recognized Israel's legitimate existence as a sovereign state and agreed to renounce acts of violence.

1995

JOSEPH ROTBLAT (1908—), Great Britain: *A leading nuclear physicist; worked on the first atomic bomb project; a Ph.D. in physics, when retiring in 1976 he was acclaimed in the* London Times *as "a world authority on radiation"—Director of research for leading universities; co-founder and president of Pugwash Conferences on Science and World Affairs.*

Rotblat wrote over twenty books on the hazards of radiation, the consequences of nuclear war, and the social responsibility of scientists. He stressed that unless there is a change in the continuing philosophy of nuclear states keeping nuclear warheads as a hedge against unspecified dangers, there will not be a reduction of nuclear arsenals to zero for a very long time, if ever. He described the official U.S. nuclear posture as "Post-Cold War environment requires nuclear deterrence"—a national policy that will keep the world hostage to the inevitable danger of nuclear destruction.

"There is no direct evidence that nuclear weapons prevented a world war. Conversely, it is known that they nearly caused one. . . . the Cuban Missile Crisis

[1962] all hung on the decision of one man, Nikita Krushchev: would he or would he not yield to the U.S. ultimatum? This is the reality of nuclear weapons; they may trigger a world war, a war which, unlike previous ones, destroys all of civilization." Joseph Rotblat

"*I call on all scientists in all countries to cease and desist from work creating, developing, improving, and manufacturing further nuclear weapons—and, for that matter, other weapons of potential mass destruction such as chemical and biological weapons.*"

Professor Hans Bethe, Nobel Science Laureate—statement issued on the fiftieth anniversary of Hiroshima

1995

PUGWASH CONFERENCES ON SCIENCE AND WORLD AFFAIRS: *A group of leading world scientists attended the founding conference in 1957 at Pugwash, Nova Scotia, financed by Cyrus Eaton, born at Pugwash, and a leading U.S. industrialist. The Conference advocates the elimination of nuclear arms and other weapons of mass destruction. Rotblat was Chief Executive Officer of Pugwash Conferences for seventeen years.*

It was forty years since the Bertrand Russell-Albert Einstein Manifesto that new ways must be found to avoid wars, and to eliminate nuclear arms. The first Pugwash Conference issued a clear manifesto on the independent social and moral responsibility of scientists to refuse to develop weapons of mass destruction. Following up this conference, the Pugwash movement made significant contributions to the change of mentality that was essential to nuclear disarmament. During the Cold War, Pugwash Conferences provided an important channel of communication with the U.S.S.R. Methods of verification first discussed at Pugwash produced technical ideas that helped lead to the Partial Test Ban Treaty of 1963.[5]

Subsequent Pugwash Conferences have continued to address many serious dangers to peace:

- tens of thousands of nuclear weapons were still deployed, in U.S. and Russia, but also in undeclared nuclear weapon states;
- the U.S. and Russia failed to ratify continuing key agreements to reduce nuclear arms;

- increasing nuclear, chemical, and biological weapons were developed in more and more nations;
- stocks of surplus nuclear and chemical weapons were not being reduced and dismantled under safe controls;
- local armed conflicts increased the killing of soldiers and civilians alike, including widespread crimes of genocide;
- large populations endured poverty, environmental degradation and economic despair, as populations increased.

"Over 200 Pugwash conferences have now been held, broadened in personnel and in agenda. Social scientists and other scholars as well as public figures have joined the discussions, as have representatives from the less developed regions. The elimination of all nuclear weapons has remained a more distant goal, while attention has turned to practical methods of halting the arms race, and to problems of chemical and bacteriological warfare, economic development, and preservation of the environment. "[6]

1996

CARLOS BELO (1948—), East Timor: *Fought for the rights of the people during the 1975 invasion, occupation, and oppression by Indonesia; Bishop of East Timor and foremost representative of efforts to protect his people and secure a just settlement based on their right to self-determination.*

Bishop Belo and his Catholic Church have made all possible efforts for over twenty-five years to support his people, standing fast to secure their freedom and human rights.

"We declare that one's value and dignity does not depend on the individual's belief, religion, politics, philosophy, race, or color of skin . . . . What the people want is peace, an end to violence, and respect for their human rights." Carlos Belo

1996

JOSÉ RAMOS-HORTA (1949—), East Timor: *International representative of East Timor independence movement; Minister of External Relations of first provisional government of East Timor in 1975; from exile a leader in challenging the invasion and in developing a peace plan; East Timor representative to the UN; university lecturer in Australia.*

In his Laureate lecture he gave a heart-felt tribute to Bishop Belo— "The people of East Timor owe almost everything to their church."

Ramos-Horta's vision for the future is an independent East Timor with fraternal relations to Australia and all the countries of South East Asia.

"Our society will not be based on revenge. Indonesians now living in East Timor will be invited to stay on. A voluntary resettlement plan will be effected to allow many tens of thousands of displaced East Timorese to return to their ancestral lands.

"East Timor is a classic study of power versus principle, of morality versus expediency, in international relations."

"By awarding this prize, we hope to contribute to a diplomatic solution to the conflict in East Timor," declared Chairman Francis Sejersted of the Norwegian Nobel Committee. "Of a population of between six and seven hundred thousand, nearly two hundred thousand have died as a direct or indirect result of the Indonesian occupation. And the violations [of human rights] are still taking place." Sejersted called this "an exceptionally brutal form of neo-colonialism" and said that "considerations of *Realpolitik* had enabled it to take place." Irwin Abrams wrote that in December 1975, U.S. President Ford and Secretary of State Kissinger reassured President Suharto of Indonesia that the Vietnam defeat would not alter U.S. Cold War policy to maintain a strong presence in the area. Suharto persuaded his guests that a newly independent East Timor must be prevented from becoming a communist "Cuba." The day after his guests left Jakarta, Indonesian armed forces moved against East Timor, slaughtering defenceless civilians with weapons which had been supplied by the U.S. on condition that they were to be used only in self-defense.

Irwin Abrams brought the tragic history of East Timor up to date.[7] In 1998 Suharto resigned, and in 1999 the next government agreed on a UN referendum for the East Timorese to decide whether they wanted independence or to remain with Indonesia—78.5% voted for independence. Then pro-Indonesian paramilitary forces . . . went on a spree of uncontrolled terrorism, killing, raping, and forcing thousands of refugees to flee. The UN brokered a ceasefire in 1999, sent in a peacekeeping mission, and administered East Timor's transition period, preparing it for elections and full independence.

(The first free election in East Timor was held in 2002, under UN administration and supervision. The turnout was estimated at over ninety per cent, a strong vote in favor of a free and democratic East Timor. The UN will provide help in setting up the new state.)

1997

JODY WILLIAMS (1950—), United States: *Founding co-ordinator of the International Campaign to Ban Landmines (ICBL); ICBL International Ambassador; chief strategist and organizing officer of over 1,000 volunteer organizations affiliated with the ICBL and working together in over sixty countries.*

1997

INTERNATIONAL CAMPAIGN TO BAN LANDMINES (ICBL): *Launched by six non-governmental organizations in 1992.*

A joint award was given to Jody Williams and the ICBL for their work for the banning and clearing of landmines. It was estimated that in 1997 there were over one hundred million landmines contaminating approximately seventy countries. Such mines maim and kill indiscriminately and are a major threat to the civilian populations whose social and economic development cannot progress in areas too dangerous to farm or to utilize for small local industry or infrastructure.

The first group to urge a ban on landmines was the International Committee of the Red Cross. In 1980, an ineffective Landmine Protocol was added to the Conventional Weapons Convention of the UN Disarmament Conference. There was very little progress with humanitarian organizations at work in removing mines, and in victim rehabilitation. New landmines continued to be used in wars.

In 1991, two humanitarian leaders joined to go after the root cause of the scourge of the anti-personnel landmine—Bobby Muller, founder of the Vietnam Veterans of America Foundation, and Thomas

Gebauer, founder of the Medico International of Germany. Jody Williams had co-ordinated a number of projects in education and medical aid to the poor in Central America. In 1991, she was appointed co-ordinator of six humanitarian groups which called for an end to the use, production, trade, and stockpiling of landmines, and for help from governments to provide more resources for humanitarian mine clearing and victim assistance. Soon groups from Sweden, Afghanistan, Cambodia, South Africa, and Kenya were added.

Support of governments was sought at the UN Disarmament Conference in 1996, but U.S. President Clinton withdrew his support given in 1994 and 1996, on pressure from the Pentagon, claiming that landmines were needed to protect its 36,000 troops in South Korea. The U.S. withdrew from an Oslo, Norway, Conference in 1997 to ban landmines, where eighty-nine countries had negotiated the draft of the first Ban Landmines Treaty. Later that year, 121 countries came to Ottawa, Canada, and many signed the treaty. Canada's Foreign Minister, Lloyd Axworthy, challenged all other governments to sign and ratify the treaty. By early 2002, the treaty was entered into force when over sixty countries had ratified the treaty. The enormous task of ending the production and sale of landmines, destroying existing landmines, and providing aid and support to the victims of landmines had begun.

Soon new members of the co-ordinating committee of the ICBL came from Japan, Columbia, Inter-African Union, the Landmines Survivors Network, the Lutheran World Federation, and the Norwegian People's Aid. By 2002, all the NATO states had joined, except for the U.S. and Turkey. This achievement shows the power of public opinion and activist volunteer organizations worldwide to mount a major peaceful humanitarian appeal. The ICBL treaty negotiations were historic, as stated by Jody Williams in her Peace Prize acceptance lecture.

"It proves that civil society and governments do not have to see themselves as adversaries. It demonstrates that small and middle powers can work together with civil society and address humanitarian concerns with breathtaking speed. It shows that such a partnership is a new kind of "superpower" in the post-Cold War world . . . . It is recognition of the fact that NGOs have worked in close co-operation with governments for the first time on an arms control issue, with the

United Nations, with the International Committee of the Red Cross . . . . This is historic because, for the first time, the leaders of states have come together to answer the will of civil society . . . together we have given the world the possibility of one day living on a truly mine-free planet. " Jody Williams

Professor Francis Sejersted, on the occasion in 1997 of the award of the Peace Prize to the ICBL and Jody Williams, stressed the lessons learned from the international campaign to ban landmines.

"It is interesting to watch this [Ottawa, October 1997] initiative apparently feeding back into the UN and the whole system of international negotiations, and giving them new life. Effective political action is dependent on co-operation of several levels . . . . Representative political bodies cannot carry on politics in a vacuum. They need in some way or other to be rooted in public opinion. And public opinion must be formed and directed by the active involvement of individual members of society in society's manifold organizations or associations. These are the fundamental institutional elements of what we have learned to know as—a civil society.

"The problem at the international level is that no global civil society has existed. Perhaps it is not so surprising that the UN has not always been able to be as effective as we might have wished. But in the extensive co-operation we have been registering between the multitude of non-governmental organizations, the many national governments, and the international political system, first and foremost the UN, we may be seeing the outline of what may turn into a global civil society . . . . We see promising signs of a more peaceful world . . . . An important step has been taken. The vast problem of landmines has effectively been placed on the international agenda. The worldwide opinion has been formed that something must be done about the problem. And the practical work of freeing the world from landmines has begun." Francis Sejersted, Retired Chairman, Norwegian Nobel Committee

1998

JOHN HUME (1937—), Northern Ireland: *Leader of the Social Democratic and Labour Party (SDLP) of the Catholic minority, a leading party committed to reconciliation and non-violence.*

1998

DAVID TRIMBLE (1944—), Northern Ireland: *Lawyer; leader of Northern Ireland's largest party, the Ulster Unionist Party (UUP); Member of Parliament; First Minister, Northern Ireland Assembly; shared the 1998 Nobel Peace Prize equally with John Hume; Trimble's Ulster Unionists were Protestant Loyalists, strongly attached to Northern Ireland, a part of the United Kingdom.*

JOHN HUME, head of the SDLP since 1979, and David Trimble drafted and signed the Good Friday Agreement of 1998. It was voted for by overwhelming numbers from both North and South. Hume has a distinguished record of awards and honorary doctorates for work in human rights, peace negotiations, the Northern Ireland Assembly, and the European Parliament.

"European Union is the best example in the history of the world of conflict resolution . . . . All conflict is about differences, whether the difference is race, religion, or nationality. The European visionaries decided that difference is not a threat; difference is natural and the essence of humanity. Difference is an accident of birth and it should therefore never be the source of hatred or conflict. The answer to difference is to respect it. Therein lies a most fundamental principle of peace—respect for diversity.

"We are two neighboring islands whose destiny is to live in friendship and amity with each other.

"Bloodshed for political change prevents the only change that truly matters: in the human heart." John Hume

Hume concluded with "a quotation of total hope," the words of Martin Luther King Jr., his great hero: "We shall overcome."

DAVID TRIMBLE entered politics in 1975. In 1998 he was elected First Minister (Designate) in the new Northern Ireland Assembly, responsible for implementing the Good Friday Agreement. The leading mediator, U.S. Senator George Mitchell, said, "Without Mr. Hume, there would have been no peace process, without Mr. Trimble, no agreement."

Trimble and his party were insistent that the Irish Republican Army would have to start decommissioning illegally-held weapons in the possession of paramilitary groups before Sinn Fein is included in the executive of the Assembly. He is a believer in the practical politics of the possible, and that each reformist group has a moral obligation to deal with its own fanatics. "In Northern Ireland constitutional nationalists must take on Republican dissident terrorists, and constitutional Unionists must confront Protestant terrorists." He said, " . . . . all that I have asked for is that they say that the 'war is over'."

"What we democratic politicians want in Northern Ireland is not some Utopian society but a normal society. The best way to secure that normalcy is the tried and trusted method of parliamentary democracy.

"None of us are entirely innocent. But, thanks to our strong sense of civil society, thanks to our religious recognition that none of us are perfect, thanks to the thousands of people on both sides who made countless acts of good authority, thanks to a tradition of parliamentary democracy which meant that paramilitarism never displaced politics, thanks to all these specific, concrete circumstances we, thank God, stopped short of that abyss that engulfed Bosnia, Kosovo, Somalia, and Rwanda." David Trimble

1999

DOCTORS WITHOUT BORDERS/MÉDICINS SANS FRONTIÈRES

(MSF): *An international relief organization dedicated to providing medical aid to populations who are in danger, victims of civil warfare, disease, or natural disasters; headquartered in Brussels; awarded the Nobel Peace Prize in recognition of its humanitarian work on several continents.*

The organization was founded in 1971 by a group of French doctors formed under the leadership of Dr. Bernard Kouchner, who were frustrated with the complications of international relief efforts. The group sends medical personnel, medical supplies, food, fresh water, and other necessities to regions where people are at risk. MSF is a private, non-profit organization that arranges medical relief in more than fifty countries each year.

MSF adheres to the fundamental principle that all disaster victims have a right to medical aid and humanitarian assistance, and to human rights. Its policy is always to give aid first to the most vulnerable, which is often not the state policy. National boundaries and politics must have no influence on who is to receive help. By intervening rapidly and maintaining impartiality, MSF calls attention to human catastrophes, and helps to form bodies of public opinion opposed to killings and oppression. "Advocacy and witnessing," they say, "are integral to our humanitarian mission." The doctors often put their own lives at risk in areas of massacres and lawlessness. Every year MSF sends out over 2,500 doctors, nurses, and other professionals to countries in need of medical assistance, where they co-operate with more than 15,000 local helpers. It is the world's largest medical relief agency. They go wherever need is greatest—often to massacres such as Rwanda in 1993-1995, or to a great flood in Bangladesh. They reserve the right to intervene, irrespective of prior political approval. They demand freedom to carry out their mission. To keep their independence, MSF has insisted half their revenues must come from private donors.

The changed nature of war has necessitated more humanitarian assistance for armed casualties and for civilians. Some brutal regimes deliberately drive out refugees and attempt to exploit MSF aid resources. In the case of Rwanda, MSF had to appeal to world opinion for military intervention to stop the brutality, but the UN was not able to persuade the main powers to send in military intervention until it was too late. In some cases, such as Bosnia, and Somalia, inadequate military intervention increased the risk to MSF workers.

The President of MSF, James Orbinski, during his acceptance lecture of the Peace Prize said, *"I appeal to the Russian government to stop the bombing of civilians in Chechnya . . . . If conflicts and wars are an affair of state, violations of humanitarian law, war crimes, and crimes against humanity apply to all of us."*

Orbinski alerted public opinion to the struggles of all oppressed, street children, and illegal refugees, saying, *"We speak not into the wind, but with a clear intent to assist, to provoke change, to reveal injustice.*

"The framework of state responsibility is today clearly dysfunctional . . . access to victims of conflict is often refused . . . humanitarian assistance is even used as a tool of war by belligerents . . . . We are seeing the militarization of humanitarian action by the international community.

"MSF is a civil society organization, and today civil society has a new global role, a new informal legitimacy that is rooted in its action and in its support from public opinion. It is also rooted in the maturity of its intent, in for example the

human rights, the environmental and the humanitarian movements, and, of course, the movement for equitable trade. Conflict and violence are not the only subjects of concern. We, as members of civil society, will maintain our role and our power if we remain lucid in our intent and independence.

"Today, a growing injustice confronts us. More than 90 percent of all death and suffering from infectious diseases occurs in the developing world. Some of the reasons that people die from diseases like AIDS, TB, sleeping sickness, and other tropical diseases is that life-saving essential medicines are either too expensive, are not available . . . or because there is virtually no new research and development for priority tropical diseases. This market failure is our next challenge . . . for governments, International Government Institutions, the pharmaceutical industry and other NGOs to confront this injustice. What we as a civil society movement demand is change, not charity.

"The UN Charter obliges states to intervene sometimes by force to stop threats to the international peace and security . . . in Rwanda, MSF spoke out to the world to demand that the genocide be stopped by use of force. And, so did the Red Cross. It was, however, a cry that met with institutional paralysis . . . the genocide was over before UN Operation Turquoise was launched.

"Srebrenica was apparently a safe haven in which we were present. The Blue Helmets were there, but the Security Council refused to support the Blue Helmets or to provide armed military intervention as the people of Srebrenica were massacred . . . . There must be a reform of peacekeeping operations in the UN. Member states of the Security Council must be held publicly accountable for the decisions that they do or do not vote for. Their right to veto should be regulated. Member states should be bound to ensure that adequate means are made available to implement the decisions they take.

"We want to thank the Nobel Committee for its affirmation of the road MSF has chosen to take: to remain outspoken, passionate, and deeply committed to its core principles of volunteerism, impartiality, and its belief that every person deserves both medical assistance and the recognition of his or her humanity."
James Orbinski

2000

KIM DAE-JUNG (1924—), South Korea: *President of South Korea. The Nobel Peace Prize recognized his lifelong work for democracy and human*

rights in South Korea and in East Asia, and for his great personal and political
courage in reaching out to North Korea for peace and reconciliation.

Kim Dae-jung entered politics in the 1950s and was first elected
in 1960, despite opposition of the police regime of a military
dictatorship. When he won forty-six percent in a presidential election
he was held in prison for many years, then house arrest and exile to
Japan and the U.S. He faced many kidnapping and assassination
attempts. Dae-jung was elected President in 1997 in a democratic
revolution. His early reforms stressed forgiveness and reconciliation,
reform of the legal system, rights of organized labor, human rights,
and support for the oppressed people of East Timor and Myanmar.

Kim Dae-jung pursued an active program of co-operation with
North Korea, called his "sunshine policy," going there in 2000 for a
historic meeting with Chairman Kim Jong-il. After very difficult talks,
it was agreed that unification must be achieved independently and
peacefully, a pre-unification stage of a confederation of "one people,
two systems, two independent governments," and that the presence
of U.S. military forces would continue for the stability of the Korean
peninsula and Northeast Asia.

The humanitarian issue of the separated families was promptly
addressed, economic co-operation was planned, and 500,000 tons of
food and 300,000 tons of fertilizer were sent as aid to North Korea.
Kim Dae-jung worked for democracy as the absolute value that makes
for human dignity and as the only road to sustained economic
development and social justice. He believed "without democracy the
market economy cannot blossom," and without market economies,
economic competitiveness and growth cannot be achieved. A further
basic mission was a system of productive welfare for low-income classes.

He warned of the hugely-growing wealth gaps between and within
countries as a serious threat to human rights and peace. He is deeply
religious, believing that God and Jesus Christ are always with him,
and have continued to save his life despite death threats and
imprisonment.

Kim Dae-jung made a moving comment in his Peace Prize
presentation lecture to the Norwegian Nobel Committee:

"A national economy lacking a democratic foundation is a castle built on
sand. Therefore, as President of the Republic of Korea, I have made the parallel

development of democracy and market economics, supplemented with a system of productive welfare, the basic mission of my government.

"Allow me to say a few words on a personal note. Five times I faced near death at the hands of dictators, six years I spent in prison, and forty years I lived under house arrest or in exile and under constant surveillance. I could not have endured the hardship without the support of my people and the encouragement of fellow democrats around the world. The strength also came from deep personal beliefs.

"Another faith is my belief in the justice of history. In 1980, I was sentenced to death by the military regime. For six months in prison, I awaited the execution day. Often, I shuddered with fear of death. But I would find calm in the fact of history that justice ultimately prevails. I was then, and am still, an avid reader of history. And I knew that in all ages, in all places, he who lives a righteous life dedicated to his people and humanity may not be victorious, may meet a gruesome end in his lifetime, but will be triumphant and honoured in history; he who wins by injustice may dominate the present day, but history will always judge him to be a shameful loser. There can be no exception." Kim Dae-jung

2001

UNITED NATIONS, KOFI ANNAN (1938—), Ghana: *Secretary-General of the UN; university education in Ghana and Minnesota, a degree in economics, followed by post-graduate work at the Institut des Hautes Études Internationales in Geneva and an M.A. in Management at the Massachusetts Institute of Technology. He joined the UN in 1962 with the World Health Organization in Geneva, and has devoted almost his entire working life to the UN.*

For one hundred years the Norwegian Nobel Committee has sought to strengthen organized co-operation between states. The end of the Cold War has at last made it possible for the UN to perform more fully the part it was originally intended to play. Today the UN is at the forefront of work to mobilize nations to co-operate in building world peace.

Kofi Annan has been pre-eminent in "bringing new life to the UN." While clearly underlining the UN's traditional responsibility for peace, security, and human rights, he has worked to meet new challenges such as HIV/AIDS and international terrorism, and has brought about more efficient utilization of the UN's limited resources. In an organization that cannot become more than its members permit,

Annan has worked to ameliorate the problems of member states using their sovereignty as a shield behind which to conceal their failures to co-operate in causes for peace and humanity which require commitments for international security at the expense of national sovereignty.

The Norwegian Nobel Committee gave Kofi Annan and the UN a shared 2001 Peace Prize, saying that it wished, in its centenary year "to proclaim that the only negotiable route to global peace and co-operation goes by way of the United Nations."

Chapter 8—United Nations, World Peacemaker—addresses the highlights of the UN. In view of the importance of readers having an understanding of the recent thinking of the Norwegian Nobel Committee and of Kofi Annan, Appendix D presents the speech of Gunnar Berge, Chairman of the Norwegian Nobel Committee, and the lecture of Kofi Annan, Peace Laureate, on the occasion of the 2001 award ceremony in Oslo.

"From [our] vision of the role of the United Nations flows three key priorities for the future: eradicating poverty, preventing conflict, and promoting democracy. Only in a world that is rid of poverty can all men and women make the most of their abilities. Only where individual rights are respected can differences be channelled politically and resolved peacefully. Only in a democratic environment, based on respect for diversity and dialogue, can individual self-expression and self-government be secured, and freedom of association be upheld.

"Peace must be sought, above all, because it is the condition for every member of the human family to live a life of dignity and security.

"This era of global challenges leaves no choice but co-operation at the global level. When states undermine the rule of law and violate the rights of their individual citizens, they become a menace not only to their own people, but also to their neighbors, and indeed the world. What we need today is better governance—legitimate, democratic government that allows each individual to flourish, and each state to thrive." Kofi Annan

Gunnar Berge, Chairman of the Norwegian Nobel Committee, said at the 2001 Peace Prize presentation ceremony:

"The UN's Millenium Declaration . . . [has] an ambitious agenda: to put an end to poverty, to provide better education for the world's billions of people, to reduce HIV/AIDS, to protect the environment, and to prevent war and armed conflict.

"The strong position of democracy today gives grounds for optimism. But much remains to be done, not least in the economic field. We have made very few advances in solidarity between countries that are growing ever richer, and the many countries and individuals who either are not benefiting to the same extent from globalization or are even suffering from its economic and social consequences. The number of poor people in the world is ever-increasing.

"As globalization expands, the question will be asked even more loudly than at present of who is to manage this development and by what means. In the view of the [Norwegian] Nobel Committee, that will be the task of the UN . . . as the more efficient global instrument which the world so sorely needs." Gunnar Berge

2002

JIMMY CARTER (1924—), United States: *President of the U.S. (1978 to 1982). His presidency was notable for the Panama Canal Treaty, and the Camp David Accords (1978) which he brokered between Anwar Sadat of Egypt and Menachem Begin of Israel. An active human rights campaigner, he has been a leader of international observer teams, has hosted peace negotiations in Ethiopia, and was a UN ambassador to Rwanda in 1996.*

The Norwegian Nobel Committee awarded Jimmy Carter the peace prize "for his decades of untiring effort to find peaceful solutions to international conflicts, to advance democracy and human rights, and to promote economic and social development."

"I was asked to discuss, here in Oslo, the greatest challenge that the world faces. Among all the possible choices, I decided that the most universal problem is the growing chasm between the richest and the poorest people on earth . . . the separation is increasing every year, not only between nations but also within them. The results of this disparity are root causes of most of the world's unresolved problems, including starvation, illiteracy, environmental degradation, violent conflict, and unnecessary illnesses that range from Guinea worm to HIV/AIDS.

"War may sometimes be a necessary evil. But no matter how necessary, it is

always an evil, never a good. We will not learn how to live together in peace by killing each other's children.

"*Tragically, in the industrialized world there is a terrible absence of understanding or concern about those who are enduring lives of despair and hopelessness. We have not yet made the commitment to share with others an appreciable part of our excessive wealth. This is a potentially rewarding burden that we should all be willing to assume.*" Jimmy Carter

"A good German cannot be a nationalist . . . He knows that he cannot be other than a good European . . . My country is no longer a great power and can never be one again but we are an economic and scientific power . . . prepared to work together with other nations."

Willy Brandt (1971)
Chancellor, The Federal Republic of Germany

Chapter 4

THE LAUREATES' LEGACY OF PEACEMAKING

Chapter 3 presented the lives and guiding principles of all Nobel Peace Laureates, twentieth century leaders in work for world peace. The world needs many different peacemakers: dedicated volunteer workers at the grass roots; leaders and organizers of peace societies and associations; humanitarians reaching out to the destitute; workers for human rights; statesmen and international jurists working to prevent and resolve armed conflicts; leaders working to eliminate nuclear arms and other weapons of mass destruction; and countless volunteers of civil society and workers in non-governmental organizations.

The Peace Laureates may be of any race, nation, creed, or color, world leaders or social workers, educated in universities or in their trade or service. They have advanced the cause of peace among peoples of many countries, serving all mankind without discrimination.

It is of interest to look for the main common influences linking together the lives of the Peace Laureates. They grew up in families devoted to religious and ethical values; to the importance of education and intellectual achievement; to working to realize one's best potential; and to the dedication of making a meaningful contribution to society. The study of the lives of the Peace Laureates shows that a large majority of them made frequent references to their deep religious faith and the importance of this faith throughout their lives.

In addition, there were anonymous religious men and women who were active as leaders of the associations and organizations that won the Peace Prize. Irwin Abram's book, *The Words of Peace*, emphasizes that the work of all the Laureates in organizing peace movements, in humanitarian work, in political leadership, and in advancing human rights is not of itself enough. Nobel's "fraternity between nations," the spirit of human brotherhood, must undergird any political or social structure of peacemaking if it is to last. Archbishop Söderblom (1930) referred to this spirit as the "soul" of such a structure; Albert Schweitzer (1952) spoke of it as "the ethical spirit." The common factor in their lives was that "they were all men and women of great faith." They were thinkers and philosophers as well as working activists dissatisfied with the status quo, pioneering new peacemaking processes, reaching to fulfil the deepest desire of all peoples for "peace on earth and goodwill to all mankind." From the first to the most recent Laureates, the concept of peace was not only the prevention and stopping of armed violence, but also the ensuring of universal human rights enabling mankind to live with safety, justice, equality, fraternity, equal opportunity, and free of discrimination, fear, and want. Many worked to provide humanitarian help wherever needed.

The essential interconnection of the many building blocks of peace was made from the first Laureate, Henri Dunant (1901) to the most recent, Jimmy Carter (2002), former President of the U.S. It is the "one world, one peoples" concept of peace expressed by Ralph Bunche (1950)—"Peace is no mere matter of men fighting or not fighting. Peace, to have meaning for many who have known only suffering in both peace and war, must be translated into bread or rice, shelter, health, and education, as well as freedom and human dignity— a steadily better life. If peace is to be secure, long-suffering and long-starved forgotten peoples of the world, the underprivileged and the undernourished, must begin to realize without delay the promise of a new day and a new life." Unfortunately, mankind has delayed giving full support to Ralph Bunche's invocation, for another fifty years.

It is important to compare the similarity in the motivation of the Peace Laureates, most of whom had not met one another. They were

initiators and self-starters, unwilling to wait for solutions coming down
from authorities on top, skillful achievers of their various missions for
peace, and totally committed to a lifetime of service. They had a
common philosophy expressed best by Albert Schweitzer (1952)—
see Appendix E. "Peace starts with the ethical character of man . . .
taking root in compassion for mankind and in reverence for life . . .
the ethical spirit alone has the power to generate a prevailing spirit
directed toward peace . . . . It abides within them like tinder waiting
to be lit, waiting only for a spark . . . the human spirit is capable of
creating in our time a new mentality, an ethical mentality . . . . Only
when an ideal of peace is born in the minds of the peoples will the
institutions set up to maintain this peace effectively fulfil the functions
expected of them." The *mission* of peacemakers is summed up by Albert
Schweitzer—"to build peace based on fraternity, the unity of mankind."

The Peace Laureates followed a new mentality of rejecting war for
an ethical reason—that war makes us guilty of the crime of inhumanity.
They followed the guidance of this ethical spirit, as illustrated by the
life of Nelson Mandela (1993) who believed that "a person who
witnessed an injustice becomes responsible for it. He must then
decide whether to act against the injustice or to let it continue." The
Peace Laureates made the choice to act against injustice as a matter of
personal conscience.

In the years before the First World War the decisions about war
and peace had been made mainly by the governments or rulers of the
nation-states. The leading powers of Europe, entangled in futile
alliances, stumbled inexorably toward war. During the last half of the
1800s, many peacemaking groups and writers had organized to protest
the follies of war. They were called the "Peace Movement," but
unfortunately they did not have the popular support of the masses.
Their first political success resulted from the International Peace
Conference at The Hague in 1899, which gave worldwide recognition
of the principle of settling conflicts between states through
negotiation and arbitration, and established the Permanent Court of
Arbitration at The Hague.

A brief outline of the work of each Laureate was shown in Chapter
3. It will now be of interest to present a broad overview of the major

trends influencing the selection of Laureates by the Norwegian Nobel Committee, themes that reflect a widening emphasis on all aspects of peacemaking. Only a few Laureates will be identified with each theme, to exemplify their special contribution to peacemaking and the wide scope of their work.

Nobel's will stated his conviction that there was an urgent need for action to build world peace based on "fraternity between nations." He placed responsibility for disarmament clearly on statesmen and political leaders, and on the leadership of dedicated peacemakers to hold and promote peace congresses. He clearly did not intend to limit the search for peace to these two areas. He had stated an idea, leaving it to others in whom he had confidence to execute it. This approach encouraged the Norwegian Nobel Committee to consider it their duty to watch for *all* developments that had a potential for advancing the cause of peace.

The largest category of Peace Prize winners included thirty-seven statesmen and political leaders. (See Appendix C, Table 1 for a summary of Peace Prizes by category.) They showed outstanding courage to become leaders in peacemaking when popular opinion was often against them. Leaders such as Woodrow Wilson (1919), Willy Brandt (1971), Anwar Sadat (1978), Lech Walesa (1983), Mikhail Gorbachev (1990), Nelson Mandela (1993), Yitzhak Rabin (1994), and Kim Dae-jung (2000), put their political and physical lives at risk to lead their countrymen in new efforts for peace and international understanding.

The Norwegian Nobel Committee gave increasing support to encouraging an ongoing political process, such as the achievement by Arias Sánchez (1987) of the declaration of Costa Rica to be a military-free nation. He gave the leadership to achieve the signing of the Central America peace plan whereby El Salvador, Guatemala, Nicaragua, Honduras, and Costa Rica agreed to end wars between their countries.

The earliest years of the Peace Prize emphasized the organized peace movement whose primary efforts were directed to influencing public opinion in favor of peace through their societies, writings, and public lectures, and to pressuring governments to follow peaceful policies. The organized peace movement has grown steadily, until today the Peace Laureates represent a wide area of work for many causes of highest priority for world peace. They have been leaders in building campaigns up from the grass roots, achieving worldwide success in influencing governments. The following group of many growing and successful peace movements represents the best work of activist volunteers of civil society: Amnesty International (1977); International Physicians for the Prevention of Nuclear War (1985); International Campaign to Ban Landmines (1997), and its International Ambassador, Jody Williams (1997). All showed the difference that sacrifice and struggle by one or two persons along with grass roots helpers can make to the peacemaking process.

Twenty-three Peace Laureates represent the humanitarian movement. The connection between peace and humanitarianism was recognized right from the beginning. Henri Dunant (1901) won the Peace Prize for his dedication to the humanity of all people as founder of the Red Cross Society. Later peace awards to the English and American Quakers (1947), Mother Teresa (1979), and Doctors Without Borders (1999), paid tribute to leaders who dedicated their lives to helping the poorest and dispossessed of humanity.

The most significant trend of emphasis by the Norwegian Nobel Committee is the conviction that human rights and humanitarianism are integral parts of peacemaking. Human rights have been a basic concern of Peace Laureates, including outstanding peacemakers such as: Martin Luther King, Jr. (1964), Pérez Esquivel (1980), Aung San Suu Kyi (1991), Rigoberta Menchú Tum (1992), Carlos Belo and José Ramos-Horta (1996).

Fridtjof Nansen (1922) of Norway organized the repatriation of over 500,000 prisoners of war and a million and a half refugees during the ten years after the First World War. The relocation of refugees received three more peace prizes—the Nansen International Office for Refugees in 1938, and the UN Office for Refugees in 1954 and in 1981. There is a greater need for aid for refugees every year, due to the increasing level of armed violence and crimes against humanity, and a corresponding greater need for peacemakers with Fridtjof Nansen's dedication to peacemaking.

President Woodrow Wilson (1919) is an outstanding example of the leadership of statesmen in the cause of peace. He advocated a conciliatory peace with Germany, which if adopted could possibly have prevented the tragic rise to power of Hitler, and the Second World War. Without Wilson there would not have been a League of Nations, the first effort of the world to establish an international organization of governments dedicated to solving their problems peacefully. The subsequent failure of the U.S. to join the League of Nations, the resurgence of virulent and destructive state sovereignty, and the failure at Versailles of the victors to give the League any power to carry out its mandate sealed the inevitable failure of the League.

Cordell Hull (1945), U.S. Secretary of State for twelve years, was called the "father of the United Nations." He laid the foundations for the "good neighbor policy" among the North and South American countries. He wore himself out working on the planning and implementing of the UN, from 1940 to his death in 1955.

Lord Boyd Orr (1949) was the first scientist to win the Peace Prize, not for his scientific discoveries, but for the way they were employed to promote co-operation between nations. He was the first director-general of the Food and Agriculture Organization (FAO) of the UN, and found nations willing to discuss for the first time a movement to provide the foundation of peace by increased food production for the people of the world.

Martin Luther King, Jr. (1964) led the civil rights movement in the U.S. from 1955 until his assassination in 1968. He was committed to achieving freedom, justice, and human rights based on non-violence, saying, "Our actions must be guided by the deepest principles of the Christian faith, injecting new meaning and dignity into the veins of civilization."

The work of R. Cassin (1968) led to the UN Declaration of Human Rights in 1948. In Cassin's words—"It is the first document of an ethical sort that organized humanity has ever adopted . . . . It proclaims as principles the whole body of rights and options without whose exercise man cannot fully realize his physical, moral, and intellectual individuality . . . it applies to all human beings without any discrimination whatever."

D. Hammarskjöld (1961), Secretary-General of the UN, developed the first major response to the need for a UN international peacekeeping force. UN troops had been used earlier to establish buffer zones between warring parties, and after 1956 were deployed equipped with light arms for self-defence. On accepting the Peace Prize to UN Peacekeeping Forces in 1988, UN Secretary-General de Cuellar said, "Peacekeeping uses soldiers as servants of peace rather than as instruments of war. It introduces to the military sphere the principle of non-violence."

Progress was made in the process of conciliation in Europe by initiatives of Willy Brandt (1971). The Cold War was gradually disappearing as a spirit of détente developed between the U.S. and the U.S.S.R.

A large group of Laureates was part of sweeping political and social changes, achieving major peacemaking advances by indomitable faith and courage. Mandela (1993) deserves special mention as a peacemaker who was able to lead his people forward with the banners of faith, hope, and forgiveness to a new land of democracy and human rights, stopping short of the feared revenge and bloodshed.

Despite all the disarmament talks, the active resistance of civil society to nuclear weapons, and agreements of the nuclear powers to reduce nuclear weapons, the world is still sitting on a powder keg that could explode at the press of a button and destroy every living thing on earth. Thousands of organizations of civil society were working to eliminate nuclear weapons. Peace Laureates who led the movement against nuclear arms include Schweitzer (1952), Pauling (1962), Sakharov (1975), Myrdal (1982), International Physicians for the Prevention of Nuclear War (1985), Rotblat, and the Pugwash Conferences on Science and World Affairs (1995).

The speech of Gunnar Berge, Chairman of the Norwegian Nobel Committee, in Oslo on December 10, 2001 (see Appendix D), gives an important assessment of the role of the UN as the international organization that is even more essential today than ever before. He stressed the truth that mankind has common interests which are being increasingly demonstrated in this age of globalization, and that this should find expression in some form or other of shared government.

The main mission of the Norwegian Nobel Committee is to strengthen international co-operation between states. The history of the Committee emphasizes the theme of hope for a better organized and more peaceful world. Chairman Berge stressed that "nothing symbolizes that hope, or represents that reality, better than the United Nations."

The Norwegian Nobel Committee has been encouraged to see the many successes of the UN in humanitarian and social fields, and since 1945 thirteen of the Peace Prizes have had links to the UN. The present Secretary-General, Kofi Annan, has been vigorous in efforts to resolve a whole series of international disputes: the repercussions of the Gulf War; the wars in the former Yugoslavia and especially in Kosovo; the status of East Timor; the war in the Congo; and the implementation of the UN resolutions concerning the Middle East and the Israeli and Palestinian war.

Since 1960, the Committee has given increasing awards to peacemakers in the field of human rights. Much more needs to be done to influence states to support the International Declaration of Human Rights, and to cease human rights abuses.

The inability of the UN to get support from the Security Council for early intervention to prevent armed conflict within states and to use international military force to secure a cease fire is a major factor in the escalation of wars in recent years. This will be addressed in Chapter 8 on the UN.

The question may be asked—*what has been accomplished by the Nobel Peace Prize to honor the leading peacemakers of the world, and to enable outstanding peacemakers to continue to work in the cause of peace? The Peace Laureates have been dedicated peacemakers—a few examples of their missions that have been active over the past one hundred years in building the foundations of an enduring world peace are outlined below:*

- The Red Cross;
- International peace societies, too numerous to mention;
- International arbitration and legal jurists, now seeking justice in international criminal courts to prevent future crimes against humanity and ethnic butchery;

- Prime movers to support an international organization for collective security and protection of universal human rights;
- Support for refugees;
- Support for human rights and humanitarian workers for peace;
- Support for non-violent reconciliation of potentially explosive racial and political conflicts;
- Support for the UN, increasingly needed for conflict resolution and human rights reforms;
- Support for elimination of nuclear arms;
- Armament reduction—a major theme in many campaigns of the Laureates;
- Protection of the environment;
- Support for dissidents against oppressive governments.

Irwin Abrams summed up his assessment of the work of the Norwegian Nobel Committee with these words: "What Nobel's will said explicitly was that the Peace Prize, like the others, was to be given to persons who 'shall have conferred the greatest benefit on mankind.' To this highest aim of Alfred Nobel, the Committee has tried to remain faithful throughout its long history, however the circumstances and the thinking of the time may have influenced a particular award, and whatever the criticisms from advocates of different conceptions of peace . . . . That the Committee has largely succeeded in this effort is attested to by the high prestige the Peace Prize enjoys in the world—no other award for service to peace and human brotherhood is ever mentioned in the same breath. Today in the nuclear age, peace has a most urgent meaning. But survival is not the only goal. Again and again in its selections, the Norwegian Committee has emphasized the positive meaning of peace, pointing to the foundations on which a true peace must rest. And through its happiest choices, the Committee has set before us an array of inspiring human beings, who sustain in the rest of us what they themselves had in such abundance, what Martin Luther King, Jr., called 'an audacious faith' in humankind."[1]

"We are like a big fish that has been pulled from the water and is flapping wildly to find its way back in. In such a condition the fish never asks where the next flip or flop will bring it. It senses only that its present position is intolerable and that something else must be tried."

Anonymous Chinese saying, quoted by
Perry Link in *China in Transformation,*
Daedalus, Spring 1993.

"Nationalism of the worst sort was displayed in the last two wars, and it may be regarded today as the greatest obstacle to human understanding between peoples. Such nationalism can be repulsed only through the rebirth of the humanitarian ideal among men which will make their allegiance to their country a natural one inspired by genuine ideals."

Albert Schweitzer (1954).

Chapter 5

OBSTACLES TO PEACE

The root causes of armed conflicts and wars are fundamental and universal—the accumulation of combustible materials of mankind's poverty, ancient enmities, territorial claims, ignorance, lack of human rights and democracy, ethnic rivalries and hatreds, megalomania, and brutish inhumanity. The direct or precipitating causes, such as the invasion of Poland by Hitler in 1939, or the massacre of over 800,000 Tutsis by Hutus in Rwanda in 1994, were the flaming torches thrown into the fuel.

Armed warfare between states can be avoided by the peaceable acceptance of mutually agreed conditions or by peaceful and orderly transformation of conditions by negotiation and agreement. The maintenance of international peace between states after the major wars of the past two centuries depended mainly on the acceptance of signed treaties by the powers involved. But in the 1930s neither Germany, Italy, Japan, or the U.S.S.R. were content with the status quo of global power and with the conditions of the Treaty of Versailles of 1919. Their political goals of more territory, resources, exploited labor, and economic power fed their greed and aggressive actions. They were "revisionist" or dissatisfied powers, and were willing to take huge risks by threatening war and backing up their threats with invasion to achieve desired changes. Great Britain, France, and the U.S. were satisfied powers, expecting no benefit from a change in treaty conditions. From the Japanese invasion of Manchuria in 1931 to the outbreak of the Second World War in 1939, military force was used by those who were willing to upset international order, but avoided by those who wished to maintain it.

Another underlying cause of war in Europe before 1939 was the instability of the international *political process* for preventing wars. There was not enough effort by the major sovereign states to increase overall stability by reconciliation with the states who were dissatisfied with the political settlements of conflicting claims after the collapse of Napoleon's empire, after Bismarck's continuing wars to build a united Germany into the dominant military power in Europe, after the First World War, and after the Yalta and Potsdam "Agreements" following the Second World War. The settlements contained the seeds of future wars, and the diplomatic agreements were more conducive to future wars than to peace.

Following the first and second world wars, the break-up of defeated world empires, such as the Turkish empire, resulted in many new state boundaries being imposed as "arbitrary lines on the map" ignoring ethnic and economic realities, creating millions of refugees and the breeding grounds of hatred, revenge, and in some cases the rising power of dictators. A key element of future peace and prosperity must be the equitable and realistic settlement of issues affecting the viability of states and the welfare of people.

Preceding sections in Chapter 1 reviewed many changes in the nature of warfare. Up to 1945, major warfare was traditionally *between states,* referred to by historian Kalevi Holsti[1] as "wars of a *first kind.*" Strategic doctrines, including the discredited balance of power, arms control agreements, and the structure of international organizations such as NATO and the UN were designed to prevent wars between states. Since 1945, the number of wars between states has been declining, while the number of wars *within single states* has been increasing. The predominance of "total war" between states has largely been replaced during the last decades of the twentieth century by "peoples' wars," or wars of a "third kind," the description used by Holsti. His book, *The State, War, and the State of War,* is the source of much of the reference material summarized here which analyzes the wars that occur between and within states. Wars of a *second kind* were described as state-nation wars which included armed resistance by ethnic, language, and/or religious groups, often with the purpose of secession or separation from the state (e.g. the Tamils in Sri Lanka). Holsti's summary of 164 wars, 1945-1995, excluding anti-colonial wars of national liberation, shows only twenty-three percent were state versus state, the remaining seventy-seven percent were mainly wars of a third kind, split evenly between wars of secession and resistance, and wars due to ideological or factional hatreds. A typical war of the third kind is described by Holsti as very different from state versus state wars: "No single crisis precipitates them . . . . Decisive battles are few. Attrition, terror, psychology, and actions against civilians highlight 'combat' . . . wars are fought by loosely-knit groups of regulars, irregulars, cells, and not infrequently by locally-based warlords under little or no central authority." Wars of the third kind have occurred most frequently in the Middle East, South East Asia, Africa, Central America/Caribbean, the former U.S.S.R., and the Balkans. Many wars since 1945 took the form of "national liberation" or wars of de-colonization to transform a colony into the prototype of a European state.

Eighteenth century philosopher Jean-Jacques Rousseau developed the theory that war is inevitable under the political system prevailing in Western Europe—a system called *anarchy*. Anarchy in this context does not mean chaos. It is the literal Greek meaning of the *lack of stable governance*. States are legally equal and sovereign, and each seeks to maximize the collective benefits and loyalty of its subjects. Where there is good governance it is rational and beneficial to co-operate in international relations. Holsti writes, "Everyone gains through peaceful contact, including trade. If there were less threat of war between states . . . how much more could the developing and industrialized states gain by investing in health, education, . . . rather than in weapons and preparations for war?

Rousseau concluded that the defensive build-up of any individual state inevitably causes distrust among other states. As states cannot rely on others for their own security, they must have the insurance of arms for their own defense. Any aggressive means that states develop for their survival constitute a threat to other states. Competitive arming results. The price of a system of non-co-operating sovereign states is permanent insecurity, an escalating arms race, and war. Alternatively, if states can develop and maintain collective security based on mutual trust and wise and beneficial national governance, the permanent insecurity and warfare inevitable under anarchy can be avoided."

Many statesmen have focussed on the political philosophy of the individual states as the imperative driving states toward war. For Stalin it was capitalist states that became imperialist and inevitably made war. For U.S. President Wilson (1919), militarism, autocracy, and absolute sovereignty were the culprits. He viewed democracies as fundamentally pacific and proposed that the League of Nations restrict membership to democracies, affirming the belief that only a covenant between peace-loving democracies having good governance could guarantee peace.

Holsti identifies state strength not in military terms but in the capacity of the state to earn loyalty and retain the right to rule, to extract the resources necessary to rule, to provide services, to maintain a monopoly over the legitimate use of force within defined territorial limits, and to operate within the context of a consensus-based political community. He places states on a continuum of strength. At one extreme are *strong states*. At the other extreme are *failed states*, political entities that suffer the anarchy of despotic, corrupt, and plundering governance and have collapsed, and where communal war and local rule by warlords, gangs, and factions are the order of the day. Most states, most of the time, fall between the two poles. As random examples only, Switzerland, the Scandinavian states, the U.S., New Zealand, Australia, Germany, France, and Japan are *strong states* at one end of the pole. At the other end of the pole the roster of recent *failed states* includes Yugoslavia, Lebanon, Somalia, Chad, Liberia, Mozambique, Rwanda, Afghanistan, Iraq, and Cambodia. The roster of *weak states* includes Myanmar, Sri Lanka, India, Pakistan, Bangladesh, and "candidates for future collapse—Democratic Republic of the Congo, Algeria, Burundi, and even Russia."[2] Russia falls into the category of weak states due to the secession of many regions. Racketeering and widespread corruption have become common, while the quality of services in health and old age security has deteriorated seriously since the late 1980s. One observer estimates that forty percent of private business and sixty percent of state-owned companies have been corrupted by organized crime. The Russian mafia may own one-half the country's commercial banks. Corruption in the Russian armed forces is similarly widespread. Most of the Mafia profits leave the country to be invested abroad.

The character of all states changes over time. During the 1990s, threats to peace were greatest from the failed and weak states. Some states may survive, but others will sink due to the destructive actions of the country's rulers and/or citizens and predatory neighbors. Wars of the third kind, of genocide, secession, communal war, and various forms of armed violence will begin as national events, but are soon transformed into international problems. After the terrorist attacks on the U.S. of September 11, 2001, wars of well-trained and financed secret "cells" of terrorist groups such as al-Qaeda are the latest threat to world peace, along with the renewal by North Korea of its nuclear development program.

One problem of future wars of the third kind is that groups at high risk of armed conflicts among competing communities and *ethnic* populations are spread extensively through areas populated primarily by weak states (a main reason they are weak.)[3] Wars of a third kind will persist for generations, despite indications of progress toward a new world order in strong and medium-strong states. There will be many patterns of external involvement in these wars. "The conditions of failed and weak states almost guarantee armed conflict, particularly among those states whose trajectory is toward failure and collapse."[4] The UN has been called upon to provide a large number of peacekeeping troops as part of the efforts to sustain and resuscitate weak and failed states. Chapter 8 on the UN will review this.

It is commonly assumed but has never been proved that violence and warfare are inherent in human nature, and that continuing wars are inevitable due to human nature having an automatic inborn reaction to escalate quarrels to armed violence. Family feuds have escalated to tribal wars since the records of history. Militarism, imperialism, aggressive nationalism, and racism are called a basic part of human nature. This theory is not generally accepted by psychologists, nor is it borne out by history. Scotland's clans no longer settle quarrels by war. Since the Second World War the peoples of many nations are committed to peace between neighbors who were once enemies. With these nations it is no longer an option to consider war as "a continuation of politics by other means." Combatant nationalism is on the wane. Willy Brandt (1971), former Chancellor of Germany, stated in his Nobel Peace Prize acceptance address: *"My nation is no longer a great power and will never be one again. I am now a European."* France and Germany and other states of the European Community, North America, Scandinavia, almost all Central and South America, and Oceania, are committed to settling quarrels peacefully with neighboring states. They are revolted by the cruelty and destruction of war, which solves nothing. The "peace with your neighbors" states will still have disputes between states and within states, but the resort to armed force will be the exception. The progress of mankind in achieving peaceful solutions to conflict shows that, while conflict is inevitable, recourse to war is not an inevitable human compulsion, whereas the love of peace is.

Another common misunderstanding is that religion is one of the main causes of war. The progress of mankind in developing peaceful solutions to conflict shows that the basic tenets of religions, that are common to many peoples, are based on the belief that everyone has an inborn love of peace, a reverence for life, and an instinctive hatred of conflict. Albert Schweitzer lived the last fifty-two years of his life among the natives of the Congo. In his Nobel Peace Prize lecture he stated that he had been made acutely aware that *"all persons, . . . are, as beings, capable of compassion, able to develop a humanitarian spirit . . . . It is my profound conviction that the solution lies in our rejecting war for an ethical reason; namely, that war makes us guilty of the crime of inhumanity."*

Even as a major cause of disease is due to the neglect of the health of one's body, a major cause of conflict is due to the neglect of one's heritage of living together peacefully. This is a "health" given to us by our family, training, and experiences. We all know what it is to live peacefully with one another, to treat one another as we would like to be treated, to have compassion for a stranger in distress, to share with others in need. These are key principles of all great religions. We know with complete certainty that these principles have guided the life of Nelson Mandela, that he has lived what he said—"*A joyful peace will triumph, because of the common humanity that bonds both black and white into one human race . . . . Thus we shall live, because we will have created a society which recognises that all people are born equal, with each entitled in equal measure to life, liberty, prosperity, human rights, and good governance.*"[5]

These basic religious principles are not a cause of war—they are a cause of peace. The lack of these principles is a cause of conflict, and if we allow conflict to escalate into bloodshed and war, then *we* and our lack of these principles are the cause of war, not religion. Wars are man-made and not caused by the malevolence or so-called "commandments" of a deity. Combatants often find it compelling to fight under a false banner of religion, but they are brought into battle by their leaders who use this banner for their own deadly purposes— purposes that are not a part of religion as it is known today. Mankind has followed this false banner through centuries of wars. But this is gradually becoming a discredited history of mankind, and one day mankind will confirm that the banners of true religion will not fly over future wars.

In the foreseeable future there will be wars fought when states break up, as with Yugoslavia, the U.S.S.R., and Indonesia, when new but weak states such as in ex-colonial Africa are formed, but have not learned to settle tribal or political aggressions without armed violence. Newly-formed states usually have a variety of political, social, economic, and legal problems and quarrels between groups competing for power, led by men who have had no training or experience in directing the affairs of a sovereign state.

Many fundamental underlying worldwide conditions contribute to a lack of peace in its broadest concepts: the denial of the human right of all peoples to enjoy life and liberty; social, political, economic, and legal inequality; poverty and ignorance; deplorable living conditions and lack of jobs; living in fear of the scourges of terrorism and war. Most UN member states have adopted the Universal Declaration of Human Rights passed by the Assembly of the UN in 1948, one of the most ethical statements of recent history. Slow progress is being made to protect human rights, but it will take many generations to eliminate violations of human rights in many states. The major work of the UN to advance human rights is reviewed in Chapter 6.

The advancement of western civilization enjoyed by the more developed regions has steadily enhanced the welfare of its citizens to enjoy the beneficial rights of peace, but not their right to freedom from war. This right is denied to many peoples involved in wars within states and with wars against other states. There is a fundamental longing for peace among "all people, one world," but this is still a distant hope in many regions of the world.

The steadily widening gap between the rich and the poor both within nations and between nations is a major basic cause of war. The more developed regions of 1.2 billion people enjoy personal, social, economic, legal, and political rights that are not available to the less developed regions of 4.9 billion people. The marginal conditions of life in most of the less developed regions are the breeding grounds of future wars. The generation of young people brought up in ghettos, refugee compounds, and squalid poverty are the masses most susceptible to war and terrorism against the privileged of the world. Many are supporters of professional terrorists from wealthy states (Japan, Saudi Arabia) and are also a major recruiting ground of large terrorist organizations such as Hamas and al-Qaeda.

The explosion of shocking social problems in both rich and poor societies has been covered in Chapter 1. It is not possible in this book to deal with the broad scope of social deterioration of recent years, except to reflect on the influences of special importance for the creation of a more peaceful society in the future. It is a major obstacle to peace if families are unable to raise their children with compassionate and honest ethical values, with little regard for truth, and for the Golden Rule of treating people the way one would like to be treated. Peace is being diminished in many countries due to social inequalities and politics that promote violence and erode peacemaking. The problems cause deep anxiety about the future prospects of mankind, but can only be listed here as evidence of the decline and deterioration of institutions which build the character and cohesiveness that civilize society. There is ample evidence that the social and ethical values which undergird peace at home, in school, in business, finance, politics, on our highways, and in our crowded cities and slum ghettos are not as strong today as in recent generations. Slowly but steadily humanity is losing touch with spiritual and moral values. There is a marked decline in the influence of religions, a decline of social interaction in cities. There is more dishonesty, theft, drug trafficking, abuse of women, children, and minorities, and more homeless and destitute. Our children are bombarded with media and advertising messages crowded with violence, dishonesty, and the exploitation of sex.

War crimes continue to be a major obstacle to peace. In 2001, war crimes were investigated by the UN Commissioner for Human Rights in a number of states: terror and slaughter by Indonesia in East Timor have been stopped by UN intervention. Progress was made with Cambodia for an international court to try former Khmer Rouge leaders; the Security Council voted unanimously for a war crimes tribunal for Sierra Leone; an International Tribunal for the former Yugoslavia is seeking justice for crimes committed by Serbian, Croatian, and Bosnian armed forces. The ratification of the UN treaty establishing the International Criminal Court is discussed in Chapter 6.

In November 2001, the UN calculated that worldwide twenty-nine million had died from AIDS and that an additional thirty-six million were infected with the HIV virus. This scourge is destroying the ability of families and countries to look after their people, creating breeding grounds of future armed conflict.

A list of prevalent obstacles to peace in the political field is long and discouraging. State reluctance to support international co-operation which infringes on state sovereignty is examined in Chapter 6. White-collar crime, corruption, and fraud is prevalent. The power of multinational conglomerates has grown without a corresponding increase in the observance of public relationships and responsibilities toward investments which have given them power over foreign peoples, resources, and governments. The power and crimes of the worldwide drug trade are out of control, due mainly to demand in the more developed regions. U.S. President Eisenhower warned the world in the late 1950s of the threat to peace of the growing and all-pervasive power and demands of the military-industrial complex of superpowers. The arms race continues, in nuclear weapons, in chemical and biological weapons, and a deluge of small arms for military and personal use. The growing consumption excesses, hedonism, and the pervasive influences of money and power in the more developed regions threatens non-renewable resources, the ecological balance of the universe, and the moral balance of peoples. The new post-colonial states have, for the most part, not achieved satisfactory democratic governance under the rule of law and protection of human rights. Enormous expenditures for aid from the more developed regions have been wasted on wars, corruption, political and economic inefficiencies, graft, and plundering by the wealthy and powerful, often by military regimes. These issues are assessed in Chapter 10.

"*Sooner or later, all the peoples of the world will have to discover a way to live together in peace . . . . If this is to be achieved man must evolve for all human conflict a method which rejects revenge, aggression and retaliation. The foundation of such a method is love.*"

Martin Luther King, Jr. (1964)

"*War may sometimes be a necessary evil. But no matter how necessary, it is always an evil, never a good. We will not learn to live together in peace by killing each others' children.*"

President Jimmy Carter
Nobel Peace Prize Presentation Lecture, 2002

Chapter 6

BUILDING AN ENDURING WORLD PEACE

Over the past one hundred years the Nobel Peace Laureates have borne witness to their faith in the ability of humanity to confront the problems of war and to find ways to continue the difficult uphill struggle of building an enduring world peace. The search for peace starts in the hearts and minds of men and women, in the ethical spirit of the individual. In the words of Albert Schweitzer (1952) this spirit "created the humanitarianism which is the origin of all progress toward some form of higher existence." In every great faith and religion the humanitarian spirit is expressed in language comparable to the same ethical spirit of the Golden Rule. The seeds of this ethical spirit are in every human being. The growth of these seeds to full maturity is nurtured by the guidance and love of the family. Here is where the family members learn to love one another, to resolve conflict, to share, and to give whole-heartedly all help needed to bring happiness to other members of the family. These same precepts of the Golden Rule can bring peace to all humanity. People have found since early history that their spiritual and family growth is nurtured best when they joined together in religious bodies which met the needs of the people. While the number of adherents of religious bodies is declining in some regions of modern society, eighty-five per cent of the world population of 6.128 billion are recorded as adherents of religions.[1] When the spiritual ethic of compassion for all humanity guides the lives of a village, state, and the world, there will be peace.

In all peaceful societies the families bond together to respect and love other families and friends. The villages, cities, regions, and states provide all the components of civilized life required by the citizens of a state. The love for family and friends is extended to the nation-state. World peace will depend finally on the growth of the ethical bonds of citizenship of a state being extended to other states and to all humanity. An essential component of the welfare and peace of a village or a state is the many volunteers that belong to co-operative organizations committed to work for peace in fields such as religious witness, education, health care, human rights, rule of law and justice systems, humanitarian causes—known as *civil society*, to differentiate these citizens from those whose activities are funded by governments. The campaigns to influence governments include non-governmental organizations of civil society, such as the International Physicians for the Prevention of Nuclear War, International Campaign to Ban Landmines, and Doctors Without Borders. The role of civil society as it relates to state governments will be reviewed in Chapter 7, and in Chapter 8 on the UN.

The building of an enduring world peace in a democracy is the responsibility of all citizens of a state. They are the grass roots of society, from which grow the multitude of volunteer workers who provide intiatives and support for work for peace of civil society and governments. The linkages of support systems between the peacemaking responsibilities of society at the local level and the peacemaking responsibilities at the state level roughly parallel the functions which have to be carried out by each level of society. The citizens of a village, city, or state need the following political and justice systems if peace is to be enjoyed:

- a bill of rights ratified by statute that all persons are born equal under the law to live in peace, security, freedom from fear and want, with equal opportunity to enjoy all fundamental and universal social, economic and political human rights;

- philosophers and religious, social, and political leaders to provide the citizens with ethical guidance by practice and example;

- education, media, and citizenship functions and duties to ensure society has well-informed and socially-motivated citizens;
- councils of elected citizens to administer a village, city, or state and pass laws and regulations as required;
- communication processes—local citizenship meetings, media, libraries, access to computers and the Internet;
- legal and judicial processes, with policing at the local and state levels to ensure order under the law.

The international government, the UN, requires comparable functions and linkages with state governments:

- ethical guidance and leadership by political and administrative bodies and by international peace research organizations;
- education and communication systems to ensure well-informed "citizens of the world;"
- a legal and judicial process for settling international disputes;
- a "policing process" to ensure that states and citizens within states have collective international support to stop military aggressors and bring the aggressors to justice. It is stated often that "the U.S. cannot be the world's policeman." It is necessary that there be village, state, and international policemen. Questions concerning the role of international policing to build enduring world peace are discussed in Chapter 7— Peacemaking by State Governments.

The media are another very important link between villages, states, and the UN. People today communicate with all society of all countries on an hourly and daily basis. A free, comprehensive, and informed media at all levels is essential to the growth of peaceful societies. The words of the Peace Laureates since 1901 have been published in many books and occasionally in magazines and newspapers, but have not been remembered by many people except in special cases, such as the insightful words of Martin Luther King Jr., Nelson Mandela, and Albert Schweitzer. Today, however, the words of Peace Laureates are available by e-mail or the world wide web, and are often quoted by newspapers and other media. This will become an increasingly important element in building a peaceful world. The trend of the television, film, and advertising media to portray pornography, violence, sex, abuse of women and children, drug and liquor abuse, immorality, and degenerate dress and social customs is increasingly a cause of the breakdown of peace in the family, village, and state. Many parents raising future generations, with teen suicides, school shootings, youth crime and violence, feel that society will have to find its lost moral compass before it is too late.

The failures of state leadership to provide peace are reviewed in Chapter 5. Any aggressive escalation of means of defense that states develop for their own survival constitute a threat to other states. An escalating arms race results, and throughout history this has led to war. The only alternative is for states to develop and maintain collective international security based on mutual trust and beneficial state governance, removing the permanent insecurity and warfare inevitable under non-beneficial state governments. It is the responsibility of all citizens to support good governance, to ensure their democratic rights are protected, that they are well-informed on questions of war or peace, and that they act to make clear to governments their commitments to peace, human rights, environmental sustainability, and humanitarian aid for the less developed regions. Beneficial state governance is essential in a free society to provide the services which subsidiary governments of provinces or regions cannot provide as efficiently, and to form and support a world organization of states that can be the leader and co-ordinator of world peace.

A main foundation of world peace is the joining of states in an international organization, the United Nations, to meet the challenges of living in the "global village" of one world. The ethic of peace has carried humanity forward, extending from peaceful states to humanity in other countries. This has become a reality over recent centuries. New Zealanders have continuing peace with Australians, even to shared familial terms, the Kiwis and the Aussies. Similarly, there will never be a war between Americans and Canadians. They have learned to live in peace, as have the leading states of Europe, most of the countries of the Americas, and the Swiss with their neighbors. This is a growing reality in many parts of the world.

Priority responsibilities of the UN are to enable all humanity to live in peace, and to ensure that all peoples enjoy equal human rights: safety, equality, freedom from fear and want, and the social and economic benefits of modern society. The specific UN priorities in the next century are eradicating poverty, preventing conflict, and promoting democracy. There has to be an unbreakable understanding, agreement, and continuing support, between the people, the state, and the UN if the world is to build an enduring world peace. The wide scope of responsibilities of the UN is reviewed in Chapter 8.

The Universal Declaration of Human Rights was ratified through a proclamation by the General Assembly on December 10, 1948, with a count of forty-eight votes to none, with only eight abstentions. Since then over 100 new states have joined the UN, and almost all have incorporated the text of the Declaration in their constitutions.

The UN's International Bill of Rights includes three separate documents:

- the Universal Declaration of Human Rights;
- the International Covenant on Economic, Social, and Cultural Rights;
- the International Covenant on Civil and Political Rights, with two optional Protocols, one aiming at the abolition of the death penalty.

The World Conference on Human Rights, held in Vienna in 1993, adopted by acclamation the Vienna Declaration and Program of Action, welcomed the progress made in the codification of human rights instruments, and urged the universal ratification of human rights treaties.

Thus the International Bill of Rights represents a milestone in the history of human rights, a veritable Magna Carta marking mankind's arrival at a vitally important new level of civilization and a conscious affirmation and protection of human dignity and worth.

While this Declaration is not a Convention, and has only moral force, any state that joins the UN must agree with the commitments of the Declaration as a condition of membership. The Declaration included no means of enforcement, which would have proved impractical, but the basic ethic of love and respect for all humanity is slowly taking root. The Declaration had originally focussed on political and civil rights and freedom from arbitrary arrest, imprisonment, or torture. Over the years it was broadened to include economic and social human rights, and the right to be given aid and economic assistance from the more developed world. A number of states contended that "universal" rights were really "western" rights, and should be modified to fit non-western society. But a majority view maintained that human rights were a common core of values of all humanity to protect the individual against the state, and against discrimination or harassment of any kind respecting race, religion, color, sex, or social or physical handicap. Major issues currently receiving attention by the UN are criminal accountability, the growing number of refugees, the HIV/AIDS pandemic, gender-based abuses, self-determination of minority groups, racial and ethnic discrimination, and the economic and social rights of less developed regions respecting loan and trade policies of international financial institutions such as the World Bank, the International Monetary Fund, and the World Trade Organization.

A major obstacle to peace is the reluctance of states to accept international co-operation which infringes on state sovereignty. It was the practice in the nineteenth century that international commitments would be given but would be dishonored whenever a state so wished. Again in 1919, in the case of commitments to the League of Nations, the practice to dishonor international commitments continued. After the bloodbaths of two World Wars, nations still make international commitments which are not honored, using the unworthy excuse that commitments can be broken if they infringe on state sovereignty. An out-dated concept popular in 1919 in the U.S. and other more developed states was that questions of vital interest cannot be submitted to arbitration because, in the words of an American jurist and statesman, "that would be an abdication of independence and the placing of government in effect in the hands of others." When nations joined the UN, the European Union, the World Trade Organization, or the International Court of Justice they relinquished a degree of sovereignty. Kofi Annan, Secretary-General of the UN, said recently, "The sovereignty of states must no longer be used as a shield for gross violations of human rights." The effective operation of the UN as the organization to work for peace can be achieved only if states honor their commitments to it, both when it serves their national interest and when it does not serve the national interest but provides greater service to the community of all states. Unfortunately, there is a tendency of the more powerful states to hide behind the shield of sovereignty when they should be setting an example for the smaller and newer states. The cause of peace cannot be served if states make commitments to other states or the UN which they fail to honor. The excuse of absolute state sovereignty was used in 1945 as a necessary expedient, by which the five permanent members each had a right of veto in the Security Council of the UN. But this has done the UN more harm than good, and after fifty-eight years of this obstacle to peace it is time to negotiate a change to its undemocratic membership provisions.

Chapter 11 emphasizes that it is necessary to give up a substantial degree of national sovereignty in order to realize the advantages of globalization. The wealthy nations cannot deny support to UN causes by claiming that this would infringe upon their state sovereignty, and at the same time push for more support of globalization of trade and finance in order to benefit from other nations relinquishing a degree of sovereignty. Just as the sovereignty of the thirteen colonies had to yield to the sovereignty of the new state, the state now must yield a degree of sovereignty to the *new union—the UN—the new collectivity of* "*We the people.*"

Another major obstacle to peace is the failure of strong states to support the UN when a population is suffering as a result of a weak state's internal wars, often of genocide, insurgency, repression, or state failure, and the state in question is unwilling or unable to halt or avert it, or takes the stand that intervention by the UN will not be accepted as it would be a violation of the sovereignty of the state. External military intervention by the leading powers to prevent ethnic cleansing and crimes against humanity was delayed and ineffective in stopping the genocide in Rwanda of the Tutsi by the Hutu in 1994, despite several years of warning. The UN did not get the support needed to prevent massacres in Somalia, Bosnia, Kosovo, Srebrenica, and other regions suffering internal massacres. Both the Security Council and the UN General Assembly failed to prevent the massacres of unarmed civilians—men, women, and children. The Secretary-General of the UN asked the question of the international community: "If humanitarian intervention is, indeed, an unacceptable assault on sovereignty, how should we respond to a Rwanda or Srebrenica—to gross and systematic violations of human rights that affect every precept of our common humanity?" A recent report to the UN addressing this problem is reviewed in Chapter 7 and Appendix G.

There have been theories from time to time that the world would be more peaceful if the state, the initiator and the combatant in all of the full-scale major wars of the past two centuries, were to gradually shrink and disappear. Various functions suitable for devolution, or the transfer of power to a regional administration, could be turned back to component regions of separate ethnic or geographic entities. But there is ample evidence that the separate regions or ethnic groups would not be more peaceful than the present structure of states—witness the warfare that followed the break-up of Yugoslavia and Russia. The state is clearly indispensable at this stage of history, which means that ways will have to be found to make it more peaceful. The joining of states such as in the European Union will strengthen peace in Europe, and make the citizens there stronger supporters of international world peace. (The views of Peace Laureate Gorbachev in Chapter 3 on the problems of "break-away" states are of interest.)

There are many initiatives in the field of international law to strengthen peacemaking. States are being encouraged to settle more conflicts by arbitration. Proposals have been made for reforming and expanding the role of the International Court of Justice at The Hague in the context of a more comprehensive system of global justice. Since 1993, an NGO Coalition for an International Criminal Court has advocated the establishment of this court to punish crimes against humanity in the former Yugoslavia and elsewhere. The International Criminal Court is the first tribunal that can claim jurisdiction under international law over heinous crimes such as war crimes, crimes against humanity, genocide, and ethnic cleansing. In the past, the UN has relied on ad hoc tribunals, such as the Nuremberg and Tokyo trials of Nazi and Japanese military leaders, and more recently the genocide trials of former Yugoslav dictator Slobodan Milosevic and of Rwandan officials implicated in the slayings of more than 800,000 Tutsis. The new court will be located at The Hague, The Netherlands. Former U.S. President Clinton signed the International Criminal Court treaty in 2000, but U.S. President George W. Bush's administration has said it will not ratify the treaty because U.S. soldiers and officials might be subjected to politically motivated prosecutions. The treaty was finally entered into force on July 1, 2002, when ten more countries ratified it. As of September, 2003, ninety-one countries have ratified the Treaty. The U.S. insisted on and received special dispensation for the U.S. military.

The trial of Slobodan Milosevic, former president of Serbia, for war crimes and genocide, has proceeded slowly in the UN Criminal Tribunal for former Yugoslavia. In criminal trials, twenty-nine Serbs, Croats, and Bosnian Muslims have been judged guilty and five have been acquitted. There are still forty-two in custody.

International law continues to evolve in the areas of human rights, international security, trade, and "universal jurisdiction," the concept that war criminals may be punished anywhere regardless of where or against whom they committed the crimes. September 2001 terrorist attacks in the U.S. raised critical questions of how terrorists should be punished and what the rules were for taking action against countries alleged to have harbored those responsible. The International Court of Justice, The Hague, has recently heard mainly cases of individual rights. Several other permanent international courts have been established, including the European Court of Justice, the European Court of Human Rights, and the Caribbean Court of Justice. Proposals have been made for a universal and effective system of habeas corpus. Some domestic courts and regional tribunals help victims to hold abusers responsible under International Humanitarian and Human Rights laws.

The continued existence of nuclear weapons threatens the survival of humanity and all life on earth. Nuclear powers have progressed very slowly to reduce nuclear weapons in their arsenals. To meet their legal obligations of the Nuclear Non-Proliferation Treaty and the mandate of the International Court of Justice, all states are required to negotiate and conclude by 2005 a Nuclear Weapons Convention which would prohibit the production, use, and threat of use of nuclear weapons. Meanwhile, Russia has announced plans to deliver the first of two nuclear reactors to Iran. Russia bristled recently at the Pentagon's plan to downsize U.S. nuclear arsenals by putting weapons in reserve rather than destroying them. In the 1990s, a New Agenda Coalition, which included seven courageous governments— Brazil, Egypt, Ireland, Mexico, New Zealand, South Africa, and Sweden— challenged the nuclear weapons states to implement seven immediate practical steps to reduce nuclear arms, including de-alerting all nuclear forces. They presented their agenda in a UN resolution, which was adopted by the General Assemby in December 1998 by 114 votes to eighteen. Transitional steps toward nuclear disarmament include: adherence to the Comprehensive Test Ban Treaty and the Anti-Ballistic Missile Treaty (both rejected by the U.S.); de-alerting; no first use; extension of nuclear free zones; and a ban on fissionable materials for military use. See Appendix "J" for details on nuclear treaties.

In December 2001, U.S. President George W. Bush served notice that in six months the U.S. would withdraw from the Anti-Ballistic Missile Treaty, generally regarded as the cornerstone of global nuclear arms control since 1972, stating that the treaty hindered his government's ability to protect the U.S. from "future terrorist or rogue-states missile attacks." The announcement of this renewed "star wars" or National Missile Defense (NMD) project was met with scarcely-concealed dismay around the world, and denunciations that the U.S. wanted world co-operation when the projects were vital to U.S. interests, but planned to dismantle a most important multilateral disarmament program whether friends and allies liked it or not.

Chapter 1 outlined the major threat to world peace of the current population explosion. Most forecasts confirm that population growth must be slowed down drastically, but this is much harder to do in poor countries. The highest rates of population increase are mainly among the poorest peoples of the less developed regions, for many reasons. The culture of many poor areas does not support birth control, and birth control is opposed politically in many regions. There is a growing need for massive transfers of billions of dollars every year from developed regions to the less developed regions. This would achieve two fundamental goals of peacemaking—to raise the standard of living of the poorest in society to enable them to forego the economic need for more children and to give the children they do have better health, education, training for better jobs, increased productivity, and hope for a better standard of living. Prosperous countries have a duty to help the poor and undeveloped areas of the world.

The third major threat to humanity is also a major threat to world peace—the unsustainable use of the earth's resources and the continuing degradation of the environment. The environmental threat to the planet has been recognized by ecologists for many years. It was brought into the general public's attention again in 1962, appropriately by a woman's prophetic alarm bell, the book *Silent Spring* by Rachel Carson. Most environmental issues are familiar to readers, so they will not be assessed in all their ramifications here, except to give a quotation by Dr. David Suzuki in his book *Earth Time: Essays*, "We are using up the ecological capital of the planet (biodiversity, air, water, soil) rather than living off the interest."[2] The continuing trends of global warming, of pollution of land, sea, and air, and of the high rate of environmental damage by industrial society will be much harder to slow down in less developed regions, where they resent the high standard of living and conspicuous consumption of advanced industrial societies that are the greatest users of earth's resources and the greatest polluters. The less developed regions want more industrial production, not less, and will not be bought off this objective by more developed regions sending them more capital for social purposes when they want to acquire similar benefits to those flowing to wealthy societies from increased industrial production. Also, many industrial societies want to invest capital in less developed regions, and would resist this being curtailed.

In Chapter 5 it was shown that, excluding anti-colonial wars of national liberation, 126 wars, or seventy-seven percent of the total armed conflicts from 1945 to 1995 were *internal* wars of secession, resistance, or ideological/factional types of conflicts. How many of these wars could have been avoided? It can be argued that some could have been avoided if the state had lessened the appeal of separation by compromises satisfactory to both parties, as has been done successfully in several instances. Some internal conflicts are generated by both regional and international problems: arms transfers; global ethnic networks; contagion due to abuses and to political power-seeking, such as in Sri Lanka; and outside political interference.

However, the origins of most wars within states seem to be wholly domestic. It was developed in Chapter 5 that *the conditions of weak states almost guarantee armed conflict.* Many of the conditions cannot be changed—for example, Lebanon collapsed mainly due to its "minority complex" of Maronites, Druze, Shiites, Palestinians, Sunnis, Syrians, and Israelis. Secession can be violent or peaceful, as it was in the case of Czechoslovakia. The main concern of secessionist elements should be—will present and future generations enjoy better lives after the end of hostilities, whenever that is? There could be an end to the armed conflicts in Northern Ireland if both sides agreed with the statement of Peace Laureate John Hume (1998) that the friendship of the Irish and British people can transcend all narrow political differences—"We are two neighboring islands whose destiny is to live in friendship and amity with each other." Could it be that the Palestinians and the Israelis, India and Pakistan, Albania and Macedonia, Ethiopia and Eritrea, are neighboring "land islands" whose destiny is to live in friendship and amity with each other?

The wide range of work crying out for peacemakers has been covered in the horror stories of Chapter 1, the obstacles to peace in Chapter 5, and the building of an enduring world peace in this chapter. It is useful at this point to summarize specific themes that were on the agenda of a conference, The Hague Agenda for Peace and Justice for the 21st Century,[3] at The Hague in May, 1999. The Conference agenda represents views that civil society organizations and citizens consider to be some of the most important challenges facing humankind.

MAIN ACTIONS— IMPLEMENTING THE HAGUE AGENDA

The Hague Appeal for Peace Conference served as a launch pad for several major initiatives and campaigns. Following are some of the key actions that were highlighted at The Hague. They represent initiatives by civil society and coalitions which are looking for new partners to join their global networks. Many other actions have emerged from the conference itself. [The wording of this section is based on extracts from the conference records.]

INTERNATIONAL ACTION NETWORK ON SMALL ARMS (IANSA)

The International Action Network on Small Arms is a global network of NGOs dedicated to preventing the proliferation and unlawful use of small arms by pushing forward the boundaries for international action. The IANSA is looking at the devastating impact of the spread and misuse of small arms, outlining the need for a global campaign and encouraging civil society organisations to join together to tackle one of the great humanitarian challenges of our times.

GLOBAL CAMPAIGN FOR PEACE EDUCATION

A culture of peace will be achieved when citizens of the world understand global problems, have the skills to resolve conflicts and struggle for justice non-violently, live by international standards of human rights and equity, appreciate cultural diversity, and respect the earth and each other. Such learning can only be achieved with systematic education for peace.

The Hague Appeal for Peace Conference launched a call and a campaign to support the United Nations Decade for a Culture of Peace and Non-violence for the Children of the World and to introduce peace and human rights education into all educational institutions, including medical and law schools. The campaign is being conducted through a global network of education associations and regional, national, and local task forces of citizens and educators.

INTERNATIONAL CAMPAIGN TO BAN LANDMINES (ICBL)

The International Campaign to Ban Landmines stressed the need for public support of the Ottawa draft treaty and renewed the call for its universal ratification. (It was ratified by over sixty nations in 2002.) The next steps of the ICBL include universalisation and implementation of this treaty which bans the use, production, stockpiling, and transfer of landmines. The ICBL also seeks to hold states which are parties to the treaty to their commitment to increase mine clearance and victim assistance efforts around the world.

ABOLITION OF NUCLEAR WEAPONS

Building on the adoption of a resolution on abolition of nuclear weapons by the General Assembly, a campaign to get nuclear and non-nuclear weapon states to commence negotiations toward the rapid conclusion of a convention to abolish nuclear weapons, as mandated by Article VI of the Non-Proliferation Treaty and by the International Court of Justice, was launched at The Hague Appeal for Peace Conference by many worldwide NGOs, including the International Physicians for the Prevention of Nuclear War, Abolition 2000, and Middle Powers Initiative.

GLOBAL ACTION PLAN TO PREVENT WAR

At The Hague Appeal, the Institute for Defence and Disarmament Studies, Union of Concerned Scientists, and World Order Models Project launched a Global Action Plan to Prevent War. This is a comprehensive, multi-stage program for moving toward a world in which armed conflict is rare.

Global Action urges a mix of enhanced conflict prevention, peacekeeping, disarmament, and measures promoting human rights, non-violent solutions, and the rule of law. It seeks to contribute to the formation of a coalition, including those concerned with non-violent means of conflict resolution and peace education, with tackling root causes of war arising from social and economic injustice, with humanitarian aid, economic development, conflict prevention, peacekeeping, and disarmament, both "conventional" and nuclear.

STOP THE USE OF CHILD SOLDIERS

The Coalition to Stop the Use of Child Soldiers was formed in May 1998 by leading international NGOs seeking an end to the military recruitment and use as soldiers of all children under eighteen years of age, whether by governmental armed forces or armed opposition groups. At the Hague Appeal for Peace Conference, the international Coalition, in co-operation with UNICEF and the Dutch Coalition to Stop the Use of Child Soldiers, renewed its call for an end to the use of children as soldiers around the world and to promote increased action by government and civil society, particularly in countries where child recruitment and participation in armed conflict continues.

TWO MAJOR OBJECTIVES

Two major, all-encompassing, long-term objectives to advance the cause of peace involve many broad sociological and political considerations which are beyond the scope of this book:

- land reform, especially in tropical rural societies where the vast majority of families eke out a marginal existence without economical opportunity and land ownership;
- the slow transformation of nationalism, with the gradual development of emotional and social convictions growing in the hearts and minds of all individuals who live both as proud and peaceful members of a national society and a world society, the "one world" community of all humanity. The Greek philosopher Diogenes, when asked where he came from, said: "I am a citizen of the world."

The many centuries of exaggerated and aggressive patriotism and chauvinism are slowly drawing to a close. In the words of Kofi Annan . . ."People of different religions and cultures live side by side in almost every part of the world, and most of us have overlapping identities which unite us with very different groups . . . . We can thrive in our own tradition, even as we learn from others, and come to respect their teaching." (Appendix D-2.)

"The responsibility of great states is to serve and not to dominate the world."

Harry S. Truman
33rd President of the U.S.

"And if we cannot now end our differences [with China and Russia], *at least we can make the world safe for diversity. For in the final analysis, our most basic common link is that we all inhabit this small planet. We all breathe the same air. We all cherish our children's future. And we are all mortal."*

President John F. Kennedy, 1963.

"A balance of interests rather than a balance of power, a search for compromise and concord rather than a search for advantages at other people's expense, and respect for equality rather than claims to leadership . . . these elements should be readily acceptable for reasonable people informed of the experience of the 20th century."

Mikhail Gorbachev (1990)

Chapter 7

PEACEMAKING BY STATE GOVERNMENTS

The state government is an all-important peacemaking organization, the hub which links to the grass roots, out to its neighbors and to all other states and peoples, and beyond to the UN. The UN acts as the deputy of world states and peoples, to implement and administer the mandate given to it by the nations of the world. The state is an organization which is constantly changing and evolving in its legal, political, social, and economic powers and responsibilities, but there is one concept which remains as its guiding compass—to act in the best interests of all its citizens, to have and to hold loyalty, a secure foundation of legitimacy, sovereignty, and the right to rule. The three essential elements of the state are interconnected: the idea of the state; the physical basis of the state; the institutional expressions of the state—the laws, norms, and operation of official office. To carry out its mandate, the first and foremost responsibility of the state is to maintain the safety of its citizens against attack from within or without.

The peacemaking responsibilities of a strong state are essentially the same as those of a village: essential services; ethical values and education; peaceful resolution of anger and conflict; sharing and help freely given as needed; respect for justice and laws; fighting poverty, ignorance, discrimination, disease; protecting the environment; humanitarian concern for all peoples; and good governance and citizenship. If government leaders, when faced with a problem about peacemaking, would ask themselves, "What would we do if this were our neighbor?"—there would be a radical change in the governance of a village or state.

The city and state could do a great deal more in meeting all the essential responsibilities of peacekeeping if they were more than putting out fires, and if there was a constant effort to remove the combustibles that are the fuel of conflict. The state can do much more to utilize the resources of the grass roots, done very successfully during the Second World War; NGOs can be given more support; businesses could be much more productive if co-operation and fairness could be the watchwords of business owners and employees; and everyone could work more vigorously to eradicate poverty, ignorance, and disease. The state, its citizens, and the UN are the key components of peacemaking, and the great need is to have these components motivated by the same ethic and all "singing from the same page."

It is obvious from the complexity of the main obstacles to peace and the main foundations of an enduring world peace that the state responsibilities for peacemaking can be listed here in summary form only, focussing on priority concerns for the general public, the NGOs, and the governments of cities, regions, and states. The informed public is familiar with the peacemaking needs in our cities and states, but often fails to realize that every domestic action, favorable or unfavorable, affects the ecology of the planet and all therein—the relation of organisms to one another and their surroundings, and the interaction of people with their environment. The abuse of women and children, the increase in dysfunctional families, violence and anti-social behavior, affect humanity everywhere. The excessive consumption of resources in wealthy societies affects the use of resources in less developed countries, where there is a major need for land and agriculture reform, fuel, power, jobs, disease control, sanitation, and all the amenities of modern living. The tragic plague of the increasing use of hard drugs worldwide tears at the fabric of peace everywhere. A peace worker anywhere sees the reality that there are peacemaking needs everywhere, not just in the many areas of armed conflict and of abuse of human rights. There is an old maxim—

"We have met the enemy, and it is us." *The work for world peace is up to us.* We cannot have peace if it is left up to city or state governments. It must begin in the hearts and minds of the family and be carried out into the world as a philosophy and action program of peace.

The peacemaking "action brigades" of the grass roots are the NGOs of volunteers—religious groups, social workers, doctors, scientists, lawyers, humanitarians, welfare organizations. They belong to independent organizations that are not organized or directed by government. Many have roots that have been growing for centuries: the Red Cross, Salvation Army, activists for women's suffrage, the stopping of the slave trade, the YMCA and the YWCA. Strong states have many thousands of organized societies of peacemakers. Many millions of volunteers work at food banks, social services, charity funding canvassing, and shelters for the homeless. Case histories of some of these volunteer organizations are reviewed in Chapter 9.

A basic obstacle to peacemaking by states is excessive and bigoted nationalism which feeds on the antagonisms separating people of different race, color, creed, religion, region and national, economic, and political identity. The things that separate humanity due to the scourges of "jingoism," hate literature, and race riots are slowly subsiding, with century-old prejudices giving way to the thing that all mankind has in common, the love of humanity. The state cannot legislate the thoughts of mankind, but progress towards rejecting public expressions of hate and encouraging multiculturalism is being made by cities and state laws against hate propaganda. This is progress which has endured and grown since it was made manifest in the life of Jesus Christ and other religious teachers to *love your neighbor as yourself.* This is the bedrock of peacemaking, and will slowly relegate bigoted nationalism and warmongering in all its hateful and obscene forms to the dustbin of history.

States continue to support multinational and regional organizations which are essential for progress and co-operation in regional, economic, and political affairs, such progress presenting major dividends to peacemaking. Mercosur, the Common Market of Argentina, Brazil, Paraguay, and Uruguay, is the world's third largest market. The Organization of American States has drawn nations together in peace and democracy. The Commonwealth of Nations of the former British Empire, the Association of Southeast Asian Nations, the Asia-Pacific Economic Co-operation Forum, the Organization of African Unity, the Commonwealth of Independent States of the former U.S.S.R., the Arab League, the Organization of the Islamic Conference, and other organizations continue to work for regional security against terrorism and for regional economic development and peace.

The tragic increase of wars *within* states, with the brutal killing and maiming of millions of civilians, crimes against humanity and ethnic butchery, have required the intervention of international peacemaking and peacekeeping armed military. The Security Council, hampered by the argument that the UN did not have a mandate to intervene in wars within states, did not act in time and in strength to prevent the Rwanda, Somalia, Kosovo, or Srebrenica massacres where 7,000 Bosnian civilians under the "protection" of UN peacekeepers were killed in 1995. In 1999, Secretary-General Kofi Annan challenged the member states of the UN to "find common ground in upholding the principles of the Charter, and acting in defence of our common humanity." He warned that, "If the collective conscience of humanity . . . . cannot find in the United Nations its greatest tribune, there is a grave danger that it will look elsewhere for peace and for justice." Humanitarian intervention was needed—how else could the UN respond to "systematic violations of human rights that offend every precept of our common humanity?"

Mr. Lloyd Axworthy, Minister of Foreign Affairs of Canada, initiated in 2000 the establishment of the International Commission on Intervention and State Sovereignty to consult with the widest possible range of opinion around the world and submit a report that would help the UN and state governments to find some new common ground as guidance for states who wanted no more Rwandas. The Commission report *The Responsibility to Protect*, summarized as follows, is outlined more fully in Appendix G:

- State sovereignty has the primary responsibility for the protection of its own people, but where internal massacres occur which the state cannot or does not stop, the principle of non-intervention yields to the *international responsibility to protect;*

- The Security Council, under Article 24 of the UN Charter, is responsible for the maintenance of international peace and security—*the responsibility to protect all mankind;*
- The responsibility to protect includes—(a) the responsibility to prevent both root causes and direct causes of crimes against humanity, (b) the responsibility to react, including coercive measures and military intervention if necessary, and (c) the responsibility to rebuild—with measures of recovery, reconstruction, and reconciliation, addressing the causes of the armed hostility.

The mandate to prevent crimes against humanity is the single most important dimension of the responsibility of the UN to protect. The need to protect the victims of internal wars is of major importance to prevent planting the seeds of future wars.

The principles for military intervention are spelled out in the *Responsibility to Protect* report. In summary, when warfare within a state cannot be justified, and the state cannot protect its citizens, the UN has the responsibility to intervene militarily if necessary, with clear agreement on the best timing, command, and resources to stop the carnage as quickly as possible. It has been suggested that the UN should have a military force as a permanent component, separate from national forces. There is convincing experience from other armed interventions to conclude that this would be inefficient on many counts, that it would be wrong to make this one more responsibility of a UN coping now with increasing responsibilities, and conceptually and philosophically wrong to combine the functions of waging war and peacemaking. The "policeman" should not be the UN, the deputy of the states, but the states themselves, under international law and authority, as agreed to by the UN.

The peacemaking effectiveness of the state starts with the ability of citizens to elect governments which provide good governance, including strong and dedicated peacemaking as one of its major priorities. Electing good governments must be supported by effective two-way communication between the grass roots, volunteer organizations, and the government. Here the importance of an educated, well-informed public and media comes into play. This starts with developing peacemakers in our schools and universities, youth organizations, and all components of the media. Governments are influenced to a major degree by the media, and it is the responsibility of peacemakers to ensure that the media and government are influenced by peacemakers. It is obvious that the media are influenced by profits, and have found a part of the public that will support violence, killing, drug trafficking, dishonesty, abuse and degradation of men, women, and children, pornography, and other social cancers. Gresham's law, that bad money drives out good, applies also to morality. Bad morality drives out good morality. Good morality cannot become strong and prevalent unless citizens and government do all that is reasonable and ethical to reduce the flow and effect of the bad morality that is gaining more influence in today's society. Committed peacemakers are resisting a continuing downhill slide into an immorality that will degrade society, and there will be no peace for the people or the state. Wherever enormous amounts of money are easily obtained there are violent criminals, sales of arms and drugs, and terrorism, all sensationalized on the front page and the screen. When peacemakers have no influence on the media, they will have little influence on the peacemaking decisions of the village or state.

Regarding the peacekeeping role of the state, recently Matthew Stepanek, an American eleven-year-old poet, was interviewed on TV by Larry King. Matthew spoke with the maturity of an adult. He has an incurable disease, and is the 2002 national goodwill ambassador of the U.S. Muscular Dystrophy Association. He stressed that his religion was a constant companion, giving him continuing strength and hope, and made the profound remark of a modern prophet—"You cannot separate church and state." We know that the separation of church and state is a sound legal and political principle, but Matthew was surely right when it comes to something more important—how we live our lives, how we train our children, and how we hope to be dedicated peacemakers. These responsibilities are functions of religion and of the family, which is the basic unit of a civilized society and is usually endorsed and supported by the state. The communist leaders of the U.S.S.R. tried for over seventy years to wipe out religion and to minimize family influence on the education of children. History has confirmed the folly of this when the U.S.S.R. collapsed.

The work of peacemakers to achieve a world free of nuclear weapons has been an ongoing campaign. Head-on, non-violent confrontation will have to continue, as governments are too slow to respond to the urgent need to eliminate nuclear arms. The threats and risks of war would surely diminish if the peacemakers of the world unite and bring their force to bear on governments.

The campaign to increase the production of power from the sun, wind, fuel cells, and other sustainable and non-polluting sources is another objective of peacemakers. Peacemakers and environmentalists are working to achieve the same objective—a peaceful world. They start from different philosophies, proceed with different methods, and use different means to support their different campaigns, but they are both working toward the same end, to have sustained peace in a sustainable "green" world.

It has been emphasized that an increasing massive transfer of funds from the rich and developed nations to the poor and less developed regions will be necessary if the world is to become more peaceful. Humanitarian aid has grown over the centuries, with religious groups, doctors, and humanitarians leading the way. This was done originally by the aid of people and money flowing directly from the givers to the receivers. The money was never enough, and was spent as frugally as possible. The people delivering the aid were prompted by moral zeal, and lifted the hopes and spirits as well as the standard of living of the poorest of the poor. Governments were involved in humanitarian aid mainly in the relief of catastrophes. Continuing aid was provided by organizations of volunteers. Due to the magnitude of human loss and suffering during the two World Wars, public opinion forced governments to come to the rescue of refugees and the destitute. The Marshall plan of the U.S. and many other government aid programs were designed to do two things—to rebuild the political and economic base of war-torn countries, and to give sufficient humanitarian aid to save countries from collapse by rebuilding the health and living conditions of war-torn societies.

Government aid in the past fifty years has been carried out in a manner that is separate from the channel of volunteer aid by civil society, which has been described as giving more emphasis to the importance of providing aid by age-old practices in traditional societies. Humanitarian aid was first developed by voluntary participation of local citizens who gave social aid through established volunteerism working from the bottom up.[1] Government aid and volunteer aid of civil society is a necessary and vital partnership.

A large part of government aid is for economic development, often for massive projects requested by the governments of states emerging from colonial status. These governments have frequently been riddled with graft by politicians, the wealthy, and the military. In many cases large capital projects and trappings of power, such as personal aircraft and military facilities, are agreed to by the politicians and industrial military complexes of the wealthy nations. Figures are not available, but massive capital aid to poor nations has often been tainted by the self-serving studies of consultants, politicians, and industry for political and military expenditures which corrupt the givers and the receivers and do very little to raise the living standards of the poor.

There are many examples of graft and waste of international development funds. Many actual cases have been reported that involve high level international financing arrangements for projects that were not feasible, but proceeded due to political pressure by receiving governments and donor governments which wanted to benefit from engineering and capital construction projects carried out by the donor industry. In many cases receiving governments diverted millions to wealthy local supporters and the military, and waste at all levels of government and the private sector resulted in widespread graft, corruption, and political bribery, in small development projects and on projects involving over hundreds of millions of dollars.

An example of the waste of development grants to less developed regions involves a grant to a tropical country to build a plant to make low cost rough building panels using waste fibres from sugar mills.

The recipients used the grant to build a very large warehouse many miles from both the nearest sugar mill and the port necessary for export to potential markets. It can only be assumed that local financial fraud was involved in the use of aid money in a way that was not part of the authorized plan. At the time of the last visit by donor country nationals, about twenty women were working in a small corner of a very large building using sewing machines to make a low volume specialty line of ladies clothes for the U.S. market. No information is available on what happened to the rest of the grant money.

The Globe and Mail, Canada, reported on August 28, 2002, that the Environment Minister of Canada stated—"We've tried in the past to have development [grants] through government-to-government [aid] *and that didn't really work,* and then we worked with the non-governmental organizations as delivery vehicles *where governments were corrupt and that hasn't worked either. If we limit ourselves strictly to levels of Official Government Aid I think we miss the boat in terms of opportunities for sustainable development."*

The Canadian International Development Agency (CIDA) is the federal agency responsible for administering most of Canada's Development Assistance Programs. CIDA gives government grants to support projects that help to reduce poverty in poor countries by providing assistance to create jobs and build up the industrial capabilities of the recipient. In addition, CIDA provides humanitarian relief to victims of emergencies such as floods, droughts, and earthquakes. CIDA also provides funding to partners who deliver the assistance, including Canadian universities, the Red Cross, Oxfam Canada, CARE Canada, private sector companies, agencies like UNICEF and the World Bank, and volunteer agencies with field staff in developing countries. Many kinds of assistance are funded: immunizing children; HIV/AIDS treatment; educating children; rebuilding homes, schools, and health-care facilities; helping victims of natural disasters; family planning and reproductive health care; environmental protection. CIDA total expenditures in 1950 were thirteen million dollars (Canadian). In 1999 total expenditures were almost three billion dollars (Canadian).

It is most important that the planning, delivery, and results of development and humanitarian aid to less developed countries be scrutinized very carefully by both the UN and donor countries to restore trust in the integrity and efficiency of the organizations involved, both donor and recipient. There are a great number of illegal diversions of aid funds and supplies. The spending of someone else's money leads inevitably to inefficiency and graft. It is a common experience that the bigger the amount of easily acquired money, the bigger the activities of criminals. The aims should be to send development aid only on agreement of donor and receiver that the project is feasible and meets the priority of doing the most to raise the standard of living of the poor in less developed countries. The process should eliminate graft and corruption wherever possible. Regarding humanitarian aid, the more it flows directly from the donating citizen to the receiving citizen at the grass roots, the better. The present system of government-to-government aid is ridden with politics, graft, and inefficiency, and must be reformed. The financial and delivery controls in place now with respect to foreign aid will not be sufficiently effective, honest and well-organized to avoid massive mistakes and graft when the greatly expanded needs for financial transfers to the less developed regions must be met.

The needs of the poor and displaced are staggering. Shipments of food aid to Afghanistan alone totalled a record 114,000 metric tons in December 2001, enough to feed six million displaced persons for two months. On a worldwide basis, in 2000-2001, the UN Children's Fund provided food and water to help an estimated 1.5 million children survive. Total shipments of food aid worldwide in 2001 totalled 8.5 trillion metric tons. In all recent years the shipments of food and medical aid, and the distribution facilities of the recipient, have fallen lower than the needs. One third of sub-Saharan Africa and three-quarters of Somalia have on-going chronic hunger, prevalent diseases, and deaths due to lack of food and sanitation. This is repeated in many areas of the less developed world.

The progress of Europe in developing continental organizations of alliance and co-operation is of major importance to world peacemaking. In 1952, six Western European countries joined in a form of supranational authority. In 1958, the European Economic

Community, or Common Market, began operation, with six nations and 175 million people. In 1967, the European Coal and Steel Community, the European Economic Community, and Euratom consolidated into the European Community. In 1979, members of a European Parliament took seats by party affiliation and not by nation. Final decisions still rested with the Council of Ministers representing each country, whose decisions on fundamental matters had to be unanimous. By 1986, twelve states had joined the European Community. Soon the twelve states laid plans to create a "single Europe," a "Europe without borders," confirmed by the Treaty of European Union (EU) in 1991, despite objections in several states to the loss of national control. The European Union of 375 million people was now the largest trading block in the global economy, accounting for forty percent of all international trade.

The European Union is making steady progress on the road to a united continent, preparing to expand membership to include Eastern Europe, Cyprus, Malta, and Turkey. The Common Market Euro currency was introduced in twelve member states in 2002. Riots and other anti-globalization protests at summits have exposed the great deal that the EU still has to do to win broad-based public support. The creation of a wider market and area of peace raised questions as to how to make ever-expanding EU institutions more democratic as well. Would stronger ties between national governments be compatible with the power now vested within member states? A convention in 2002 debated on reform of the EU's responsibilities and institutions to allow it to connect better with its citizens and cope with enlargement. After the September 2001 terrorist attacks in the U.S., the EU leaders emphasized that such global crises demanded a global response, but indicated that in the short term the EU would be able to make only a limited collective contribution to the war against terrorism. The EU will hopefully, however, take up more peacemaking, peacekeeping and reconstruction responsibilities to strengthen the sinews of peace in order to prevent any repetition of the tragic ethnic butchery wars of the twentieth century.

In 1991, Serbian armed forces invaded Croatia and Slovenia, and savage warfare of genocide and crimes against humanity raged unchecked. Croatia, Slovenia, and Bosnia-Herzegovina seceded to form independent states. Warfare spread into Bosnia and Herzegovina, Albania, and Macedonia. The UN tried to intervene, to stop the slaughter, but was not supported by the Security Council. Armed peacekeeping was too little and too late, and unable to even provide humanitarian relief. In 1995, the guns stopped, leaving 200,000 dead or missing and 4.4 million displaced persons. The mass crimes against civilians were the most brutal imaginable. Despite these setbacks to peace in Europe, the careful steps over fifty years towards integration and co-operation continued, with the objectives of security, prosperity, and social harmony to bring all the benefits of a peaceful Europe at last.

Globalization of the economy, political movements, military affairs, cultures, and government policies is not new. But as globalization accelerates, the welfare of individuals is increasingly affected by global market forces beyond the control of nation states, and by international organizations outside the control of domestic and international political processes. Institutions such as the World Trade Organization, the International Monetary Fund, the World Bank and the Group of Eight became targets of criticism and protests from all sides. The public were not part of the planning process, and generally did not understand the issues. Too many economic decisions have been delegated to these elitist institutions and governments. Powerful groups, such as trade unions and environmental activists, believed they should be given greater responsibility for solving the world's international problems of environment, labor, immigration, and human rights. The consequences of globalization can be both advantageous and devastating from a personal, social, and political viewpoint. Workers in one country often have to emigrate to find employment, leaving behind dying towns and their traditional social and cultural background. Workers arrive in new countries with a loss of identity and traditions, and often find discrimination and open hostility. This transition has a major impact on world peace. Both governments and the people do not understand the future impacts of globalization, and what could be the long-term consequences. State governments have ceded a large degree of economic power to the global jurisdiction of international institutions by opportunistic acceptance of the best arrangements that could be obtained according to the bargaining clout of the strongest and biggest power.

An article in the Britannica summarizes the public confusion about globalization: "Clearly, the reality of globalization has outstripped the ability of the world population to understand its implications and the ability of governments to cope with its consequences. At the same time, the ceding of economic power to global actors and international institutions has outstripped the development of appropriate global political structures. As a result, probably many more years of public confusion and unfocussed protests can be expected as the stable new global world order takes shape."[2]

Research of a representative sample has shown that many less developed regions, globalized since 1980, have benefited strongly from rising incomes and a reduction of poverty. The debate on whether further liberalization of world trade is desirable continues. In 1999, the annual meeting in Seattle, U.S., of the World Trade Organization was disrupted by violent protests. Since then several more violent protests disrupted meetings of international organizations. Host countries' costs of security have risen sharply. In 2001, a meeting to expand the multilateral trading system was held in Qatar amid the highest security. Estimates for security costs alone for a meeting in 2002 in Alberta, Canada, exceeded $325 million—money that in a peaceful world would have great benefits if spent on schools or health care.

It is important to note that globalization can succeed only if all nations honor their financial and trade commitments. If nations dishonor their commitments on grounds of protecting their sovereignty, or make commitments with "escape clauses," or force one-sided commitments by the manipulation of the more powerful, globalization will not be supported by the less powerful, and will not work to advance the interests of all mankind. Such failures will not advance the cause of peace.

In a recent book by Robert S. McNamara and Professor James G. Blight, *Wilson's Ghost*, the authors recommend the policies that must be followed by the U.S. and other governments if the twenty-first century is to be less murderous than the last century. Their probing and lucid analysis of the urgency and importance of new policies for peace is summarized as follows, and reviewed in Chapter 15.

State governments will continue to be the instrument that will finally have to find the way to meet the needs of their citizens to live in peace. There can be no cessation of wars until state governments follow policies committed to two basic moral priorities. The first policy is to ensure full support for *internal peacemaking* by the citizens of one's state—to become a nation of peacemakers. The second is to be committed to external *collective peacemaking* by joining with other peace-loving states imbued with the same moral priority—to ensure world peace by full support of collective security and full support of human rights for all peoples. The U.S., the world's leader in military, economic, and social power, has the unique opportunity and responsibility to lead in world peacemaking and peacekeeping.

"For I dipped into the future, far as human eye could see,
Saw the Vision of the world, and all the wonder that would be;

Saw the heavens fill with commerce, argosies of magic sails,
Pilots of the purple twilight, dropping down with costly bales;

Heard the heavens fill with shouting, and there rained a ghastly dew
From the nations' airy navies grappling in the central blue;

Far along the world-wide whisper of the south wind rushing warm,
With the standards of the peoples plunging through the thunderstorm;

Till the war drum throbbed no longer, and the battle flags were furled
In the Parliament of man, the Federation of the world."

Alfred, Lord Tennyson
Locksley Hall, 1837-38

"This era of global challenges leaves no choice but co-operation at the global level."

Kofi Annan
Secretary-General of the UN
December, 2001

Chapter 8

UNITED NATIONS— WORLD PEACEMAKER

Since 1945 the United Nations has been, directly or indirectly, part of the lives of virtually everyone on earth. Its mission is to meet the needs of all humanity for global peace, security, justice, human dignity, equality, and universal human rights. These aspirations of the human spirit have never been realized before by mankind. The ruling powers had failed to find the path to world peace during the horrors of the twentieth century. After the scourges of the First and Second World Wars, and after Hiroshima, it was clear that mankind had only one more chance. Mankind must stop its continuing warfare, and sow the seeds of peace to prevent future wars. We must destroy the threat of nuclear warfare, or it will destroy us.

Long before World War Two it was clear that a new international organization of world states was needed. The League of Nations had failed, but collective security was still the only feasible option to secure peace for all peoples. At a meeting in London in 1941, leaders of countries occupied by Hitler signed an Inter-Allied Declaration to "work together, and with other free peoples, both in war and peace," toward worldwide social and economic security. U.S. President Roosevelt and Great Britain's (now legally the United Kingdom) Prime Minister Churchill signed the Atlantic Charter in 1941, pledging mutual support and for "a peace which will afford all nations safety and freedom from fear and want." On January 1, 1942, twenty-six nations signed the Declaration of the United Nations. In 1945, fifty-one nations met for two months in San Francisco, where they debated and signed the Charter of the United Nations—to "save succeeding generations from the scourge of war," "reaffirm faith in fundamental human rights," "establish conditions under which . . . international law can be maintained," and "promote social progress." The first sessions of the General Assembly and the Security Council were held in 1952.

The primary body of the UN responsible for peace and security issues is the Security Council of five permanent members—the U.S., U.S.S.R., U.K., France, and China. Later, ten members were added, elected by the General Assembly and serving in rotation, normally for two years. The ten non-permanent members do not have the right of veto. Any nation, large or small, can refer a dispute to the Security Council. The Council can suggest terms of agreement, impose economic and diplomatic sanctions, or if necessary authorize military actions by troops from volunteering member states. These troops wear the uniforms of their countries, have blue helmets or berets, and may be armed with light weapons. The five permanent members of the Security Council each have a veto. This was necessary in 1945. Cordell Hull, U.S. Secretary of State, explained—"Unless the Great Powers agree, we cannot hope to have peace." All members of the Security Council have used their veto powers from time to time. The U.S.S.R. used its veto power extensively, which effectively prevented vigorous action by the UN for many years. In 1950, the General Assembly was given the power to act on a "threat to peace" if the Security Council failed to do so. This has helped the UN negotiate around Council deadlocks on a number of occasions.

The UN has six principal organs; the General Assembly, the Security Council, the Economic and Social Council, the Trusteeship Council, the International Court of Justice, and the Secretariat. The General Assembly represents every UN member state, with each having one vote. Decisions on important matters require a two-thirds majority—on other matters only a simple majority. This gave the same voting power to a state of 100,000 people (Tonga) and of 281 million (U.S.), resulting in prolonged debate and delay among the 191 members jockeying to build a block of supporters. Often decisions were too little, too late, without the substance worthy of a world organization, or defeated for political reasons. No organization is perfect under all circumstances, and many recommendations have been made over the years to make both the General Assembly and the Security Council more democratic and effective.

The most important job of the UN is to keep the peace. This now requires four major functions: removing basic causes of war; solving immediate disputes; working on long-range problems such as nuclear control disarmament; and after September 11, 2001, the elimination of world terrorist organizations such as al-Qaeda, led by Osama bin Laden, a Saudi Arabian. With the winding down of the Cold War in the mid 1980s by Ronald Reagan, U.S. President, and Chairman Gorbachev of the U.S.S.R., the UN was able to become more active in both peacemaking and peacekeeping. Peacemaking has included authorizing a UN alliance to fight major wars launched by aggressor nations, such as the Korean War in 1950 and the Gulf War in 1991. Peacemaking also includes enabling the international community to remove both the root causes and the short-term causes of war, and to act to defuse violent hostilities before armed hostility erupts. Peacekeeping includes sending observer missions to gather information on hostilities, securing and maintaining cease-fire agreements, and being treaty negotiation advisers. When peacekeeping failed, as during the genocide in Rwanda, it was often because there was no peace to keep.

The UN has had extensive experience in dealing with all the issues that are precipitating causes of war. For example, in 1954, Thailand, experiencing unrest following a political *coup d'état*, asked for UN observers as a protection against war. If the disputing countries cannot find a peaceful solution, the UN can suggest terms of agreement and send in experienced arbitrators. The UN has been given authority under the Charter to authorize UN members to defeat invasion of a member state, and to take action both to prevent the outbreak of armed hostility and, if necessary, to authorize policing actions by peacekeeper units from member states, armed with light defensive weapons, to act as a buffer to keep armed fighting to a minimum until a ceasefire can be secured and maintained.

Often the mere presence of a UN force has been enough to avoid war. In response to the presence of Soviet nuclear missiles in Cuba, U.S. President Kennedy launched a naval blockade against Cuba and asked the Security Council to intervene. The UN and peacemaking diplomacy on both sides of the dispute succeeded in halting Soviet ICBM deployment in Cuba. The U.S. then called off the blockades and negotiations with Chairman Khrushchev continued to a peaceful resolution. U.S. diplomat Clark Eichelberger commented about the UN's role during the crisis: "Let us picture the U.S. and the Soviet Union deadlocked in the Caribbean, without a Security Council where they could appear and where the hopes of all mankind could be expressed. It is hard to see how one or the other could have pulled back from such a perilous position. Indeed, one could say that if there had been no UN the two giants might have confronted each other with disaster."

Since 1964, UN forces have maintained a shaky cease-fire between a Greek majority and a Turkish minority on Cyprus. The opposing sides threatened violent takeovers both before and after UN intervention. UN peacekeepers are still there, a waste of UN and peacekeeping resources. Nothing has been achieved over almost thirty-eight years to settle this longstanding ethnic dispute. Greek Cypriot president Georgios Vassilou stated, "The duty of the world is not ended by setting up the peacekeeping forces. Peacekeeping is not peacemaking. The only reason for peacekeeping is to stop the killing and give time for peacemaking." This dispute must be settled sooner or later, so why not now? If peoples of different histories, such as Belgium or Switzerland, can be peaceful, why not Cyprus?

The winding down of the Cold War in the mid 1980s gave the UN many more opportunities to make and keep peace. A major activity has been to send peacekeeping missions to act as a deterrent to armed hostilities. There have been over fifty peacekeeping missions since the one to monitor the armistice between Israel and the Arab States in 1948. The number of missions has increased in frequency and scope as armed conflicts within states has increased. (See Appendix H for detailed information on current UN peacekeeping missions.) Recent peacekeeping missions are much more demanding than the routine patrolling of cease-fire boundaries. Duties have included disarming warring factions, as in El Salvador, and functioning essentially as a temporary substitute government in the absence of stable law and order, as in East Timor.

Some peacemaking missions have not succeeded in achieving their goals. UN-backed economic sanctions failed to stop Iraq's invasion of Kuwait, and the Gulf War sanctioned by the UN followed in 1991. A UN-sponsored peace accord in Angola was short-lived. UN peacekeepers were not able to disarm both sides in a long civil war before an election was held, and fighting resumed soon after the election. In Cambodia the UN had over 20,000 soldiers, police, and civilians, as part of a $4 billion operation over two years to stabilize the economy and the government, and to prevent continuing warfare between the Khmer Rouge guerrillas and the government forces. For many years the UN has had to literally "govern" Cambodia as a protectorate.

Peacekeeping is rarely easy. Some UN members resent UN "meddling," while others want early intervention to solve political disputes. Some of the problems hampering peacekeeping are self-inflicted. Peacekeepers are often not equipped for, nor allowed to take, military action, except in self-defense. In 1993, for example, heavily armed Serbian gunmen killed a Bosnian official travelling in a "protected" UN convoy. In Rwanda UN peacekeepers were incensed by being under orders not to fight off guerrillas killing civilians in a "UN protected safe haven." When Somalia collapsed after prolonged clan warfare the UN was too late to prevent fighting and looting of UN food and medical supplies, and finally was forced to ask in late 1992 for U.S. troops to intervene. They got some supplies delivered, and stemmed the violence to some degree, but in May 1993, U.S. troops were replaced with a UN force which was under-armed, outnumbered, and unable to prevent further bloodshed, because the troops were able to fire only in self-defense. A Transitional National Government was formed, sat in the UN, and was backed by the Organization of African Unity and the Arab League. But the government enrolled guerrilla gunmen, and most of Mogadishu, the capital, remained in chaos. A peace agreement was signed in December 2001. Fighting was resumed by a number of tribes and small secessionist regions. The UN High Commission for Refugees commented, "If UN forces are going to fight their way into a place, humanitarian organizations delivering aid are going to have a very hard time carrying out their mission because their credibility as impartial organizations would be undermined." Recently, in Afghanistan, a U.S. shipment of food and medical aid was set on fire by an anti-U.S. mob.

The Universal Declaration of Human Rights was one of the first objects of UN study in 1946 and was formally adopted in 1948. The Declaration encourages respect for "the highest aspirations of the common people . . . faith in human rights, in the dignity and worth of every person, in the equal rights of men and women and of nations large and small." It mandates "human rights and fundamental freedoms for all, without distinction as to race, sex, language or religion." Specifically, the declaration affirms the right to equal protection against discrimination, arbitrary arrest or exile, slavery, cruel or inhuman punishment; equal opportunity under the law, a fair trial; the right to privacy, freedom of residence and movement within a home country, political asylum, freedom to marry without restriction of race, nationality, or religion, and the freedom to own property. Subsequent articles affirm the universal right to freedom of thought, conscience, religion, opinion, speech, assembly, and participation in one's own government.

Currently the main focus of the UN protection of human rights is on topics of genocide, slavery and forced labor, the persecution of refugees, racial discrimination, discrimination against women, hostage taking, and torture. There is also concern for the rights of ethnic minorities, native or indigenous peoples and migrant workers, concern about economic globalization, the HIV/AIDS pandemic which exceeded twenty-five per cent of the population in many sub-Saharan countries, child trafficking, and terrorism. Military action erupted in Macedonia in 2001 when frustrated ethnic Albanians fought for repatriation. In El Salvador, killings of judges, kidnapping, and police brutality continued. Prison abuses were reported in Brazil, Chile, Morocco, Malawi, Mozambique, and Turkey. In Malaysia harsh measures were taken to limit the rights of assembly and free speech.

Throughout 2001, Nigeria had ethnic and tribal violence, leaving about 50,000 persons displaced from their home villages.

Recently there were about twenty-two million refugees, including twelve million recognized refugees, 800,000 returnees, and eight million miscellaneous refugees. In the Congo 1.8 million are displaced. Afghanistan has a staggering refugee problem. Columbia's refugees increased to about 125,000. Tens of thousands of refugees fled Sierra Leone and Liberia. Many countries reduced their contributions to refugees, leaving a shortfall of $100 million, forcing Rud Lubbers, the High Commissioner for Refugees, to reduce his staff by 800. The resettlement of refugees in other countries has been tried, with little success.

The responsibilities of the UN cover a very wide range of human activity. The organization's comprehensive agenda has been developed by many different agencies and programs. It is a channel for world funds to be allocated to meet the UN mandate, an organization for service, research statistics and information dissemination, and a place for communication and advocacy respecting international problems and solutions. (See Appendix I for a list of the main 2002 priority activities of the UN.)

In addition to securing world peace and human rights, the UN has the objective to improve daily life in developing countries with environmental, social, and economic programs. Problems of famine, shelter, population control, drug abuse, health care, and maintaining a sustainable, healthy, and economic environment are addressed by the UN Educational, Scientific, and Cultural Organization (UNESCO). The UN does this with help from hundreds of governmental agencies as well as the volunteer NGOs of civil society.

The Globe and Mail, Canada, reported on March 25, 2002—"'Of the 600 million children in the world, 150 million suffer from malnutrition,' say UN officials. 'Almost 11 million die each year of preventable disease.'" Annual income in the forty-one poorest countries is well below $300, compared to about $15,000 for developed countries. Seventy percent of the world's income is produced and consumed by fifteen percent of the population. Living standards in Latin America are lower today than in the 1970s, and

African living standards have slipped to the level of the 1960s. Over 900 million adults worldwide are illiterate. A UN executive has written—"The gap in living standards between the world's rich and poor has steadily grown . . . Industrial societies . . . have prospered, but a billion people [still] live in absolute poverty".

UN Environment Programs operate in many areas, assisting in monitoring the results of environment management by local government, industry, agriculture, and management of water, and scarce resources. An environmental adviser notes, "Poor people can be stopped at borders, but poverty can't be stopped. Poverty travels in the form of drugs, terrorism, ignorance, and AIDS."

The UN has been a major supporter of global environmental conferences. At the 1992 Earth Summit at Rio de Janeiro, Brazil, a large majority of world governments signed a pact to reduce global warming. In 1997, at a follow-up world conference in Japan of 116 nations on global warming, eighty-four signed the Kyoto Protocol. By 2002, fifty-four nations have ratified or exceeded the commitment of industrialized countries to reduce the emission of six polluting gases by an average of 5.2 percent (below 1990 levels) by 2012. Some large industrialized countries have still not ratified the Kyoto Protocol. This problem was the main item on the agenda of the 2002 Earth Summit at Johannesburg, South Africa.

The interrelationship between peace, environment, health, living standards, and development was stressed by Ms. Gro Harlem Bruntland, Director-General of the World Health Organization, a medical doctor and three times Prime Minister of Norway, in an article in the Britannica 1998 edition:[1] "Concerns about environment, health, population, women, and development . . . [these] are global in nature . . . [and] can be overcome only by intensified global co-operation and by strong, efficient, and forward-looking international institutions underpinning our common efforts . . . In 2000, almost three billion of the world's six billion lived in urban areas. A failure to manage the urban infrastructure will lead to further mushrooming of settlements having insufficient access to essential facilities such as clean water, sanitation, food supplies, transportation, education, health care, and other public services. We know what that means:

overcrowding and a disease pattern linked to poverty and an unhealthy environment."

UN short-term emergency aid of food and basic needs for victims of famine or natural disasters is handled by the UN Disaster and Relief Organization (UNDRO). The UN Food and Agriculture Organization (FAO) is concerned with supplying food and training to developing countries over the long-term. FAO co-ordinates international programs to provide donated food to needy countries or store it for an emergency. In a recent year, FAO's World Food Program shipped $1.1 billion from one hundred countries in cash and commodities, sent to seventy-nine operations in thirty-two countries, affecting some fifteen million people. Food aid deliveries are often hampered by local chaos, slow response, overlapping agencies, and poor delivery efficiency. These were factors in a critical worsening of the famine in Somalia. The UN also provides advisers, education programs, and materials to improve techniques and results in agriculture, fisheries, forestry, livestock, and land reform.

The critical health situation, especially in the less developed countries and urban slums, is of major concern for the UN and its chief agency, the World Health Organization (WHO). Nearly half the world's population live in areas where malaria, AIDS, cancer, measles, heart disease, and tetanus are major killers. Every day about forty thousand children die of preventable disease and starvation—a total of fourteen million every year. WHO provides assistance to local health agencies and to field volunteers of medical services organizations, such as Doctors Without Borders. An estimated one million people in developing countries are reached each year by WHO programs. The UN Children's Fund (UNICEF) reaches many millions of children through age fifteen in 162 countries every year. A major UNICEF program provides vaccinations to over eighty percent of the world's children exposed to infectious diseases and to AIDS. The challenge for the future will be to maintain and expand the fight against disease and poverty while securing a clean environment.

Experienced observers of the UN stress that there are pervasive causes of the world's increasing inhumanity, mass misery, and violence. They have examined how the UN responded to achieve its goals despite these negative trends and what needs to be done to improve its effectiveness. A summary of many different views and recommendations is constructive:

- The UN is basically the universal extension of ourselves, our national behavior. We are citizens of both our nation and the United Nations, and have as "dual citizens" the ultimate responsibility for the UN;

- Governments too often allow the UN to function only in uncoordinated fits and starts, without enough sustained effort against root causes. Neglected causes are now producing crises and human suffering on an increasing scale, placing massive burdens on the limited capabilities of the UN to respond. *We citizens therefore have no choice but to tackle both the causes and the consequences of human neglect and suffering;*

- Governments should provide trained Rapid Response forces available instantly to the Secretary-General, as urged by Sir Brian Urquhart,[2] to prevent such horrors as occurred in Rwanda *before* they expand into genocide;

- The UN General Assembly and Security Council should vote to approve the authorization procedure recommended on page XII of *The Responsibility To Protect* report of the International Commission on Intervention and State Sovereignty (see Appendix G);

- It is hypocritical for governments that are promoting their own arms sales to criticize levels of military expenditure in other countries;

- The ultimate form of hypocrisy in arms issues is the attitude of nuclear powers toward nuclear "proliferation," while refusing to forego the very weapons they themselves introduced to the world;

- We must find a truly ethical standard in national and international decision-making to replace the unethical practice of the powerful demanding their own aggressiveness be accepted, while that of others is punished. Major powers have used outright economic intimidation of impoverished countries to secure their votes or their silence on many UN issues. The Charter invokes the best in all of us when it asks that we "practice tolerance and live together in peace with one another as good neighbors." We must be more vigilant and resolute in demanding that our decision-makers act according to this principle;

- There is too much tangled overlapping of separately-operated humanitarian relief funds and machinery, which could be consolidated into an efficient Operations Branch of the UN Department of Humanitarian Affairs, organized to best help the front-line volunteers of all the NGOs;

- One report states that all official "aid" from the North to the South amounts to about $56 billion a year. The trade, monetary, and financial policies of the same donor governments are currently depriving developing countries of over $500 billion in *income* that they could be earning each year if restrictive trade practices against the less developed world were stopped;[3]

- To lay solid foundations of trust the General Assembly and the Security Council should adopt clear criteria and rules of engagement for interventions by the UN with or without the request of a state. The efficiency of the UN command systems should be improved to the point where no major power will have an excuse for refusing to place its forces under a field commander approved by the UN, while expecting all other countries to do so;

- It is unconscionable for governments that were responsible for, or complicit in, the total destabilization of countries like Angola and Mozambique, to expect the UN to try to cope with the chaos with little or no special assistance;

- The major industrial powers have refused to create an equitable International Trade Organization. The International Monetary Fund (IMF) focuses only on the poorest countries, imposing conditions that have contributed to one upheaval after another. Too often, the "global economy" is in reality the economy of North America, Europe, and Japan. The costs of putting band-aids on the mass abject poverty in less developed areas are staggering, and will increase exponentially unless addressed. The more developed areas will have peace only when the needy of the less developed areas have the purchasing power to achieve an equitable standard of living. An urgent, new Marshall Plan alliance of wealthy nations for massive aid to the poorest nations may be the only sensible way to give the poor nations a civilized standard of living, and to prevent uncontrollable masses of the poorest nations overwhelming the ability of the affluent nations to absorb them without disasters to both emigrants and receiving nations.

The criticisms that the UN has not been able to eliminate the scourge of warfare, and that there is still a worldwide denial of justice, human dignity, and universal human welfare and rights for all people, are not valid. The UN is in reality a deputy of the nation states, and has achieved an amazing degree of success despite the failure of the nation states and the general public to give the UN the direction and the support required to carry out its duties. The leaders of modern society are faced with finding a new approach to building world peace. The fatal flaws of war and inhumanity of the last one hundred years have degraded our humanity, and it may well require another hundred years for civilization and humanity to work its way out of the abyss of mankind's inhumanity toward one another which is manifest in today's society. The reform and renaissance of the ethical spirit for peace must start with "we, the people," the world nation states, and the UN. To meet the dreams of the founders of the UN is the most urgent and demanding task facing mankind today. The continuing evolution of the progress since the end of the Second World War toward the unity of mankind and our co-dependence on one another as citizens of "one world," the "global village," has made the work of the UN the main cohesive entity to serve all nations and all mankind. The UN is now indispensable as the only organization unifying the political and social future of mankind. Without the UN there is no prospect of peace, goodwill, and the continuation of raising and sharing the standard of living of all mankind.

"Advocacy and witnessing are integral to our humanitarian mission."

James Orbinski, President
Doctors Without Borders/
Médicins Sans Frontières

We appeal, as human beings, to human beings. Remember your humanity, and forget the rest. If you do so, the way lies open for a new paradise; if you cannot, there lies before you the risk of universal death . . . . "

Bertrand Russell
The Russell-Einstein Manifesto, 1954

Chapter 9

VOLUNTEER PARTNERS IN PEACEMAKING

We have reviewed the role of state governments and the UN in building the foundations of peacemaking and peacekeeping. The main underpinning of these foundations is the citizens—or grass roots—the base on which the foundations of peace are built. Every person shares a universal longing for peace with all of humanity. In every society there are volunteers who join groups working for peace—members of religious bodies such as the Quakers, the Salvation Army, and hundreds of thousands of humanitarian causes, from block parents to canvassers for donations to food banks and rummage sales. NGOs have grown out of the grass roots as organized special interest volunteer groups who build up massive media and international support for peace organizations such as the International Physicians for the Prevention of Nuclear War, Médicins Sans Frontières (Doctors Without Borders) and the International Campaign to Ban Landmines. NGOs have raised worldwide concerns for peace and have influenced agendas at the state and UN levels. They are activist organizations of *civil society*, all part of the common ground of the grass roots in working for peace. It is important to note that ideas and actions flow mainly from the bottom up, from the grass roots to state decisions, and not from the top down—the traditional procedure in peacemaking legalities. In Canada there are more than seven million volunteers for charitable causes. Twenty-two million give donations annually to 80,000 registered charities and an endless number of non-registered social welfare causes. Most countries of developed societies have comparable involvement of their citizens in working for peace and humanitarian causes.

The outstanding work of both Save The Children, founded in the U.K. in 1919 by Eglantyne Jebb and Dorothy Buxton, and of Oxfam, founded in 1942 by a small group including Professor Gilbert Murray and Canon T. R. Milford, is legendary. These organizations have inspired thousands of volunteers and brought aid to the world's most needy.

It is important to look at several examples of the growth and enduring strength of present day volunteer peacemaking organizations which started with one person and a small group of friends. The Nobel Peace Prize of 1947 was awarded to two Quaker organizations, the Friends Service Council of Great Britain and the American Friends Service Committee of the U.S. The Quakers are best known for their good works. They were nominated for the Nobel Peace Prize after the First World War for their field ambulance and war-relief work, and again in the 1930s for their assistance to refugees from Nazi oppression. Many leading peacemakers have been Quakers. William Penn, a Quaker and founder of Pennsylvania, said, "True Godliness does not take men out of the world, but leads them into it, to mend it . . . Let us then try what love can do." Many Quakers were in front line hospital units in the two world wars. Many joined Quaker relief units in Europe, India, China, and Japan after the Second World War.

The Quaker religion was founded as the Society of Friends in the seventeenth century by George Fox who "*trembled* in the spirit of the Lord." In the words of Irwin Abrams, Nobel Peace Prize historian, "Quaker pacifism has never been a mere refusal to join the armed services; to Quakers it is a way of life with which war is incompatible, an outward expression of the Inward Spirit of Truth and Love and Goodness, with which every person is endowed and which is to be nurtured and translated into action."[1] Peace Laureates Philip Noel-Baker (1959) and Emily Balch (1946) were Quakers. U.S. President Herbert Hoover, a Quaker, created an American Relief Administration which distributed food to over one million destitute German and

Austrian children during the great depression of the early thirties. Quakers are currently active volunteers in a number of social causes, such as prison reform, care of the mentally ill, and support for abused women and children. Total Quaker membership in the U.S. and Great Britian is about 200,000, doing relief work made possible by the thousands of additional volunteers who support Quaker projects. During addresses on receiving the Nobel Peace prize on behalf of the Quakers, they were described as "common folk, not statesmen, not generals, but just simple plain men and women . . . a few thousand Quakers and their friends, if they devote themselves to resolute insistence on goodwill in place of force, even in the face of great disaster . . . can do something to build a better world."[2]

The essence of service to peace by volunteers is that it usually starts in the mind and soul of one woman or man inspired to make a contribution to the human family. The Salvation Army is familiar to all—on the street, rain or snow, with a cheery greeting for all as money is dropped into a red kettle to provide a Christmas dinner for the homeless. The "Sally Ann" canteens went overseas with the young soldiers. At home they ran thrift shops, provided hostels with shelter and food, collected used clothes for the needy, and became one of the largest religious philanthropic organizations in the world. The Salvation Army was founded in Great Britain in 1865 by William Booth. He attracted street-corner groups of the homeless down and out, with a small band of women and men singing hymns, with tambourines, a drum, and a trumpet, followed by a religious message. The basic unit of the Salvation Army is the corps community centre. In addition to social service activities, it operates drug and alcohol rehabilitation programs, boys' and girls' camps, senior citizens' hostels, day-care centers, family assistance programs, and the rehabilitation of prisoners. Much of the worldwide service of the Salvation Army is in less developed countries, providing education, basic needs, vocational instruction, and disaster relief.

The Salvation Army's U.S. arm has an annual budget of $2 billion of which $1.4 billion comes from volunteer fund-raising, and is managed by a head office of less than one hundred people. It has been called the most effective organization in the U.S., with eighty-seven per cent of income going directly to programs to assist all who come for help. In the U.S., there are over 28 million such calls yearly. Its substance-abuse treatment centers have success rates that are the envy of the field. Their mission statement is, "To preach the gospel of Jesus Christ and to meet human needs in His name, without discrimination . . . . The Salvation Army stands for hope; that, when every other light is extinguished, and every other star has gone down, this one gleam shines steadily and clearly out of a darkened sky."— William Booth, Founder.

There are many other organizations that have started with one person and have grown to very large organizations which do their part in building a better world of the "fraternity among nations," to use the words in Alfred Nobel's will. The Young Men's Christian Association (YMCA) was founded in London in 1844 by George Williams and a group of friends. Today, the YMCA is in 120 countries, serving about thirty million persons yearly. There are 2,400 branches in the U.S., and many maintain contact with other countries. Membership is open for all, to participate in physical, educational, social, and religious programs, including strong emphasis on citizenship and world affairs.

The Young Women's Christian Association (YWCA) was founded in 1887 in Great Britain by Emma Roberts and Lady Kinnaird, who opened homes, clubs, and institutes for young women in business or in need of shelter and welfare. New programs have been developed to meet new needs, such as computer skills, drug abstention, and community outreach. There are now about twenty-five million members in over 100 countries, with ninety-four national YWCA associations.

The Young Men's Christian Association and Young Women's Christian Association are among the largest non-profit organizations of volunteers in the world, serving about fifty-five million members in over ninety countries. One of their main goals is increasing international education and volunteer exchanges. They have programs in adult education, outdoor activities, community and youth services, guidance and counselling, refugee resettlement, child-care centers, employment placement services, and leadership training.

The Boy Scouts were founded in Great Britain in 1907 by Lord

Baden-Powell to train boys in outdoor skills, citizenship, and personal achievement. The movement has always encouraged a multicultural approach, and soon spread rapidly to all parts of the world. During both world wars Scouts under military age volunteered for essential duties on the home front. World jamborees are held every four years in various countries, bringing together the youth of all nations.

The Girl Guides movement had a spontaneous beginning by the girls themselves, in admiration of their brothers in the Boy Scouts. Lady Baden-Powell organized the Guides to promote good citizenship and service to others. Here again Guides under eighteen did service work on the home front during the two world wars. There are now about ten million Girl Guides, Girl Scouts, and Campfire Girls in 140 countries. Their mission is to encourage girls to develop their fullest potential as responsible citizens of the world.

The Peace Corps is an independent volunteer organization supported by the U.S. government, working overseas with people in less developed countries. The chief goals of the corps are to help the poor obtain everyday needs, to promote world peace, and to increase the understanding between peoples of all nations. The Peace Corps was established in 1961 by U.S. President Kennedy. It selects, trains, and supports American men and women for two years of service, sending them to the less developed nations that request them. Agencies similar to the Peace Corps have been organized in about twenty-five other countries, all enlisting volunteers from among their young people to serve overseas. Projects are selected by host countries. Most are designed to raise the living standard of people who dwell in villages. The corps works to improve agriculture, health care, education, to promote local leadership and management of community resources, and to develop small businesses.

The Red Cross, founded in 1863 by Henri Dunant and one of the largest and best known volunteer organizations in the world, has received four Nobel Peace Prizes since the first was awarded to Dunant in 1901. It is the primary supplier of blood and blood products in many countries. In the U.S., they collect blood from about 4.5 million donors each year. A nationwide network of tissue centers supplies tissue used for transplants, such as heart valves, ligament, tendon, bone, and blood vessels. The Red Cross also conducts research to improve the safety of blood supplies and develop potentially lifesaving medical products. They provide first aid and safety training, instructions in using medical emergency equipment, and HIV/AIDS prevention. In Muslim nations the Red Crescent Society is an independent volunteer organization which operates along the same lines as the Red Cross.

The list of Nobel Peace Awards to Institutions and Associations (Appendix C, Table 3) presents an amazing record of the dedication and unconquerable determination of the work of individual peacemakers who presented an idea and followed through to organize a worldwide power for peace. The seventeen organizations are all still active, which is an outstanding tribute to the strength and universal appeal of associations that fill an essential need in building world peace. The Nansen International Office for Refugees (and Nansen Passport), Red Cross, Quakers, Amnesty International, International Physicians for the Prevention of Nuclear War, Pugwash Conferences on Science and World Affairs, International Campaign to Ban Landmines, and Médicins Sans Frontières (Doctors Without Borders) were all launched by volunteers.

The UN and state government activities in peacemaking are part of established and formalized procedures, with little opportunity or initiative to involve the grass roots in innovative solutions to international problems of peace and security, economic and social responsibilities, human rights and humanitarian challenges, financial and trade matters. The words of the UN Charter gave hope to saving succeeding generations from the scourge of war, and of developing international machinery for the promotion of economic and social advancement of all peoples. The Charter states that "conditions of stability and well-being [are] necessary for peaceful and friendly relations among nations based on respect [for] equal rights and self-determination." A new world order committed governments "to contribute to the expansion of the world economy and to liberate humanity from hunger." The World Health Organization (WHO) declared that "the health of all people is fundamental to the attainment of peace and security." The UN Educational, Scientific, and Cultural Organization (UNESCO) stated that "since wars begin in the minds of men it is in the minds of men that the defences of peace must be constructed." Taken together, the constitutional structures of the UN have developed into a new *world system* giving all humanity a comprehensive international social contract for the first time.

Following the Second World War the trend toward concentrating all peacemaking discussion and policy making in a small group of powerful countries had to be reversed. A wider and more democratic system of participation was introduced, necessary in a highly interdependent world wherein many issues of international scope were beyond the capacity of powerful states, acting alone, to resolve. These problems could, however, be approached by dedicated volunteer activists from a wide diversity of backgrounds and nations, who banded together to form NGOs to influence state governments and the UN. Formal mechanisms for NGO participation at the UN level are very limited compared to the breadth and depth of NGO involvement in world affairs. Mainly, however, NGOs are able to contribute their insights, experience, and expertise to UN decision-making and policy-setting at the national level. "The shape our societies take does not depend exclusively on governments. Individuals, families, community groups, international foundations, trans-national corporations, the communication media—these and many others help mould civil society. There are thousands of NGOs operating nationally and internationally, monitoring human rights, organizing humanitarian aid, and promoting the interests of such groups as women, the disabled, or indigenous people. New organizations emerge each year, often sprouting up spontaneously in response to felt needs and forming new alliances for change. They can powerfully influence government policies, as many women's organizations and environmental groups have demonstrated."—*UN Development Program Human Development Report, 1994.*

NGO work takes many forms, including information dissemination, projects, collaboration with UN Agencies, advocacy, and lobbying of governments. The Economic and Social Council (ECOSOC) of the UN, a fifty-four-member body, co-ordinates and oversees work in the economic and social fields, following formal procedures and arrangements used also with other agencies and programs. The UN has a Department of Public Information (DPI) to service public relations, including NGOs. In the mid nineties there were 411 NGOs with UN consultative status, 1,096 on a general roster, and 1,312 with general consultative/roster status.

NGO participation at major UN conferences has increased in recent years, particularly in issues relating to sustainable development and in lobbying national governments as a basic form of popular representation. NGOs face a dilemma. Recent demands require more policy work at the international level, leaving less time to implement programs at the local level. NGOs are mainly special interest groups, but broad public participation is essential for liaison and effectiveness. They are a specialized group of civil society building bridges between civil society, the UN, and state governments. One example of this was the strong support of the Canadian government for the NGO campaign to secure ratification of the International Protocol to Ban Landmines. U.S. Senator Leahy noted this important support of the Canadian government whereby the objectives of civil society were given preference over some governments' objections. "I would like to have my government signing today more than anything else in my political life . . . [a product of the] blend of the best of civil society, individual advocacy, and government action."

Everywhere in the world today NGOs have been unavoidably drawn into the industrial development process, as described by Erskine Childers in *Challenges to the United Nations*.[3] In Zimbabwe an NGO "credit union" now links together local savings clubs, government agencies, and fertilizer corporations to improve agricultural practices. In Kenya an environmental NGO network is developing a national biomass energy policy. In Brazil, NGOs are defending the Amazonian Indians against the pollution from mining. In Mexico City NGOs are defining policies to help the poor cope with earthquakes. In Sri Lanka and Indonesia NGOs have moved the state to support funding of NGOs demanding sustainable logging practices. NGOs organize housing co-operatives in Uruguay, provide transport to market for local producers in Africa, address drug-related problems in Columbia and Ecuador, and are a partner with the Association for Progressive Communication in setting up information links between nine countries in Europe and Central America.

NGOs are involved in an increasing number of campaigns protecting the environment. They are active in the Council for Sustainable Development (CSD), a UN forum to assist "we the people" in prosecuting violators of environmental and developmental rights, much as Amnesty International is a forum to protest against state violence and abuse of human rights. The CSD presents an opportunity for NGOs to build a global constituency for earth issues through a new Earth Council, which publishes monthly "alerts" on the environment, human rights development, and peace movements. The Earth Council promotes a free flow of information, giving the UN a broad basis for public participation, as envisioned in the Charter.

The involvement of NGOs in becoming an essential new component with state governments, the UN, the business community, and the grass roots is gaining ground rapidly in the opening years of the twenty-first century. NGOs have been successful in presenting the concerns of civil society at international meetings. The signing of the Kyoto, Japan, global warming treaty in 1997 was achieved by intense pressure from environmental NGOs. Here, for the first time, smaller and middle-sized powers did not yield ground to intense pressure to weaken the treaty to accommodate the policies of a few large powers. Kyoto could not have happened without the worldwide environmental movement. New global rules were negotiated on climate warming. A list of fifty key issues was discussed at The Hague Appeal For Peace and Justice Conference in 1999; all involved initiatives by NGOs to secure actions by state governments. Examples of current issues are appeals for low cost medicines and for an increase in foreign aid in the worldwide fight against poverty and insecurity in the less developed world. The NGO proposals are summarized in Chapter 6 under Main Actions—Implementing The Hague Agenda.

Sustained NGO pressure has gained support for structures that allow a wider cross-section of the public to participate in making the rules that govern potentially destructive behavior, whether in the form of pollution, trade warfare, or terrorist networks. While NGOs cannot replace the functions of elected governments, they provide essential ideas, information, pressure for results, and the leverage to implement solutions on the ground, all necessary to solve global problems. This is especially true at the global level, where very few elements of global processes of state government exist. Better ways to build international consensus between grass roots peacemakers, NGOs, and state governments must be developed, not by creation of new organization structures, but with the support to full co-operative efficiency of the peacemaking potential we have now.

NGOs will be more effective if they have an iron clad non-violent code of conduct as a prerequisite to discussion, if they work harder to bring in rarely heard voices of the less developed world, and if they are transparent, accountable, and honest in what they say and do. "This is the future of global citizen action: not gas masks and gasoline bombs but a disciplined democratic commitment to the responsibilities—as well as the rights—of global citizenship . . . . The boundaries between direct and representative democracy, and between local, national, and global governance, are being tested and re-arranged. Where this will end up, no one knows, but the question for governments, business, and civil society is already clear: Do they have the courage and imagination to work out new answers in partnership together, or only the mindset that sees a new space to be fought over for their own power and profit? The stakes are very high."[1] (Michael Edwards) - *Globe and Mail*

"The ballot is stronger than the bullet."

Abraham Lincoln,
1856 Address,
16th President of the U.S.

"We can have democracy in this country, or we can have great wealth concentrated in the hands of a few, but we can't have both."

Louis D. Brandeis
Judge, U.S. Supreme Court

Chapter 10

WORLD PEACE AND DEMOCRACY

World peace and democracy are two essential components of modern civilization, part of an interwoven mosaic affecting all areas of society. The gradual evolution of western civilization toward peace and democracy has progressed slowly since the Middle Ages. Unfortunately, progress respecting peace during the twentieth century could only be described as three steps forward and two steps back. The longing for peace continued to grow slowly up from the grass roots of mankind, nourished by the ethical spirit of humanitarianism, and by the development of social, economic, legal, and political advances of a society based on the common bonds of humanity. The universal love of all peoples for peace has motivated increasing millions of peacemaking volunteers of civil society, activist NGOs, responsive state governments, and the UN, which unites all peoples in a collective and universal pledge to work for peace. During the last two centuries the same influences have enhanced the growth of democracy, until today it is the main sustaining hope for a political system that will advance the capability of peoples and of states to free mankind from the scourge of armed conflict and to advance the cause of economic and human rights for all peoples.

The Secretary-General of the UN, Kofi Annan, stressed the link between peace and democracy: "The lesson of the last century has been that where the dignity of the individual has been trampled or threatened—where citizens have not enjoyed the basic right to choose their government, or the right to change it regularly—conflict has too often followed . . . . Three key priorities of the UN in the next century are: eradicating poverty, preventing conflict, and promoting democracy . . . . Only where individual rights are respected can differences be channelled politically and resolved peacefully. Only in a democratic environment . . . can individual self-expression and self-government be secured, and freedom of association be upheld."[1]

U.S. President Abraham Lincoln described democracy as government of the people, by the people, for the people. Sir Winston Churchill defended democracy in the British House of Commons: "No one pretends that democracy is perfect or all-wise. Indeed, it has been said that democracy is the worst form of government except all those other forms that have been tried from time to time." In brief, the essence of democracy is one man, one vote; regular periodic elections; human rights for all; a free media; parliamentary procedures as established by a constitution of democratic principles; justice and legal institutions; historical traditions and cultures endorsed by peace-loving peoples; institutionalized party politics, including an independent official opposition; and formalized and fair voting systems. The aim is to have honesty, clarity, integrity, transparency, fairness, and due diligence in all matters affecting government for the people. As perfection in human endeavors is not achievable, so it is with democracy. The British *Mother of Parliaments* has had many advances and retreats since 1215 when King John of England was forced to sign the Magna Carta to confirm and guarantee key historic liberties for his subjects. Many improvements in democratic principles and procedures have been developed over the past almost 800 years, so it is manifestly unreasonable to expect a tribal society to become a strong modern democracy in one or two lifetimes. It is also important to remember that democracy was developed by hard work, struggle, sacrifice, and a willingness to risk all to make the necessary advances, one step at a time. Mature democratic societies have a basic responsibility to help new democracies by giving all necessary support during a long period of trial and error, and by showing by example the best that democracy can be. Democracy is essential for world peace. Without democracy, those with dictatorial power have waged violence and wars to achieve the ends of the ruling elite rather than the welfare of society. The common people bear in war "blood, toil, tears, and sweat,"[2] the destruction of their homes and meagre resources, the loss of their young men. They have slowly learned that the ordinary citizen must be the final decider of all key matters of peace and war, as these issues are too important to continue having key decisions made by despots, politicians, or generals. Unfortunately, many strong nations have governments that have allowed democracy to be down-graded from its full potential, and many weak governments, especially of ex-colonial emergence, are in reality savage dictatorships under the guise of democracy.

The words of Nelson Mandela show how far the ethical spirit of humanitarianism has come in support of democracy: "We will have created a society which recognizes that all people are born equal, with each entitled in equal measure to life, liberty, prosperity, human rights and good governance. This must be a world of democracy and respect for human rights, a world freed from the horrors of poverty, hunger, deprivation, and ignorance, relieved of the threat and scourge of civil wars and external aggression and unburdened of the great tragedy of millions forced to become refugees . . . . [We must] demonstrate in practice that the normal condition for human existence is democracy."[3]

Since 1990, forty-two of the forty-eight countries in sub-Saharan Africa have held multi-party elections. Not since Africa began shaking off colonial rule has the continent witnessed such broad political change. In the early 1980s, only four countries held multi-party elections in a continent dominated by autocrats and military juntas. Now, despite evidence of vote rigging, intimidation, and killings, most Africans have the right to vote, but in many new democracies voting is not without obstruction, intimidation, and violence. However, despite the attacks on democracy in many states, governing parties in Senegal, Mauritius, Ghana, and Mali have recently handed power over peacefully to opposition party rivals, a brave and essential act of democratic principle.

In sub-Saharan Africa political and economic changes are often accompanied by bad governance, corruption, crime, and deepening poverty. In Zimbabwe, Kenya, and Republic of the Congo, for example, national leaders, supported by rival militias, have been accused of manipulating the electoral process and continuing to persecute or silence their critics. Democracy has often been followed by deteriorating living standards. Many Africans are now freer but poorer than they have been in decades. Free enterprise reforms have not yet increased the standard of living to an acceptable level. Foreign aid has dropped to its lowest levels in several decades. In practice, the recognition and granting of statehood by the UN has been based primarily on the right of colonial people to self-determination, irrespective of their actual capacity and/or readiness to govern. Under this policy, many new African nations have not been ready for self-government. Some countries, such as South Africa, Mozambique, and Senegal, are making progress toward democracy. In 2002, Sierra Leone had its first election since the end of its civil war throughout most of the 1990s. In Lesotho, after an attempted coup in 1998, a peaceful election has been held.

In June of 2002, at a meeting of G8 leaders in Canada on foreign aid, African leaders tried to persuade Western governments to open markets to African produce, and to give more foreign aid and investment to Africa's fledgling democracies. The presidents of South Africa, Nigeria, and Senegal are confident that a new generation of African leaders is committed to good governance and respect for human rights. They have endorsed a plan called the *New Partnership for Africa's Development,* which includes the creation of a peer group review system to speed up African compliance with democratic principles. "We must not be complacent," said the UN's special representative for Africa. "There are still seventeen ongoing [armed] conflicts. Africa is still the poorest continent in the world, the biggest sufferer of HIV and AIDS, the continent with the most external debts and the least foreign investment. But we are a lot more hopeful than we were five or ten years ago."

In a recent survey of public opinion in twelve African countries, seventy percent of the respondents said democracy was "always preferable" to non-democratic forms of government, despite the failure of the new democratic political systems to deliver economic benefits to the masses. The World Bank reported that per capita income in sub-Saharan Africa—about $474 per year—is less in 2002 than it was at the end of the 1960s. In Nigeria, where democracy returned in 1999 after sixteen years of military misrule, rising lawlessness and government corruption have overshadowed real advances in personal freedom. Even in Africa's most stable and prosperous countries, such as South Africa, competitive multiparty systems are still struggling to achieve maturity. In the Congo Republic, only one real candidate stood for election on voting day. A new residency law barred two candidates from running, and a former prime minister dropped out two days before the vote, saying the elections were rigged.

Strong democracies give the highest priority to providing external security, law and order, and internal protection. The state must protect communities against each other, individuals against individuals, and individuals against predatory or discriminating actions of the authorities. Democracies must provide essential services, but must refrain from taxing too much compared to the services offered. To do otherwise would diminish the legitimacy of a democracy. Tax and price increases are a constant reality in the environment of economic decline that has prevailed in Africa for many recent years. It is perhaps not accidental that the erosion of democracy in Africa correlates strongly with poor economic performance. Building strong democratic traditions requires favorable economic progress and strong consensus and adherence to the "fair and honest rules of the game" of democratic politics.

Weak democracies often experience one powerful group "capturing" the state and using its authority to exclude others from participation and equal access to government benefits and resources. Often the military, warlords, or guerrillas, gain power. The average less developed African state has spent more than one-half of its years of independence since 1946 with the military in power. Another weakness is the ability of integrationist and/or secessionist groups to seize control for purposes that are fundamentally incompatible with the existence of a democratic state. Marginal democratic states are seriously weakened by internal divisions, with decisions often made and enforced by a small group in power and not by state institutions. It appears to be inevitable that weak states will be the breeding grounds of war and massacres of civilians and soldiers alike for many years to come. Weak and failed states have not been able to establish adequate democratic processes. Somalia collapsed amidst a failed attempt to create a state on the western model. The list of failed and failing states (see Chapter 1) is a very long and tragic one. Most failed states had hoped to develop a democracy after release from colonial powers, but the survivors have not been able to establish democratic customs and processes, and cannot be considered healthy democracies.

During the last half of the twentieth century, the lessons of the futility and horror of war were finally learned by many autocracies. Italy, Germany, and Japan, for example, the most warlike of nations under despotic rule, have decided democratically to settle any conflicts without war, whereas the dictatorships of Yugoslavia and the U.S.S.R. were not able to avoid collapse and murderous internal wars. When the voice of democratic people is heard there is a far more cautious and conciliatory approach to settling international conflicts than is the case with a dictatorship wanting to maintain power at any cost. The link has finally been established that the peoples of the "global village" are dependent on one another to act together to ensure the best future for all mankind, and the greatest threat to this is the continuation of wars. The peoples in a democracy will be guided toward peaceful solutions, whereas the peoples in an autocracy will not be able to counter the narrow nationalistic focus of the rulers of the state. The spread of democracy will encourage the harmony of international relations between peoples. This has not been the case under autocratic rule, as has been continually shown by the failure of ex-colonial weak states to avoid internal wars, or wars with neighboring weak states.

There have been no wars between South American states since 1941, despite the fact that many governments were not democratic. South America illustrates that states which had not been able to develop a strong democracy nevertheless learned that armed hostilities had not solved anything. All of them have decided that it is much better to live in reasonable harmony with each other. Since

1900, eight territorial conflicts were settled peacefully, and only two were resolved by war. South America has solved most conflicts peacefully for many years, except for the continuing drug and guerrilla wars and conflicting territorial claims of military rulers. South America is clearly not yet a zone of peace, but it is a predictably peaceful, if not demilitarized, no war zone. The probabilities of conflict are substantially lower now. It is notable that one Central American country, Costa Rica, had declared itself a "no war zone" and disbanded its military. Needless to say, it is a successful democracy. With the co-operation and help of all countries of North, Central, and South America, it is reasonable to expect that less developed regions will see more stable and people-oriented democracies gradually develop and become free of conflict and abuses of human rights.

Many of the failing states in the less developed world call themselves democracies but do not provide democratic governance. The recent elections in Zimbabwe and Kenya were fraudulent. The actions of many so-called democracies among the new ex-colonial states are a complete denial of both peace and democracy. Since 1990, forty-two of the forty-eight states in sub-Saharan Africa have held multi-party elections, but most of them are not governed with prevailing western democratic standards. Corruption and poverty still cloud political changes.

Some democracies have frequently subverted popularly elected external regimes through clandestine actions, arming of opposition groups, and economic coercion. Former colonial powers have supported armed intervention to sustain collapsing military despots in parts of Africa *against* popular movements, and in Chile in 1972-3 by the destabilization of the elected Allende government. By and large, however, western democracies do not usually war against each other, but they have often acted militarily or by proxy to veto the politics and policies of emerging democracies. Needless to say, this has not been helpful for the long-term growth of true democracies.

The UN was created in 1945 with a necessary compromise between the great powers of democratic states—the U.S., U.K., and France— and non-democratic states—the U.S.S.R. and China. However, a large majority of the original fifty-one members were democracies, and democracies are substantially the largest membership today. History has confirmed that in order to have peace and equality for all peoples *within* a state there must be democracy *within* the state. The continuing challenge for strong democracies is to demonstrate that in order to have peace *between* states there must be mutual understanding between states that share democratic principles and customs, a free and equal society, and a system of economics that enhances the freedom, equality, and standard of living of all peoples involved.

A large number of democracies have become complacent and non-reforming. It is constructive to list some of the key concerns today about the poor political health of many large and small democracies:

- Low voter turnout;
- General lack of public trust in the honesty, integrity, efficiency, and accountability of governments and politicians;
- Low level of education in and commitment to political affairs by the majority of voters;
- The media, opinion polls, and demagogues have more power to influence votes than parliamentary debate of elected representatives. At the end of the twentieth century the media were a more important component of the political process than parties and electoral systems. An ethical and honest media is an essential part of a healthy democracy, but the media of many countries fail to meet these standards;
- Graft, corruption, bribery and coercion continue "as usual," in both high and low offices of government;
- *The Globe and Mail*, Toronto, reported on June 19, 2002, statements of Jesse Ventura, Governor of Minnesota, "Career politicians are more interested in self-service than in public service. That's the downfall of our political system . . . the buying and selling of politicians. We have a political system based on bribery. In the private sector, you're arrested. In the public sector, it's the norm.";
- "Dirty tricks" and "personal smearing" are often used as campaign tactics;

- The appeal of politics as a career for public-spirited and highly qualified candidates is declining;
- Reform of campaign financing is overdue;
- Protection of minorities is often not good enough;
- Frequent abuses of lobbying by special interest groups;
- Lack of support for the basic ethical principles of the free enterprise market economy (discussed in Chapter 11);
- Excessive growth of bureaucracy and "big government";
- Excessive government spending, often "out of control" and to "bribe the voters";
- Inadequate progress toward equality of women in politics and government;
- Continuing growth of the power of big corporations to secure political favors from government;
- Military-industrial complexes of many powers have secured advantageous treatment by governments;
- Domestic ethical and legal democratic principles have often not been practised in foreign affairs;
- Tendency of politicians to show greater concern about the next election than for the need for timely action to address major long term problems, such as threats of population growth, nuclear armaments, environmental degradation, aid to less developed states for progress in human rights, sustainable economic development, cancellation of debts of the underdeveloped world;
- Excessive expenditures on defence when more money spent on aid to less developed countries is an urgent necessity, and will do more to advance the cause of peace than escalating rearmament;
- Abuse of power under many democratic parliamentary systems, whereby there are very few checks and balances to limit the power of the Prime Minister and the government. Many constitutions do not provide for checks and balances between legislative, administrative, and legal authority. In the U.S., the American founding fathers established this essential provision to ensure prevention of abuses by the government in power;

- Politicians often give lip service to the support of free trade and the reduction of domestic subsidies and tariffs, but frequently fail to do this in practice;

- The power of special interest groups in legislation and court decisions often subverts the best interests of society as a whole, especially with respect to the protection of young people and families from the degrading promotion by many of the media of pornography, violence, extreme sexual exploitation and permissiveness, the increasing acceptance of drugs, abuse of women, children and minorities;

- Many expenditures of government are not in the interest of the general public, but are in the interests of getting the incumbent politician re-elected, often tainted by a practice known as "pork barrel" legislation;

- Many leading democracies are testing, manufacturing, stockpiling, and selling weapons of mass destruction and standard military equipment, at the expense of spending to build peace;

- The party system, while necessary, is being discredited by the general practice that all party members must support party loyalty and vote for every important item of legislation proposed by the leadership of the party, whether it serves the broad public interest or not. Democracy would have more integrity if elected members voted as a representative of all the people, rather than only representing the wishes of their local constituency and the dictates of party leadership. Is a dictatorial party voting machine the only answer to the many failures of democracies if too many legislatures break up into small splinters with resulting weak governments and "revolving door" leadership?;

- Democratic leaders are expected to be honest. One of the major weaknesses of our political society is the tendency of some leaders to be devious or dishonest when their power or wealth is threatened, and for the media to cater both to the powerful and the publicity-seekers. An extract from the *Warriors of the Rainbow* shows how misleading statements and distortions soon become accepted by the media. "While the original crew [of the first Greenpeace boat] had not really believed in its own propaganda, and had, in fact, understood perfectly that we were engaged in a propaganda war, the bulk of the second crew was composed of people who had accepted our propaganda as truth. It was not that we had ever lied—that's one thing you must never do in modern propaganda—but we had painted a *rather extravagant* picture of the multiple dooms that *would be unleashed* if [the nuclear test] went off: tidal waves, earthquakes, radioactive death clouds, decimated fisheries, deformed babies. We never said that's what *would* happen, but that it *could* happen . . . we had nothing more than images to hurl against the AEC [U.S. Atomic Energy Commission], so we threw the heaviest, most horrifying images we could. By the time those images passed through the mass communications system, they had assumed tremendous proportions."[4] This must sound familiar to leaders of society today, and the media. With today's constant polling to ascertain "public opinion," how much of this opinion has been based on distorted and misleading statements by the media, politicians, businessmen, lobbyists, special interest groups, and individuals—by all ranks of society?;

- Democracies cannot function without freedom of speech, assembly, expression, and free media. However, democracies have established legal responsibilities that have priority over these individual freedoms when it is necessary for the protection of all members of society. For example, it is agreed by all that, "You cannot shout 'fire' in a crowded theatre." The right to free speech is not an absolute, and can be limited if this is necessary for the greater good of society. Democracy today is faced with a comparable problem of protecting society from the exploitation of children, women, minorities, and the handicapped—in brief, all those who need protection for the good of an ethical and moral society. If democracy fails to protect its fundamental basis, that all men and women are created equal, and therefore must be treated as equal, democracy can fail from rot within and from attack from without, military or non-military.

Citizens of democratic societies are required to be constantly vigilant to protect their liberties from the abuses of power by governments and big business. For example, is it democratic for powerful entities to control TV, broadcasting, and the press? A large conglomerate in Canada controls a TV network and thirty-three percent of the total newspaper circulation. Was it "power politics" when the publisher, for sixteen years, of a subsidiary of this media chain was "retired" over an editorial calling for the resignation of the Prime Minister of Canada?

The actions and support for peacemaking carried out by government begin generally with appeals from individuals and groups committed to work for peace, and with appeals from special interest organizations of civil society, such as NGOs. When the advocacy of these appeals wins wide support, the power of public opinion commands the attention of government. This process led to the conference in 1999 of *The Hague Appeal for Peace*. It was attended by a large number of leading organizations of civil society. It is of interest to report two of the main agenda themes respecting democracy, with ad verbatim extracts:

A—Democratic International Decision-Making

"The United Nations system and other multilateral institutions have the capacity to be a unique and universal force for peace. Too often, however, they have been treated with cynicism, politicized, and under-funded. The international system must be revived, democratized, and provided with resources if it is to realize its potential in peace-building. In particular, we call for a Security Council that can serve human security rather than Great Power interests, and for a radical reorientation of international financial institutions to make them more transparent and accountable to serve human rather than corporate needs."

B—Promote International Democracy and Just Global Governance

"The promotion of democracy at all levels of society is a prerequisite for replacing the rule of force with the rule of law. Establishing more representative and democratic decision-making processes is a prerequisite to achieving limited, accountable regional and global governance with binding, enforceable, and equitable legislative mechanisms."

The Hague Appeal for Peace endorses:

- The reform and democratization of the UN, including democratic strengthening of the General Assembly and extending consultative rights to civil society representatives, non-governmental organizations, and parliamentarians at all levels of the UN;
- The promotion of regional institutions to advance peace through adherence to international law;
- The modification of the weighted voting formulas utilized by the International Financial Institutions (IFI's) to protect the interest of small nations;
- The recommendations of the Commission on Global Governance, including the participation of civil society in global governance;
- The reform of the UN Security Council to make its composition more democratic and its decision-making process more transparent.

A major problem facing democracy in the world context is whether parliamentary democracy and free market economies should be promoted as the desired normality for other cultures and civilizations such as China and Islam. Eminent political scientists have written a profusion of articles and books that present a challenging framework for understanding the realities of global politics in the twenty-first century. This debate is most important regarding peace in the years ahead, but is beyond the scope of this book.

Another major problem of world peace currently facing all democracies relates to the devastating attacks by the al-Qaeda group of Muslim terrorists on September 11, 2001, killing about 3,000 people in New York City, Washington, and in a Pennsylvania field. The main motives were reported to be revenge for the invasions and killings in

Palestinian territory, an attack on the U.S. as the "great Satan" and ally of Israel, to strike against the power and arrogance of the U.S. military and society, and to create fear and panic in the U.S. of an implacable and invisible enemy. The U.S. launched a war against all Muslim terrorist groups, and urged all countries to stamp out the common enemy of Muslim terrorism and to denounce an "axis of evil" of Iran, Iraq, and North Korea for supporting terrorists and producing chemical, biological, and nuclear weapons of mass destruction. Many western countries rallied to support the U.S. leadership in a war against worldwide terrorism, but most Arab and Muslim countries held back from supporting the U.S. to see if it would restrain Israeli aggression and cool down angry street mobs denouncing the U.S. and being stirred up by the Mullahs. The prevalent view of western statesmen was that it would be a major catastrophe to have an escalation of hostility between the Muslim world and the West. Any analysis of this complicated confrontation falls outside the scope of this book. Suffice it to say that the impending threats to peace faced when Chapter 1 of this book began in March of 2001 are now magnified many times over due to the fallout from the events of September 11, 2001, and the continuing escalation of armed violence and atrocities in the Middle East. The U.S. and coalitions of allies and the UN face complex and continuing problems in assisting in the reconstruction and reconciliation of Afghanistan, Iraq, Israel and Palestine. However, this must be persevered with for as long as it takes, as the winning of peace is now the only road to stable and humane societies in the Middle East.

The Britannica Year Book of 2002, Foreward page, commented on the increasing terrorist attacks by Muslims: "The [attacks] spurred a worldwide examination of Islamic doctrine . . . . Muslim scholars pointed out . . . that terrorist violence is an interpretation of Islam that most adherents of the faith reject."

"We put our kids to 15 years of quick-cut advertising, passive television watching, and sadistic video games, and we expect to see emerge a new generation of calm, compassionate and engaged human beings."

Sydney Poitier
The Measure of a Man

"Without principles, no company deserves profits. Without profits, no company can sustain principles."

Sir Mark Moody-Stuart
Former Chairman, Royal Dutch/Shell Group

"The eternal verities of capitalism—growth, full employment, financial stability, rising real wages—seem to be vanishing just as the enemies of capitalism vanish. Something within capitalism has changed to be causing these results. Something has to be changed to alter these unacceptable results if capitalism is to survive."

Lester C. Thurow,
The Future of Capitalism

Chapter 11

WORLD PEACE, SOCIAL FREE ENTERPRISE, AND THE MARKET ECONOMY

We have reviewed the work of peacemakers; the family; the multitude of individuals who give donations and work for peacemaking causes; the grass roots peacemakers of a myriad of social, economic, and philanthropic associations such as the Quakers, the Salvation Army, Oxfam, and the Save The Children Fund; voluntary activist workers for NGOs; local and state governments; UN employees and UN project personnel; professional organizations, and peace research institutes. These are key linkages of peacemaking, starting with the grass roots of families and ordinary citizens and extending to state governments and the world assembly of nations, the UN. History has shown that without democracy there is no enduring world peace. All other forms of government fail to build peace up from the grass roots by the democratic process. Making decisions about peace from the top down has been a continuing failure. The only way to build a sustainable world peace is by the active involvement of grass roots peacemakers of ordinary citizens participating in a democratic society. Democracies cannot build world peace, however, without all people enjoying the good life that modern civilization has to offer—peace, order, good government, justice; economic opportunity to enjoy the benefits of a modern standard of living; freedom from fear and want; full support by governments and society of human rights for all; and access to a media that is free and provides well-informed, intelligent, substantive, and critical viewpoints on key issues.

In addition to the democratic process, there has to be an economic system that will provide the social and economic needs of the people. Only one economic system is compatible with democracy, and with the ability to marshal the necessary sustainable resources of brainpower, technology, efficient workers, capital, and managerial efficiency. It has been described variously as the capitalist free enterprise, entrepreneurial, or market system. It was developed by many philosophers and economists following mainly the work of Adam Smith in *The Wealth of Nations* in 1776.

Socialism was proposed by Karl Marx in 1867 in a book *Das Kapital* as a remedy to the main anti-social defects of capitalism—increasing exploitation and poverty of workers, rising unemployment, and increasing insecurity due to recurrent business recessions. To cure these defects socialists believed that a new "social individual" would trust the state to own all land and means of production and would be motivated to work hard for the state's social objectives. The Russian version of socialism was communism, the same system by different names. Communism did not work out. In the U.S.S.R. the workers finally wanted to work for themselves and not for the dictates of the state. Production and productivity fell as state spending increased, until the masses revolted in the early 1990s and the U.S.S.R. disintegrated.

Many extensions and modifications of the capitalist or market system have been developed during the last century in response to the need to curb the excesses of this system and to provide essential benefits for all in need. Some examples are: the measures of unemployment relief and family support developed mainly during the world depression of 1930 to 1933; government control of banking and regulation of stock markets; regulation of insurance, communications, and many other business functions; anti-monopoly legislation; the organization of new world capital processes at Bretton Woods and the General Agreement on Tariffs and Trade (GATT) after the Second World War; establishing the World Trade Organization and the International Monetary Fund. These represent some of the many steps taken to enhance the ability of capitalism to address social and economic needs. The developments of capitalism to optimize the efficiency of the production, buying, and selling of goods and services is commonly called the "market economy." This describes a part of the overall "social free enterprise economy," a term which encompasses the necessary melding of the social and economic needs of modern society.

The capitalist system has won out over its main rivals, socialism and communism, by exploiting the favourable economics of growth, increasing productivity in industrial and services employment, rising real wages, the advance of financial capacity and stability, and rapid technology advances. There are costs of this, including recurrent depressions, financial and social instability, inability to avoid recurrent unemployment, and a growing disparity between rich and poor.[1]

One of the major changes in the social free enterprise system has been the dynamic growth of the globalization of world production and trade of goods and services and of world capital markets. In one typical twenty-four hours the world capital markets move over $1.3 trillion, when all of the world's exports amounted to only $3 trillion per year. Electronic communication and computers have changed the way business is done, the way people live and work, the ability of strong states to compete in a global economy, and of weak states to survive, many at the sub-subsistence level. There are fundamental changes in technology, transportation, and commerce in a world where almost anything can be made and sold around the world. National economies are locked in as integral parts of the world economy. A divergence of interests often arises between global multinational conglomerates and national governments that take steps to protect domestic industries despite political commitments to free trade. Globalization has many downsides. Hardships are imposed on workers who are replaced by low wage foreign workers and immigrants, and are forced to move away from traditional communities and cultures to find jobs which often do not match the migrant's typical work experience. Such migrations are unavoidable under today's world economy, but they weaken the extended family at a time when one of the major needs is for society to support and strengthen family cohesion. *To make the global economy work requires giving up a substantial degree of national sovereignty.* The economic advantages of world trade have clearly demonstrated that the world would be impoverished if world trade were curtailed. Six years after the freeing of trade at the Uruguay meeting, exports from developing nations increased by nearly $1 trillion, to a level of $2.4 trillion. Also, globalization is a force for peace. Memoirs of Cordell Hull, Roosevelt's secretary of state, reveal that the peace interest was the chief motive behind the reciprocal trade agreements process which led to the GATT, WTO, and IMF.

There is a high price to be paid for the worldwide integration and specialization of the modern industrial economy to maximize efficiency. The supply of goods and services is often interrupted due to costly breakdowns caused by the failure of any link in the long chain from natural resource to the final consumer. Changing costs and markets, strikes, natural catastrophes, changing tariffs and exchange rates put all links in the chain at risk. In pre-industrial times, for example, all necessities of life and employment were assured as long as the individual family and village unit functioned. Today, a series of power failures or other interruptions thousands of miles away can cut off family necessities, business operations, health support systems, transportation, etc. Because of the interdependency of all modern business and industrial operations, the prevention of interruptions, large and small, and the maintenance of peace and order, in a village or a country, is dependent in many cases on government intervention, often by political rather than economic measures. It is a tragedy that the modern world is increasingly torn apart due to political, social, and economic conflicts, when the benefits of peace require co-operation by all links in the economic chain to maintain modern standards of living and major capital transfers to the less developed world.

All of the prosperous, more developed economies are market economies. Misguided intervention by governments reduces the efficiency of markets. Experience has shown that the guarantee of individual human rights by government enhances the productivity of modern societies. The leading democracies and the social free enterprise system have developed the most "profit intensive" trade, have the highest levels of per capita income, and also have developed the greatest protection of individual human rights. To paraphrase Churchill, the social free enterprise system is not perfect, but it is better than all those other forms that have been tried from time to time.

Recent studies have examined the reasons why some market economies have performed very well, whereas others have failed.[2] The transition from colonial economies to market economies has exposed less developed countries to competition with economically advanced democratic nations which have protected the individual rights of all citizens. Mancur Olson concludes in his book *Power and Prosperity* that there are two main conditions required for a market economy that generates economic success. The first is to provide secure and well-defined individual rights, such as the ownership of private property and the impartial enforcement of contracts. All citizens have secure and precisely delineated rights which are legally defensible against other parties and against the government. The second condition is the enforcement by government against predatory acts of plundering, such as illegal lobbying, cartels, collusion, price-fixing, kickbacks, market fixing, and bribery. No society in the post-war world that has fully met these two conditions has failed to prosper.

The economic deterioration throughout sub-Saharan Africa has increased since the 1960s and 1970 and has reached a crisis. A new UN report estimates that half of sub-Saharan Africa lives on less than $1 per day. The crisis has become exacerbated by wars between tribes, guerrilla bands, local warlords, street mobs, and by the HIV/AIDS pandemic. By 2005, South Africa will have one million orphans. In Botswana life expectancy was over sixty, but is now headed below forty. By 2010, Botswana will have thirty-two percent less production than it would have had without AIDS. A UN summit meeting in 2001 agreed to provide a global fund to fight AIDS, tuberculosis, and malaria, costing between $7 and $10 billion yearly. To date, only about $380 million has been disbursed. The AIDS catastrophe is killing young adults and parents, leaving no one to care for orphans and invalids.

Of the forty million HIV positive people in the world, more than twenty-eight million live in sub-Saharan Africa, where 2.3 million people died of AIDS last year. It is estimated that deaths at this rate will continue to increase unless billions are spent for drugs, hospital care, and AIDS prevention clinics and programs.

The leaders of the Group of Eight (G8) countries—the U.S., Russia, Great Britain, Japan, France, Germany, China, and Canada met in June 2002 at Kananaskis, Alberta, Canada, to discuss a long agenda of proposals for international security and co-operation, including world trade and finance; dealing with Russian nuclear weapons disposal; the Israeli-Palestinian conflict; the war against international terrorism; and aid for Africa from the developed world. The UN had asked for $10 billion a year in new aid grants, but the fund has pledges for only $2.1 billion over the next five years. The aid fund needs another $2 billion in 2003 and $4.6 billion in 2004 just to meet existing commitments. The G8 agreed that half or more of an added $12 billion of aid funds promised in March 2002 to help the Third World would be sent, but only to countries that take a tough line on corruption and human rights abuses, and engage in good governance. As many developed countries do not meet these standards, it appears the G8 group is not serious about giving massive new aid money needed by less developed countries. The leaders also pledged to top up by $1 billion an existing $30 billion plan to reduce the debt of many African countries that practice "sound economic policies and good governance." Here again the substance of G8 pledges of aid lack sincerity. G8 countries pledged to open up their markets to provide greater access by eliminating tariffs and quotas on many exports from Africa and to help Africa fight AIDS. Many developed countries have been doing exactly the opposite of this, and are unlikely to change. NGO groups assailed the African aid package as "woefully inadequate." A representative of the European Commission said private investment in Africa would ultimately be more crucial to its development than public funds. A UN advisor condemned the lack of new funds. "The implementation of the Millennium Development Goals for the world would require substantial, new, and additional resources from both domestic and external sources. The World Bank estimated that $30 billion would be required annually for a period of thirty years to meet that goal. The United Nations estimated that some $50 billion would be required annually up to 2015, of which $10 billion would be spent on stemming and reversing the surge of HIV/AIDS."[3] As far as major substantive financial assistance to less developed countries is concerned, recent G8 meetings were a disappointing farce.

A statement by Ugandan President Museveni stressed that trade was more important than aid. "For too long, Africans and their partners in the West have looked to international aid as the answer to the poverty and the economic challenges confronting developing countries . . . . While well intentioned, this overemphasis on aid has actually handicapped Africa by promoting a dependency mentality and the impression that African countries could not compete in the global economy. By itself, aid cannot transform societies. Only trade can foster the sustained economic growth necessary for such a transformation." These arguments are like a prolonged debate as to which life preserver should be tossed to a drowning man. There are many difficult questions about aid to Africa. Kofi Annan, Secretary-General of the UN, asked at a Seattle summit meeting of the W.T.O., I.M.F., and World Bank in 2000, "Why was it that many of the freer trade promises to developing countries under the Uruguay meeting have not been honored? Why was it that tariffs and quotas were much lower among developed nations than between developed nations and developing ones?" But slow progress is being made. Recently, Mr. Museveni lauded the American legislation known as the African Growth and Opportunity Act, which removes some tariffs and quotas on African exports to the U.S. Unfortunately, the U.S. is currently taking trade action against imports of South African fruit—another example of how domestic political pressures often win out over extending help to the developing world.

Recently, Nobel Prize winning economist Joseph Stiglitz charged, "The critics of globalization are right. The western countries have pushed poor countries to eliminate trade barriers, but kept up their own barriers, preventing developing countries from exporting their agricultural products and so depriving them of desperately needed export income." This criticism comes from a former chairman of the U.S. President's Council of Economic Advisers and subsequently the World Bank's chief economist. However, Mr. Stiglitz believes in globalization. "It has raised living standards in recent decades for most people in most countries. But it's the leaders of the rich countries that don't believe in it—at least, when their farmers clamor for subsidies and protection from imports. They choose hypocrisy, and the poorest countries pay the price. Jobs have systematically been destroyed— poor farmers in developing countries couldn't compete with the highly subsidized goods from Europe and America." A recent World Bank report described the enormous level of subsidies in world agriculture. The average annual value of subsidies is about sixty percent of total world trade in agriculture and about double the value of exports from developing countries. Clearly the first life preserver must be to get humans able to work again, and there should be no discriminatory tariffs on low cost farm products, textiles, minerals, and utilitarian manufactured goods.

Extracts from an article in *The Economist* of May 11, 2002, describe the problem of political leaders who support globalization and trade liberalisation, but not when domestic political interests are affected adversely:

"*Bush The Anti-Globaliser: America's monstrous new farm bill could wreck any chance of further trade liberalisation.*

Two new sources of [trade] agreements are likely to . . . severely damage the health of the global trading system. The first is steel, with the Europeans preparing next month to retaliate against America's outrageous imposition of steel tariffs in March. The second is the new farm bill that could undermine any hopes of liberalising farm trade. At recent trade summits the talk was of a new period of the rich countries making a big effort to liberalise textiles and agriculture. It was the Americans who led the charge against agricultural protection in Europe and Japan, and insisted on putting freer trade in agriculture at the heart of the Uruguay round of trade talks in 1994 and the Doha, Qatar, round in 2001. The 2002 U.S. farm bill throws all of this out the window. It raises the level of federal subsidies by over eighty percent, with increased subsidies for soya, wheat, corn, and many new subsidies. Three quarters of the cash will go to the biggest and richest ten percent of farmers. American subsidies could soon reach three or four times European levels."

Currently, the European Union spends about $46 billion yearly on agricultural subsidies. This will increase greatly to match the latest U.S. increases. It is a necessity for all developed countries to lower their subsidies of agriculture so that African and other struggling areas can compete in world markets.

The continuing revelations by large U.S. companies of massive financial and accounting fraud have shaken the trust of worldwide investors in the integrity and honesty of U.S. free enterprise and financial markets. The payment of obscenely high bonuses and stock options to Chief Executive Officers (CEOs) and other senior officers, when these companies had large losses, was a ruthless game of defrauding the shareholders. Many mergers and acquisitions have been completed at grossly inflated values, with enormous extra compensation for both continuing and retiring senior officers. This excessive greed has been "business as usual" to many senior corporate executives at the expense of shareholders. But the bubble of arrogance, greed, and gambling finally burst with the revelations of fraudulent practices when Enron went bankrupt in December 2001, wiping out employees and investors, who lost tens of billions of dollars. The extent of involvement of Enron officers and auditors, Arthur Andersen, will be probed in court proceedings. A headline in *Forbes* of January 7, 2002 read, *"How Enron concealed losses, inflated earnings, and hid secret deals from the authorities. Are criminal charges next?"* In 2000, Enron paid out $750 million extraordinary compensation to top executives, including $140 million to the CEO, when its entire net income had fallen. Enron was reported to have overstated its 1997-to-2000 profits by more than $1.2 billion using "special purpose entities" that were kept off its balance sheet. Many other corporate risks were not recorded. About 250 U.S. public companies had to restate their accounts in 2002, compared with only three in 1981. *The Economist* reported on November 30, 2002, *"Managers will be as greedy as they can get away with."* *The Economist* reported on May 24, 2003 that WorldCom had agreed to pay a fine of $500 million to settle charges it had overstated profits by $11 billion since 1999. Also, WorldCom agreed to settle with the Securities and Exchange Commission an investigation into its accounting for $1.51 billion.

After the stench of financial misconduct was out in the open, more financial fraud emerged. Nearly $2 billion in revenue disappeared at Xerox Corp. More than $3.9 billion in expenses at WorldCom were falsely reported. Merck had recorded $12.4 billion in revenue over three years that was never actually collected. Accounting and tax fraud was also alleged at other major companies, including Tyco International, Kmart, Adelphia Communications, Dynegy, Global Crossing, and Qwest Communications. *The Economist* reported on June 29, 2002, "The revelations of corporate misdeeds at Enron, Global Crossing, and WorldCom confirm that there is an urgent need to rein in greedy and overmighty chief executives, and to curb rampant abuses of stock options . . . . The audit scandals swirling around Andersen testify not only to the sins of a single firm; they also point to something rotten in the state of auditing itself. And that is where the action is most pressing." The U.S. Congress has submitted legislation to restrict Boards of Directors practices of giving excessive bonuses and stock options, and will mandate that members of the Board and of the Audit Committee must be completely independent of any conflict of interest regarding their duty to represent the interests of shareholders. It is hoped that this is just the first phase of a drastic housecleaning at Wall Street. Without honesty, integrity, and accountability, capital markets cannot be supported in a democracy.

The financial markets have traditionally regarded accounting firms as the watchdog whose duty was to scrutinize and vouch for the reliability and integrity of company financial operations and reports. Unfortunately, many accountants bend over backwards to ensure their retainer is continued as long as possible. Another serious conflict of interest arises due to accountants' overriding interest in retaining clients who provide a lucrative sideline of buying consulting services. The role of accountants is to ensure that all financial matters are honestly and clearly reported. Their duty is to refuse to certify company statements which have used "innovative accounting" to mislead the shareholders and the public. For example, many companies now include in their annual reports two different profit and loss statements—one using traditional and "as recorded" accounting practices, and one called a "Pro Forma" profit and loss statement, which is usually explained as a "more realistic" presentation. This Pro Forma statement is in the Annual Report presented to the public, and is referred to by brokerage salesmen, analysts, and promoters as "the financial statement published in the Annual Report." The Pro Forma statement is a projection of the following year's results, based on management's estimates and forecasts of enhanced sales and/or reduced costs that might be valid if various risk estimates were minimized and various favourable elements were maximized. These estimated adjustments might happen, but were provided solely to show a series of optimistic estimates that would make the public happier and the activities of selling company stock, or the company itself, much easier. If this were not so, why would the company and the auditor release these Pro Forma statements? Pro Forma statements were originally developed just as an in-house accounting technique to present reports showing a range of financial options or data variables. The public release of this data was formerly considered misleading corporate practice, as it introduced uncertainty as to the methods used to forecast the various financial variables, and profit forecasting has no legitimate role in annual financial reports. A recent report states that seventy-four percent of U.S. semi-conductor companies show pro forma accounting in their published financial statements.

The Globe and Mail, Toronto, reported on June 27, 2002—"President George Bush deplored the lack of corporate ethics in America yesterday, and called on company leaders to clean up their act or face justice after revelations of yet another massive U.S. business scandal . . . . 'We will fully investigate and hold people responsible for misleading not only shareholders, but employees as well . . . . Admissions that telecom giant WorldCom Inc. overstated [profits] by about $3.9 billion were outrageous . . . . There is a need for renewed corporate responsibility in America. Those entrusted with shareholder's money must strive for the highest of high standards.'" President George W. Bush warned the New York financial leaders again on July 9, 2002—"Americans could conceivably lose confidence in the free-enterprise system." Reports from Washington indicate that Congress does not consider these scandals the result of just a "few bad apples," but that they were the result of a system that has condoned greed, dishonesty, and illegal behavior due to incentives to get excessive rewards and pay few and miniscule penalties if caught with one's "hand in the cookie jar." The world will follow with great interest the actions by the U.S. government to regain its position of leadership and integrity in world financial and business affairs.

The free enterprise system, with its capitalist philosophy and its market economy, has vanquished its rivals of communism and socialism. But like all human endeavours, the capitalist system can fail to adjust to the interactions of new technologies and new ideologies, the forces driving the world economic system in new directions. Powerful and arrogant in its victory over its challengers, capitalism has matured, become complacent and non-reforming, and faces the danger recognized by Lord Acton—"Power tends to corrupt, and absolute power corrupts absolutely." If the democratic free enterprise philosophy is to earn continued public support, the financial markets of capitalism require drastic and urgent reform of excesses, inequalities, dishonesties, and greed. The present weaknesses of capitalism have been the subject of a heightened and alarming concern of all parts of society. Some questions asked are deeply critical: has capitalism lost its moral compass, as is often the case in many other social and economic practices? Does the industrial work place create discontent and lose the loyalty of the workers? Have we carried the "survival of the fittest," "dog-eat-dog" motivation to damaging lengths? Is the "greed is good" philosophy of the world's financial markets professionals leading to collapse of investor confidence? Have the philosophies of "win at any costs" and "the end justifies the means" led to practices that are destructive to a respected system of business ethics? Is honesty not important in high and low places; is cheating part of the game? Is money the be-all and the end-all of business and capitalism, or is fair treatment of employees, customers, and the general public more important than excessive profits going to top executives with no concept of their public relationship and responsibilities?

After the First World War, American business became the world leader, and has continued its growth until today U.S. economic society is dominated by corporations that are bigger and more powerful than most countries. General Motors has annual sales larger than Israel's GDP; Exxon's annual sales are larger than Poland's GDP. Wal-Mart's annual sales are larger than the GDP of 161 countries. General Electric has hundreds of subsidiaries. Two hundred corporations, led by General Motors, Wal-Mart Stores, Exxon Mobil, Ford Motors, General Electric, International Business Machines, Citigroup, and AT&T dominate America's economy, and that of much of the rest of the world. America's biggest companies are an overwhelming force in its national politics, pouring over two billion into recent political campaigns. Corporations can continue to flourish only if they pay close attention to their relationships and responsibilities to the public, both domestic and foreign. The future of world business is dependent on many things, with the future of world peace, democracy, and the social free enterprise system among the most important factors.

With respect to the future of the social free enterprise system, an important question is raised in much of today's literature. How long will the public support the "winner take all" mentality, in which one percent of the population holds forty percent of the total net worth of a leading industrial society? When this book was started, these questions were not as disturbing as they are now, when each day brings new revelations of fraud, greed, and dishonesty about leading public companies' treatment of their employees and shareholders. The glue that holds all banking and investing activities together is trust in the integrity of others who are in positions of responsibility and stewardship. This trust has been badly eroded during the past few years.

The linkages between peace, democracy, and the free enterprise system that give priority to the social and ethical well-being of mankind are observable in all western societies and countries today. If there is diminished democratic performance worldwide, there will be diminished social and economic well-being worldwide, accompanied by diminished peace and lack of support of human rights worldwide. There can be no peace unless mankind gives full support to true democracy, to the integrity of the social free enterprise systems, and an equitable share of all requirements for a good life for all mankind of our global village.

A further question has been raised as to whether the publics of western nations agree with the conclusions of a leading economist of the U.S., Lester Thurow, in *The Future of Capitalism*, written in 1997: "One can make the argument, as the communitarian movement does, that our societies were more efficient and human in the past and could be more efficient and human in the future if the right social values were inculcated in the young . . . . Exactly what are the right values and how do we agree with them? . . . . Values are not, and will not be, inculcated by the family, the Church, or other social institutions in either the present or the future. *They are, and will be, inculcated by the electronic and visual media.*"[4] (Italics by author.) If this assessment is true, and there is much statistical evidence to support it, and the media continues to promote the prominence now given to dysfunctional families, violence, killing, destruction, sex, pornography, dishonesty, greed, and immorality, then we are condemning our grandchildren and great-grandchildren to a debased and dangerous living. The growth of moral and social values has to start with the family. *If the family does not inculcate moral and social values in succeeding generations it will not be done.* It cannot be done by the electronic and visual media, because it is not their purpose, interest, or capability. The media will have to clean up their act, and give social values much more prominence than anti-social values, or the drift downward toward a dysfunctional society as a whole will continue.

To continue to build the foundations of world peace the family will have to continue to inculcate the moral and social values to guide our children to be peacemakers—in the family, at school, at work, and in society at large.

"I have fought against white domination and I have fought against black domination. I have cherished the ideal of a democratic and free society in which all persons live together in harmony and with equal opportunities. It is an ideal which I hope to live for and to achieve. But if needs be, it is an ideal for which I am prepared to die."

Nelson Mandela
President of South Africa
(Said during trial in 1964, when sentenced to prison for life.)

Chapter 12

NEW APPROACH TO PEACEMAKING

The world is emerging from the bloodiest, most war-ridden century in history. Progress has been made in many areas of human rights, but much more is needed before all peoples will enjoy universal human rights. Science and technology have made extraordinary advances. However, the ability of mankind to live in peace has suffered setback after setback, and future prospects for peace are much less reassuring than they were one hundred years ago. Mankind has succeeded in establishing the UN, which has made significant progress. The mechanisms for ensuring world peace based on international collective security are gradually being developed and made more effective, but are not supported in many parts of the world. It is an overriding priority for the more developed nations to find solutions to the poverty and the lack of true democracy in the world. Civil society is concerned about a great many factors destroying world peace, such as the lack of progress on the treaties banning chemical and biological weapons; in eliminating all nuclear weapons; in stopping the flow of small arms and light weapons; and in the failure of the developed world to provide the massive financial aid necessary to enable the less developed nations to avoid the abyss of war, dire poverty, and social collapse.

It is encouraging that civil society organizations have brought the demands of people directly to the international level and have created a new diplomacy of NGO interaction both with state governments and the UN. Civil society has been prodding these two partners in peacemaking for most of the last century. Now a new priority must be given to increase the empowerment of the peacemakers of the common people and their leaders. It is of interest to look at one example of a current mission of civil society—to stop the flow of small arms and light weapons. Many proposals to achieve this will be challenged due to the enormous complications of a worldwide campaign to cut off both the demand and the supply. The demand in, say, Africa arises from a long list of political and social differences: ancient grudges and tribal hatreds; clashes of race; disparities of economic resources and opportunity; political ambitions and rivalries; lack of adequate laws and justice systems; lack of ethical standards of morality; lack of safety; and cultures of ignorance and violence. To stop the demand for small arms would require stopping hostilities before armed conflict began, extinguishing hatreds built up by past wrongs, and providing economic opportunity for all classes of society. To stop the supply would mean enforcing control of the supply side of developed nations, of import and export of small arms and ammunition, effective border controls, and ultimately control of access to weapons in both supply and demand areas.

It would be impossible to stop all the flow of small arms, but major trafficking could be reduced if the demand could be curtailed by governments taking determined action to provide personal security for all, both in demand countries and supply countries. This, in turn, could be done only by building peace, the peace that begins in the soul and minds of mankind. So we are back to the beginning; stopping the flow of small arms must start with the individual and the family unit, where moral training by example begins. Many nations have developed strong grass roots of dedicated peacemakers, and it is here that renewed peacemaking must begin if we are to give our descendants a more peaceful world than we have today. It will be impossible to put out the fires of armed violence (with small arms or machetes as in Rwanda), until more developed and less developed countries take steps to remove the basic causes of violence and wars.

The obstacles to peace, and the actions required of mankind to build the foundations of peace, have been examined and solutions tried throughout history. A renewed campaign for peace must begin at the beginning—the awakening in the grass roots, the ordinary citizen, of a determination to find out what we are doing that is wrong, ineffective, or just not enough. The achievements of world leaders in philosophy, government, politics, science, and social and economic progress have been remarkable, but we have failed to develop a practical and achievable process for peoples to resolve their conflicts without war, and to achieve justice and equality for all. The existing systems of war or peace are based mainly on decisions made at the top, at the national state level, and with directions and actions *flowing from the top down. There is a disconnection between the top, the government, and the ordinary citizens, the grass roots.* The citizens are not involved as partners in peacemaking. Many excuses are made for this. Ordinary citizens are more interested in things that affect their daily lives— family, jobs, recreation, sports, amusement, scandals, tragedies, and all the trivia that appears regularly on the front page or the TV. Most ordinary citizens have scant interest in affairs of world peace and social welfare. It is natural for their concerns to be about this week or this year, and not about things that might affect society in twenty to fifty years, and longer. They feel peace problems are the business of state governments, that they do not have the power to affect government decisions, and even if they could develop this power the government would still make the usual partisan political decisions which they consider necessary to win the next election, with peacemaking deferred as a problem for the future.

Ordinary citizens are generally not interested in world peacemaking. They work hard to maximize their income. They do not want higher taxes in order to spend billions on international peace projects that would be subject to excessive waste due to inefficiency and corruption. When money passes from government to government not enough gets through to the needy. At the state government level, the powers-that-be feel that problems of world peace are too complicated for the grass roots to understand them and to make wise decisions—that peace must be left to the experts. This concept has been the process for many hundreds of years, and the record of state governments and the grass roots citizens is one of failure.

There are several critical and growing factors that have an important bearing on the thinking of both the government and the citizens. A proposal to pay more taxes now, or change one's lifestyle now, in order to leave a better world for future generations, has very little appeal for our present generation. There is, however, solid evidence that we must change our propensity for war, our failure to protect the environment, and our addiction to conspicuous consumption of non-essential consumer goods, and that we have to face up to this *now, not later when weapons of mass destruction are used or when the damage to the environment is irreversible.* Stopping continuing wars of the poor and dispossessed, and growing international terrorism, will also require very large sacrifices now, not later. Today's defense budgets will have to be reduced if the planet and the peace of the world is to be made secure. We cannot have large increases of military spending, large spending increases to save the environment, and still give massive aid to less developed regions, as we learned in two world wars. R. L. Heilbroner's reasoned conclusion in 1974 was that the odds were high against society accepting the large sacrifices that would be necessary in our lifetimes, and that strong military-oriented governments might be necessary to force society to accept such sacrifices before it is too late.

The world cannot continue with wealthy industrialized nations being separate from and unconcerned about the poverty and despair of the less developed nations. Information is now available on an hourly basis worldwide. Travel will carry diseases, explosives, and terrorists to any part of the world. Movies and TV give the poor the images of the good life in wealthy societies. The worldwide web connects all world citizens instantly and continuously. As all are now part of the "global village," the peoples of the world are faced with either living together or dying together, quickly or slowly. As Heilbroner wrote, "Ours is such a time that we must learn to live with its irreconcilable conflicts and contradictions . . . . To accept the limit of our abilities [to make sacrifices to save future generations], both as individuals and as a collectivity, seems to be the most difficult idea that . . . man must learn. But learn it he must, and learn it he will. The only question is whether the teacher will be history or ourselves."[1]

The message is clear. The free world has received its "wake up" call and must act now on the principle that the grass roots of society must bear its fundamental responsibility for peace or war, and cannot continue to leave this up to state governments and the UN. These institutions have been established and empowered by the citizens to achieve their objectives for peace, with a minimum of concern or input from us. "Leave it up to the government and the UN—they are the experts and will muddle through as always"—have been the slogans of the grass roots. Mankind is aware that a completely new era is dawning, with portents of overwhelming changes that are of such magnitude that ordinary citizens can no longer shirk their responsibility to take hold and act to cope with future threats. Major changes will replace the old with the new, but it will be up to us whether it will be by an evolutionary or revolutionary process.

The time has come to try a new approach to peacemaking, to empower the grass roots to become a partner in peacemaking with the state government, to have objectives, strategies, and decisions flow not only *from the top down*, but also *from the bottom up*. The mode of communication can no longer be *one-way*, from the top down. Realistic *two-way* communication is necessary. To achieve this the citizens must equip themselves to be an effective partner, by a renewed effort to inform and enlist the grass roots and develop the grass roots leaders who will achieve new standards of leadership and responsibilities for peacemaking. The grass roots leaders will also develop two-way communication and partnership with present and future NGOs, enlarging the constituencies that add strength to NGO organizations. Bringing new or revitalized grass roots organizations into the loop with other peacemaker organizations such as social service, humanitarian, and philanthropic groups, and with NGOs, would not produce "crowding out" or "overlapping." It is abundantly clear that the strengthening of all peacemaking groups would greatly assist governments and widen their peacemaking constituencies, and that there is an endless number of peacemaking needs to be addressed. The strengthening of the peacemaking effectiveness of the grass roots automatically strengthens the effective peacemaking of state governments and of the UN.

The conviction that peace must start in the souls and minds of the individual leads to the conclusion that the best way to revitalize the peacemaking role of the grass roots is to "start at the beginning." More grass roots peacemaking needs more men and women who are concerned about the failures of society to find sustainable world peace, and are interested in becoming better informed about the whole issue—the causes of the obstacles to peace and the obvious need for more individuals to do something about it at the grass roots level. This is not a new or infrequent decision of well-informed people. There are hundreds of thousands of examples of individuals becoming dedicated peacemakers because they yearn for peace for their families and fellow citizens. They first of all want to learn more about the need to take action to help build peace where it is most needed. Today there are urgent social needs in all more developed countries, but there the most help is available. The greatest need for help is in the less developed countries, where there is a tremendous shortage of available help and the people are in the most desperate need.

As individuals in the more developed world learn more about the growing threats to peace, they will become concerned about the need for action at the grass roots. The next step would see small groups of friends talking about peacemaking issues, about *what they can do* to support peacemaking and to develop their ideas about *how they want to do it*. Peacemaking can be a solitary effort, but the seeds of peace will grow much faster and more vigorously if team efforts are brought to bear.

> *This proposal is based not as an alternative to the millions of volunteer groups now working for peace, but on adding greatly needed reinforcements. If this renewed emphasis on small group peacemakers is successful there is no limit to the added strength that can be achieved to further the many causes of peacemaking.*

The addition of grass roots partners to the peacemaking process, based on personal commitment and group action, brings into focus another partner in peacemaking—the media. As the peacemaking activities of more grass roots groups, NGOs, and state governments are increased, communication by the media becomes much more available and important. The objective would be to have all media carry more significant messages of peacemaking as a new and revitalized civil society movement develops better methods, processes, and specific programs that will attract more media coverage. An essential way to strengthen international peacemaking is to build strong media and public support for more effective peacemaking at the grass roots, resulting in enhanced peacemaking of civil society, state governments, and the UN.

The proposal that a new partner of peacemakers groups could make an important contribution to world peace will be regarded with much scepticism. There have been many thousands of special interest organizations tilling this field for hundreds of years. Many people would assert that the proposal is not practical, not capable of "quick results." Even if peacemaker groups are formed and are active, how will they be able to raise their effectiveness in peacemaking enough to attract broader attention and support of the general public, and of government? Will this proposal be just another Don Quixote tilting at windmills? One never knows, but the only way to resolve the many uncertainties of a new campaign of peacemakers groups is to take the first step, try it, and see how far this can progress. The stakes could not be higher. The future of mankind depends on its ability to *develop the will* necessary to meet the challenges of the future. The man-made evils of war and poverty are enemies that can be defeated. The fact that the collective destiny of mankind requires unavoidable sacrifice is no reason for doing nothing. "This general admonition applies in particular to the intellectual elements of western nations whose privileged role as sentries for society takes on a special importance in the face of things as we now see them. It is their task not only to prepare their fellow citizens for the sacrifices that will be required of them but to take the lead . . . for a future in which the exercise of power must inevitably increase and many present areas of freedom, especially in economic life, be curtailed."[2] The proposal for a renewal of the activity of small peacemakers groups will be explored further in Chapter 14.

In democracies, the constituency most concerned with peacemaking is the grass roots of society. Offloading this responsibility on elected state governments by frequent general elections is not good enough, as the current history of political failures to solve peacemaking problems shows. The public, and its peacemaking leaders of civil society and NGOs, must be held responsible for peacemaking, and for ensuring that the public's reasoned principles are the general guidelines for state peacemaking. This democratic system must have, however, a public that takes its responsibilities for peacemaking seriously, and at all times as its top priority. The public cannot carry out responsibilities for peacemaking if it does not keep well-informed, study all sides of critical issues, set appropriate guidelines, and work towards influencing state governments to build up peacemaking programs in both the short and long term. The public cannot carry out its responsibilities if it allows itself to be swayed by the false rhetoric of demagogues, to be bought off by "bread and games," or to accept promises of easy short-term solutions. The aim should be to grow slowly with programs that have long-term staying power. Some of the most successful NGO programs are over seventy years old.

Peace Laureate Albert Schweitzer studied the roles of the public and political leaders of great states long and hard, and wrote these words: "Of all the will toward the ideal in mankind only a small part can manifest itself in public action. All the rest of this force must be content with small and obscure deeds. The sum of these, however, is a thousand times stronger than the acts of those who receive wide public recognition. The latter, compared to the former, are like the foam on the waves of a deep ocean."[3] This is a remarkable statement. Here is a heroic figure dismissing heroes as mere "foam" and telling us to look elsewhere—at "small and obscure deeds"—if we want to learn about making the world a better place. He suggests that we look away from grand figures, extreme situations, and moments of high historical drama, and pay attention to how thoughtful, practical men and women resolve the challenges of peacemaking in everyday life. Schweitzer's life received wide public recognition for his devotion to the sick in the Congo, his work as a professor, writer, musician, religious philosopher, and public campaigner to rid mankind of the atom bomb. He associated both with heroic figures for the last sixty years of his life and with the grass roots, the "small and obscure deeds"—a remarkable life. He was firmly convinced that the grass roots play the most important role in peacemaking.

The reader will be familiar with a long list in earlier chapters of examples of "small and obscure deeds" of dedicated peacemakers committing their lives to the founding of durable worldwide institutions of peacemaking. Most of the institutions and associations shown in Appendix C, Table 3, were started by individual peacemakers and a few friends. The brief highlights of the lives of individual Peace Prize winners show their early commitment to the direct service of humanity, resulting in peacemaking miracles. The beginnings of all modern humanitarian organizations, from the founding of the Red Cross in 1863 by Henri Dunant, Nobel Peace Laureate (1901) to the meeting in 1991 of Bobby Muller, Thomas Gebauer, and Jody Williams, Nobel Peace Laureate (1997) to form the International Campaign to Ban Landmines which shared the Peace Prize in 1997, were started by individuals with "small and obscure deeds" of service to humanity. In addition to the statesmen and the receivers of wide public recognition were the millions of peacemakers whose endeavours led them to service to humanity. The excuse that the actions of one peacemaker cannot make a difference is completely refuted by the differences to humanity made by countless numbers of ordinary citizens, the grass roots from which all peacemakers grow. The same excuse is often given that, "Whether I vote or not will not make any difference." If citizens do not carry out their personal responsibility to vote, it will make all the difference between living in a democracy and living in a dictatorship. So it is with peacemaking. If citizens do not carry out their personal responsibility to make sacrifices in the name of peace, it will make all the difference between living in peace and living in inhuman conditions of war, mass poverty, and curtailed freedom.

There are many real life stories of missions succeeding far beyond the vision of the founders. An amazing example is the growth of Greenpeace from a few unemployed young men and women meeting in 1969 in a church basement in Vancouver, Canada, with a determination to stop the U.S. from carrying out a test nuclear explosion in a 4,000-foot hole on Amchitka, one of the Aleutian Islands of Alaska. This small group had to hold concerts to raise money and to develop an action plan, but they knew that there were many thousands of potential local and international supporters who would be interested in a cause that was of utmost importance for the future of mankind. Young people had sacrificed their lives in the cause of saving the future of free peoples in two world wars, and the founders of Greenpeace were prepared to do the same to save the future of the planet by sailing to Amchitka and staying there as martyrs to stop the nuclear tests. In thirty years their campaign has grown to a worldwide movement with public support that commands the respect of all governments, industry, and society. Greenpeace has done the impossible, and a new mission of peacemakers can do the same. The Greenpeace Story is told in Chapter 13.

"It is our relationship to our planetary environment which is the most important issue of all. All human structures inevitably rest upon it."

Robert Hunter
A Founder and President of Greenpeace

Chapter 13

THE GREENPEACE STORY

The Amchitka Campaign

In the fall of 1969, the United States announced that a 1.2 megaton (unit of explosive power equal to one million tons of TNT) nuclear bomb would be detonated in autumn, 1971, at Amchitka Island in the Aleutian islands of Alaska. A smaller test had been made here in 1965.

A co-founder of Greenpeace, Robert Hunter, had written in a British Columbia, Canada newspaper *The Vancouver Sun:* "Beginning at midnight tonight, the United States will begin to play a game of Russian roulette with a nuclear pistol pressed against the head of the world. As of midnight, a blockade will be thrown around remote Amchitka Island near the tail end of the Aleutians. Sometime between tomorrow and Oct. 15, a 1.2-megaton atomic bomb will be triggered at the bottom of a 4,000-foot hole on the island.

"No one knows what the consequences will be, but scientists in Canada, the U.S., Japan, and Hawaii have warned that there is a distinct danger that the test might set in motion earthquakes and tidal waves which could sweep from one end of the Pacific to the other . . . . By setting off its underground nuclear test in the Aleutians—one of the most earthquake-prone areas in the world—the U.S. Atomic Energy Commission is taking a chance on triggering a chain reaction of earthquakes and tidal waves which would slam the lips of the Pacific Rim like a series of karate chops."[1]

On October 1, 1969 a large group of peaceful protesters, about six thousand Canadians and one thousand American draft dodgers living in the Vancouver area, demonstrated at the border crossing between British Columbia and Washington State, U.S., stopping all traffic for about one hour. Extra police detachments let protesters rant until the organizers of the blockade ordered everyone off the road. The staged "media event" was very successful. Widespread public anger was stirred up, and increased after another nuclear bomb was detonated at Amchitka two days after the mass protest.

A few Vancouver anti-nuclear activists, determined to stage more protests to stop the next Amchitka tests, held meetings in a church basement in Vancouver. Soon an ad hoc committee discussed sending a boat to stay in the forbidden zone of the bomb test, volunteering their bodies as a compelling deterrent to the next test. The media made a big news event of this and hundreds of young people volunteered to risk their lives for a dramatic anti-nuclear cause. Soon, frantic work on the "Amchitka Campaign" was underway, led by the following main organizers:

- Robert Hunter, Canadian, newspaper columnist;
- Jim Bohlen, American, Second World War veteran, engineer;
- Marie Bohlen, American, activist volunteer, brought son to Canada to avoid the draft, as did Dorothy Stowe;
- Irving Stowe, American, lawyer, a Jew who became a devout Quaker;
- Dorothy Stowe, American, Quaker, wife of Irving Stowe;
- Paul Côté, Canadian, lawyer;
- Bill Darnell, Canadian, environment activist;
- Terry Simmons, American, geographer, an organizer of The Sierra Club of B.C.

The challenge attracted a small group of additional full-time activist organizers who were co-founders of a newly-named Greenpeace Foundation:

- Patrick Moore, Canadian, university student, later Ph.D. in Science of Ecology;[2]

- Ben Metcalfe, Canadian, free-lancer for the Canadian Broadcasting Corporation;
- Bob Cummings, Canadian, writer for local underground newspaper;
- Bob Keziere, Canadian, photographer, chemistry student;
- Rod Marining, Canadian, active demonstrator for environmental causes;
- Paul Watson, American, seaman, fighting supporter of many communist front organizations and demonstrations.

The group spent over a year raising funds, staving off Canadian and American government obstructions, and searching the waterfront for a boat. Greenpeace finally chartered an eighty-foot fishing boat described as an old junk heap, with an indomitable sea-going skipper, John Cormack. An enthusiastic crew of twelve volunteers, young and inexperienced as seamen, set sail for Amchitka, over 2,400 miles away, putting their safety and their futures at risk. A daily flow of press releases from the boat, renamed *Greenpeace I*, aroused intense media and public support across North America.

After more than a month of heavy storms and repair delays the crew reached the Aleutians, but finally had to return to Vancouver when the date for the explosion was postponed. Meanwhile, the Greenpeace team in Vancouver had organized a second crusade to Amchitka on a 154-foot obsolete naval minesweeper, renamed the *Greenpeace Too*. Hundreds of volunteers turned up, and twenty-eight were chosen for the second voyage. Amchitka was now a worldwide story, with nightly TV broadcasts and daily front page reports. The *Greenpeace Too* arrived in the Bering Sea too late to enter the test area. The blast went off on November 6. The two Greenpeace crews felt their projects had failed, but they had succeeded far beyond their wildest dreams. Dramatic media coverage aroused public support all around the world. A new force for protection of the environment had arrived on the world scene, organized and carried forward by young activist volunteers. The United States announced in February 1972 that the further nuclear tests planned for Amchitka had been abandoned. This was the breakthrough that led to the leading nuclear powers later signing a pact abolishing future underground tests.

The Second Campaign—Mururoa Atoll

After Amchitka the leaders of Greenpeace decided that their aim was to be an all-purpose ecological "strike force" worldwide—at a time when their assets were only nine thousand dollars from donations! In the early 1970s, France announced a series of atmospheric nuclear tests above Mururoa atoll in the South Pacific ocean, and had created an illegal no-entry zone of 100,000 square miles around the atoll. Greenpeace saw this as another place where nuclear tests had to be stopped by sending a Greenpeace boat to stay in the no-entry zone and staging a media event that would create a storm of public opinion worldwide to stop the tests. In April 1972, David McTaggart of Vancouver sailed the *Greenpeace III*, a small thirty-eight foot ketch, into the no-entry zone with a volunteer crew of five—two Englishmen, two Canadians, and one Australian. Scientists predicted that anyone in the direct path of the fallout from an above-ground nuclear explosion would be doomed. After the *Greenpeace III* entered the forbidden zone France sent a small navy, almost crushing the ketch, and exploded a test. The fallout missed the ketch by about fifteen miles. The French announced a second test, and sent a minesweeper which rammed a repaired *Greenpeace III* and towed it out of the test zone.

The following year *Greenpeace III* sailed again from New Zealand to stop the next tests, and stirred up worldwide protests. New Zealand sent out a navy ship, and a large number of small "peace boats" entered the fallout zone, only to be driven out by the French navy. On August 15, 1973, the French sent out three warships. A commando unit boarded the *Greenpeace III* and savagely beat the crew, leaving McTaggart with a permanently blinded eye. The French publicly denied this, but were embarrassed worldwide by a media release recording the beating on a film which had been taken by a young woman crew member and smuggled past unsuspecting French guards. Three months later, in November, 1973, France announced that, after one more airborne explosion, all future tests would be done underground.

Greenpeace had achieved two incredible victories against military superpowers. The media and public opinion were alerted to the threat of nuclear annihilation. The focus of Greenpeace attention now shifted not only to protect the human race, but also to protect the ecosystems supporting all forms of life. Scientists were estimating that there were 900 species on the endangered list. In 1974, a New Zealander named Paul Spong moved to Vancouver and persuaded Greenpeace to launch a campaign to end the mass killing of whales. The seeds that would change Greenpeace from an anti-nuclear protest group to an all-encompassing environmental movement with thousands of supporters around the world were planted.

The Save the Whales Campaign

During 1974-1975, Greenpeace debated many different direct-action campaigns that would create media events. It was a time of endless meetings and leadership turnover. Greenpeace had in essence ceased to function, left with only a four-man "save the whales" committee. A rebirth came when a new plan to use high-speed inflatable two-man rubber boats called Zodiacs, to race in front of the harpoons of whaling boats, caught their imagination. It was decided to send a boat with two Zodiacs to interfere with the Japanese and Russian whaling fleets in the North Pacific ocean, from August to September, 1975.

In the next five months support poured in from radicals, students, artists, businessmen, politicians, Japanese Canadians, ethnic Indians, and miscellaneous environment activists. Two boats were refitted and supplied, with costs paid for by a lottery. Information gleaned secretly in Europe by Paul and Linda Spong indicated that the Russian whalers would be off the coast of California in late June 1975. In April a crowd of 23,000 gathered at Jericho Beach in Vancouver for a big send-off rally of the two Greenpeace boats, departing for the north end of Vancouver Island, B.C., to prepare for a move south to intercept the Russians. It was leaked by a friend in the Russian embassy in Ottawa that an agency of the Canadian government was feeding the Russians regular reports of the Greenpeace locations, presumably to avoid an international incident. To thwart this, Greenpeace sailed north to the Queen Charlotte islands, with full publicity, and then secretly turned and went south to meet the Russian fleet off California. The ruse worked.

The latest news by radio was that the International Whaling Commission had voted to increase the killing quotas. This was supported by Russia, Japan, and Canada, despite fifty-two nations voting for a ten year moratorium on whaling. Combining amateur navigation and good luck, *Greenpeace V* located the Russian whaling fleet of a large factory ship and six harpoon boats. The Zodiac crews harassed the Russians, and took pictures of the corpse of a baby sperm whale twenty-five feet long, an illegal kill, and many more kills. The Zodiacs intervened many times to stop the harpooning, with the big factory ship trying to run them down. The intervention of the Zodiacs enabled a pod of eight whales to escape.

A second day of attack followed. When the films ran later on world TV showing Greenpeace crews interfering at close quarters with the harpoon gunners, a media storm swept around the world. The campaign was a complete success in winning public support for stopping the slaughter of whales, and for the conservation of all sea creatures. A new objective was to increase the protection of sea-life by persuading governments to establish a new offshore control zone of 200 miles from shore to replace the old limit of twelve miles. Many governments opposed this, but it has now been achieved. The Quaker belief that bearing witness by working for righteous causes changes the level of commitment on the part of the bearer was now exemplified in the future lives of the Greenpeace activists.

Foundation and Empire

Greenpeace had generated increased worldwide media attention during the courageous challenge to the Russian whaling fleet—but was now some $40,000 in debt. Only four of the original founders were now full-time leaders—Hunter, Marining, Moore, and Watson. There was a dedicated hard core of roughly thirty followers. Fortunately, a Vancouver entrepreneur took charge of managing the business side and reducing the debt. Soon Greenpeace was able to finance another major campaign—to stop the 1976 pup seal slaughter on the ice floes off Newfoundland. The plan was to fly to the ice and spray the pups with a green dye to make the pelts worthless. After three months of non-stop organizing, a crew of five women and ten men went by train, bus, and ferry to the north end of Newfoundland, which was being battered by one of the roughest winter storms in many years.

Meanwhile the Newfoundland public, stirred up by local seal hunters, were incensed at losing a pup fur harvest that gave jobs to about 3,000 Newfoundlanders and significant income to an impoverished area. Crowds of angry seal pelt hunters blocked access to the staging area, and threatened the safety of the Greenpeace crew and the two chartered helicopters. The expedition was stopped dead in its tracks, until Hunter and a local leader worked out a deal that cancelled the green paint spraying program but would allow Greenpeace to fly to the distant, far-out ice where the seal-hunting foreign icebreakers were located. To maintain completely free access out to the icebreaker fleet area, the crew set up a base camp on the wind-driven arctic snow of Belle Isle, north about thirty miles. On March 15, the helicopters finally found the two icebreakers amid blood-streaked ice. The Greenpeace crew charged a number of sealers busy clubbing baby seals, but soon had to leave for base camp due to weather. The crew were trapped in a fierce arctic storm for two days, and were rescued just a day ahead of a new blizzard which destroyed the base camp. When the storm passed the crew returned to a killing ground scene of utter carnage of lifeless skinned baby seals and crazed mothers. Watson and Hunter locked arms in the path of the huge advancing icebreaker, yelling, "We're not moving." The icebreaker crunched to within ten feet of the men, pulled back, and charged again, stopping about three feet from the backs of the two men. The captain then pulled back, giving in to a superior force of muscle and will. The crew got the whole scene on some of the most dramatic real-life film of the century. The next day, March 20, the helicopters flew over a blood-soaked scene again, and then returned to base, to be charged and seized by the Royal Canadian Mounted Police. Hunter wrote, "If we had, in fact, saved any seals, it would only have been a handful. But we had made political inroads in Newfoundland, acquired allies, divided the opposition, and brought the great glass eyes of the mass-communication system to bear with more intensity than ever before."

The Second Campaign to Save the Whales

While the seal pup campaign was in full operation the Vancouver Greenpeace group was planning a second campaign to save the whales. A converted minesweeper, renamed *Greenpeace VII*, 150 feet long, was bought and re-equipped. Membership was booming, by now close to ten thousand, with twenty-eight branches in North America. The projected budget for 1976 was $300,000. *Greenpeace VII* left Vancouver with 26 men and 6 women on board, acclaimed by a cheering crowd of 16,000. A UN flag flew from the mast. The send-off celebration had raised $27,000 to cover a bank loan. The *Greenpeace I* was re-equipped and joined the *Greenpeace VII* to add to the protest expedition. The plan was to meet the Russian whaling fleet, then near Hawaii. Leaving B.C. waters was delayed by a failed attempt of the Canadian government to seize the *Greenpeace VII*.

For the first time in many years the Russian fleet stayed away from the U.S. coast, forcing the *Greenpeace VII* to search for it in the mid-Pacific ocean. After several weeks, contact was made with the Russian whaling fleet which was busy killing whales. Three Greenpeace Zodiacs raced in, blocking the Russian harpooners from a pod of five whales, which moved off safely with the three Zodiacs centred in their midst. Hunter wrote later, "In centuries to come—people would look back on these films and tapes and charts—and say: Look, here is where the turning point occurred. It was not just that humans went out to save the whales, but the whales held back to acknowledge the effort. It was a real beginning of brotherhood between living creatures."

After a refit and reconnaissance lay-over in Hawaii, the *Greenpeace VII* spent a week tracking down the Russian whaling fleet again. Three Zodiak crews interrupted the Russian harpoon boats, getting in position before the harpooners could fire. After a number of skirmishes the Russian fleet disappeared. The *Greenpeace VII* returned to Vancouver, where a large crowd of 3,000 cheered the successful confrontation at sea. Before the previous year the Russian fleet had taken up to 1,300 sperm whales annually. Greenpeace intervention had saved, by one calculation, at least one hundred whales and probably many more. The Russian and Japanese fleets had abandoned their usual whale killing grounds about 700 miles off the west coast of North America.

Greenpeace membership soon rose to 80,000, but many newly-formed groups were at loggerheads. In January 1977, politics, not ecology, dominated an organization described as a nightmare. Watson picked a "sealing attack" Committee to go again to challenge the sealers. Project organizers included only four experienced Vancouver leaders. A large majority of the committee came from money-raising groups around the world. Watson took a hard line of no negotiations with Newfoundlanders, Eskimos, or Indians, declaring only physical action would stop the hunt.

The Second Save the Seal Pups Campaign

In March 1977, a large contingent from Canada, the U.S., and Europe set up base camp at the small village of Blanc Sablon in Labrador, within helicopter range of the Belle Isle advance camp. There was complete confusion at Blanc Sablon—too much equipment, not enough helicopters, and a horde of mainly European journalists and cameramen crowded into two small and inadequate hotels. The day before the hunt twenty-one Greenpeace members were flown north to Belle Isle and set up a camp with at first only one tent. A group of U.S. media stayed back in Newfoundland, mainly covering angry crowds of local seal-hunters held back by the RCMP. The next day two helicopters from Belle Isle arrived on broken and slush ice around a big ice-breaker ship, hunters clubbing pup seals, pools of blood, and piles of pup pelts. Only five Greenpeace were able to cross the heaving ice floes. Watson charged past several sealers, and then handcuffed himself to a ship's cable, attached to a bale of pelts, yelling, "Where's the camera!" He was hoisted up and dropped back into the icy water twice before being rescued onto a small raft by one of the Greenpeace crew. A Canadian fisheries officer on the ship convinced the captain to haul Watson on deck. He was resuscitated by a Vancouver partner and flown to hospital the next day. Things now went from bad to worse. A famous world actress, sex-kitten Brigitte

Bardot, arrived to protest the hunt. Two press conferences were held, after which she was flown to Belle Isle, where she spent two sub-zero nights. She could not be flown out to the killing area for a photo due to blizzard weather.

When the hunt was over, foreign ships had taken 24,000 pelts out of their quota of 35,000; Newfoundland sealers had killed about 16,000. The media coverage in North America and Europe had been so poor it was embarrassing. Only Brigitte Bardot saved an unmitigated disaster. The new "biggest ever" concept had been beyond Greenpeace's capability at this time. Greenpeace had forgotten an earlier lesson that the operation must be professional or the message is lost.

New Planetary Consciousness

One of the most revolutionary new post-war developments was the freedom to access information of any kind by computer and media from any part of the world. A new world consciousness had emerged, affecting all human thought and action. Greenpeace was now operating in a global culture. Hunter wrote that "a genuine planetary consciousness was coming into existence, and these issues Greenpeace was tackling were the flash points of its awakening." New Greenpeace Philosophy and Greenpeace Ethics statements give insight into the thinking of the world's first popular movement guided by the basic concepts of the interrelationship of the sciences of ecology and the environment.

The Greenpeace Philosophy:

"Just as Copernicus demonstrated that the earth is not the center of the universe, so ecology teaches that man is not the center of life on this planet.

"Through the study of ecology, man has embarked on a quest toward understanding the great systems of order underlying the complex flow of life on our planet. Ecology has taught us that the whole earth is part of our "body," and that we must learn to respect it as we would respect ourselves. As we feel for ourselves, we must feel for all forms of life: the whales, the seals, the forests, and the seas. The tremendous beauty of ecological thought is that it provides a pathway to an understanding and appreciation of life itself. That understanding is vital to the continued existence of life itself. That

understanding is vital to the continued existence of our environment and ourselves."

The Greenpeace Ethic:

"The Greenpeace Ethic is one of personal responsibility and non-violent confrontation.

"According to the ethic, a person who witnesses an injustice becomes responsible for it. He must then decide whether to act against the injustice or to let it continue. The choice is a matter of personal conscience."

In April 1977, Hunter resigned as president and chairman of the board, and was succeeded by Patrick Moore, ecology guru and inter-disciplinarian. His approach was to engage ecology with the realities of human dynamics. Greenpeace had evolved into a political and an ecological party, concerned with both local and world issues. A new mantra was, "Think big, very, very big, and small, very, very small."

Campaign Against Oil Tanker Terminal

In the mid-seventies a large oil consortium proposed a pipeline terminal for oil supertankers at Kitimat, British Columbia, in the heart of over 800 miles of undeveloped coastal wilderness, including the ancestral land of the Tsimshian Indians. The oil consortium hired a large coastal pleasure cruiser to take a group of local politicians and TV cameramen to see the Kitimat area, and support the pipeline terminal. The Vancouver Greenpeace group hired a sixty-seven-foot boat to stop the oil consortium cruiser from getting through to Kitimat. A protest fleet of 25 boats of local fishermen, the Tsimshian, missionaries, union groups, and west coast ecology radicals arrived to block the water access. The cruise ship captain refused a meeting. He pushed ahead at full speed and ran down a Greenpeace Zodiac, leaving two men sucked under the wake of the ship. A small skiff pulled the men from the water, narrowly averting their death. The oil consortium cruise was a public relations disaster. After a number of hearings by west coast and Ottawa politicians, a final decision was made against an oil terminal at Kitimat. There would be no massive oil spills on the inside coastal waters of British Columbia.

The Spruce Budworm Crusade

A second campaign in the summer of 1977 was to prevent the spraying of a chemical insecticide over an area of 50,000 square miles of B.C. forest, to eliminate the spruce budworm destroying trees in the large area. The insecticide would have killed all the small birds and animals in the area as well. Moore felt the wildlife had to be protected, as research showed that the infestation was in its last year and would begin to decline. A convoy of volunteers set up dozens of camps beneath the trees to be sprayed, and hung helium balloons at random above the trees, to be in the way of the spraying helicopters. The B.C. government sent in the police to remove the protesters and block the roads to prevent any more going in. But Moore was able to get reinforcements, as he had asked the local Indian council for permission to use reservation land as a base to launch the campaign. The Premier of B.C. was defeated by a determined Greenpeace band of activists, and cancelled the program.

The Third "Stop the Whalers" Campaign

In 1977, the Hawaii Greenpeace Foundation supported a major drive to finance another campaign to stop the whalers. Two veterans from Vancouver, Paul Spong and George Korotva, brought the expertise to organize the project, including the refit of a "176 foot tin hulk," an ex-Navy sub chaser, renamed the *Greenpeace X*. She was fast—able to do 26 knots, and could carry extra fuel, a helicopter, and seven Zodiacs. The Honolulu media and fund-raising volunteers gave massive support. The U.S. national ABC network paid $60,000 to provide an eight-man TV crew, plus about $200,000 for the helicopter, charter fees, and other support costs. This major operation was falling far behind schedule, so Vancouver backed it up by sending a large volunteer crew in a refitted *Greenpeace VII*, financed by concerts as they sailed down the west coast to California.

In June 1977, the International Whaling Commission slashed the whale quotas for 1978 by 36 percent, with only Russia and Japan dissenting. Greenpeace morale went through the roof. In about two weeks *Greenpeace VII* sighted the Russian whaling fleet of killer boats and a large factory ship. When this news was heard in Honolulu the

Ohana Kai (the new Hawaiian name of the *Greenpeace X*) left in a great rush with a crew of thirty-five (only four had been on a Greenpeace expedition) and about fifteen more volunteers who jumped aboard as the ship left the dock. Unfortunately, the plan for the *Ohana Kai* to join the *Greenpeace VII* in confronting the Russian fleet was not achieved, due to further delays after departure.

On July 30, two Greenpeace Zodiacs and the *Greenpeace VII* pushed their way into the Russian fleet of nine harpoon boats and the factory ship which was pursuing a pod of whales. A long chase in rough seas was too punishing for the Zodiac crews, who had to be changed. By then the entire pod of whales was surrounded by nine harpoon boats, and all whales were killed. Greenpeace cameramen had the whole slaughter on film, which was shown on ABC and hundreds of independent TV stations. The President of the U.S., Jimmy Carter, phoned Greenpeace, saying he would send the film to the International Whaling Commission to protest the illegal killing of a fifteen-foot whale. The *Ohana Kai* made contact with a second Russian fleet. A Greenpeace delegation of four went aboard, and after a brief discussion with the captain were invited to leave. The Russian fleet left the area, and were not sighted again by the *Ohana Kai*. The *Greenpeace VII* refuelled in San Francisco and tracked down the second Russian fleet again, about 1,200 miles away. The Russian ship did no hunting as long as *Greenpeace VII* was present. Four Greenpeace crew went on board the factory ship and had a friendly talk with the Russians until ordered off. Once more, this fleet was not sighted again. The several voyages that summer won worldwide media attention. Greenpeace felt, however, that a big part of this was due to the media stressing the violent act of a harpoon fired to threaten human flesh. Hunter reflected, "Without confrontation—the risk of life and limb— the mass media could not have cared less about what we did."

The Australian Stop-the-Whalers Campaign

In the summer of 1977, Robert Hunter and his wife Bobbi flew to Sydney to organize a protest against a land-based whaling station in western Australia. Financing came from a Frenchman, M. Fortom-Gouin. With a start date two weeks away, none of the essentials had been organized. Hunter and a crew of five set out in two overloaded makeshift vehicles for the Albany whaling town about 1,200 miles away. They arrived to learn that the station was very dangerous for Zodiacs, as large sharks came in for the whale blood being discharged daily. During several weeks of confrontation with two Australian whaling ships two harpoons had been fired so close to the Zodiacs that one line snagged on a Zodiac propellor. Finally, the Greenpeace crews were exhausted and had to break off further harassment. They had not stopped the whaling nor had a dramatic media event. However, several months later, the Australian government ordered an inquiry into whaling. Soon the last whaling station in the English-speaking world was closed. While the Australian "stop the whaling" campaign ended in a draw, the media coverage around the world was a complete victory. This added to the amazingly swift transition of Greenpeace from an organization focussed on denouncing nuclear weaponry and saving threatened species, to a worldwide force of volunteers devoted to protecting the environment and the ecology.

Greenpeace, Year 2000

The current strength of Greenpeace can be summarized in extracts from the annual report of year 2000—exciting reading for all persons dedicated to saving the environment:

"Greenpeace is an independent campaigning organization that uses non-violent, creative confrontation to expose global environmental problems and to force solutions which are essential to a green and peaceful future.

"We organize public campaigns for the protection of oceans and ancient forests, for the phasing-out of fossil fuels and the promotion of renewable energies, for the elimination of toxic chemicals, for nuclear disarmament and an end to nuclear contamination, and against the release of genetically modified organisms into nature."

The following summaries of some of the main recent campaigns show the importance of Greenpeace as a force for change on a world scale:

• In Lebanon, Russia, China, and Turkey peaceful protests challenged government repression of human rights;

- Campaigns against toxic wastes, ozone-depleting CFCs (chlorofluorocarbons),[3] the dumping of nuclear waste in the oceans;
- Campaigns to protect the Antarctic;
- Campaigns to challenge pollution of water, air, land, and food;
- Campaigns to force renewable development and sound environmental policies in the Amazon and other development areas;
- Leadership against the biotechnology industry introducing genetically modified organisms (GMOs) in human and animal feed;
- Maintaining political, economic and social pressures to reduce the resource-depleting and polluting habits of all societies, rich and poor;
- An ongoing campaign to focus on climate change, a major threat facing the global environment, and to challenge the increasing burning of coal, oil, and gas;
- Challenge overfishing, the biggest single threat to marine biodiversity;
- Pressure to maintain the 1986 moratorium on large-scale commercial whaling;
- Protection of the Great Barrier Reef, Australia;
- Pressing the U.S., European Union, and Japan to ratify the Kyoto Protocol to save the climate;
- Challenging the import of illegally caught Atlantic tuna;
- In July 2000, Turkey announced the cancellation of the Abbuyu nuclear reactor project after intensive pressure from Greenpeace and other non-governmental organizations;
- Challenging the U.S. Star Wars program and the militarisation of space;
- Greenpeace policy that in the absence of a viable solution to nuclear waste disposal, the nuclear industry must be challenged.

Greenpeace—Summary

Greenpeace membership as of January 1, 2001 was about 2.65 million, an increase of over six percent on the previous year. Net income in the year 2000 was $134 million, an increase of eleven percent over 1999. Greenpeace continues to grow in worldwide public support, and in diversified local initiatives to challenge the impairment of ecosystems and the global environment. Greenpeace bears witness to the ability of dedicated individuals to associate in local grass roots organizations in support of a cause vital to all mankind and to mother earth. The strength of worldwide public opinion supports challenges to governments and the private sector to respect all mankind and the environment. A Greenpeace ethic can be summarized as follows: "Following a pathway to an understanding and appreciation of life itself is vital to the continued existence of our environment and of ourselves."

World Peace

The growth of Greenpeace is a model for individuals who yearn for world peace and are searching for a way to do something meaningful about it. The story of Greenpeace shows that individual peacemakers can work for a cause shared by millions worldwide, can co-operate in grass root groups of ordinary citizens to bear witness to their commitment to work to protect the world environment, and can energize the widespread support of public opinion that will force governments and corporations to take into account the aims of environmental peacemakers.

The organization and actions of Greenpeace can be studied by peacemakers to find common ground, starting from the grass roots and working to achieve objectives to enhance world peace for present and future generations. An organization working as peacemakers can achieve ongoing success in the cause of world peace, growing with the philosophy that peace begins in the hearts and minds of ordinary men and women everywhere who work together in small groups. Peacemakers will learn, as Greenpeace did, to "Think big, very very big, and small, very very small." Peacemakers will develop the wisdom to adopt philosophies, ethics and commitments that will attract worldwide support, help to protect the environment, and promote the cause of world peace.

There are many organizations that have been committed to principles that are fundamental to mankind's search for peace. For the most part they were not created and organized from the "top down" but from the "bottom up," from the grass roots of the social conscience of mankind. The following chapters will explore the realities that there can be no peace without respect, fairness, justice for all humanity, human rights, and a standard of living that supports a good life. They also explore the realities that without democracy, social free enterprise, respect for the environment and the ecology of the universe, without respect for human rights and equal economic and social opportunities for all mankind, there can be no peace.

"Individual commitment to a group effort—that is what makes a team work, a company work, a society work, a civilization work."

Vince Lombardi

Famed football coach

"It is of no use trying to build a new world from the top down, with political ideas of spheres of influence and so on. We have to build it from the bottom upwards, and provide first the primary necessities of life for the people who have never had them."

Lord Boyd Orr (1949)

Chapter14

GRASS ROOTS
PEACEMAKERS GROUPS

The phenomenal success of Greenpeace shows how a grass roots organization can spread rapidly worldwide with millions of supporters and by winning major public opinion support and political influence. Some key factors contributing to this success are described in Chapter 13. Greenpeace's popularity stems largely from the universal appeal to individuals of doing something to protect the environment; dramatic campaigns to achieve maximum media exposure; publicity to win powerful public support of young and old; activists dedicated to exploiting media exposure by "creative confrontation"; building a world headquarters capable of co-ordinating overall world programs and of concentrating strong professional expertise to lobby for legal and political consideration in confrontations with government and industry. Instant worldwide communication by TV and the Internet made this rapid growth possible.

The proposal to form small groups of persons willing to promote peacemaking up from the grass roots to eventually win public opinion support and political influence was explained in Chapter 12. The first Peacemakers groups could begin with a meeting of minds about what individuals can do to start a movement that is worthwhile and can lead to action plans and concrete results. It will be up to the members to gradually develop a consensus on the philosophy of the Peacemakers. Peace Laureate Albert Schweitzer has given us a profound philosophy of peacemaking as a guide, paraphrased as follows: "*We must direct our hopes and our intentions to the coming of an era in which war will have no place. Our will can have but one aim: to attain, through a change in spirit, that superior reason which will dissuade us from war. The ethical spirit alone has the power to generate a prevailing set of moral principles directed toward peace. Decisive steps must be taken to ensure peace, and decisive results obtained without delay. Only through the spirit can all this be done. The ethical spirit created the humanitarianism which is the origin of all progress toward some form of higher existence. Inspired by this spirit we are true to ourselves and capable of creating. Whether peace comes or not depends on the direction in which the mentality of individuals develops and then, in turn, on that of their nations. The time has come when governments must look on themselves as the executors of the will of the people. Only when the ethical spirit becomes a living force within us and leads us to a civilization based on the humanitarian ideal will we find peace. All men are, as beings capable of compassion, able to develop a humanitarian spirit. It abides within them like tinder waiting to be lit, waiting only for a spark. The human spirit is capable of creating in our time a new ethical mentality.*"[1]

Early members could also discuss guidelines as to how they wish to develop a common approach based on a set of moral principles to support the unity of understanding and purpose of Peacemakers groups. Examples of practical guidelines used by many established peacemaking groups are summarized as follows:

- To be guided by respect for the universal human rights of all peoples;
- To act as catalysts to encourage ordinary citizens to join Peacemakers, to become well-informed on problems of peace, and to work in support of Peacemakers projects;
- To encourage two-way communication and co-operation with all elements of civil society and government working for peace, including religious and social service organizations, non-governmental organizations, regional and national governments, and the UN;
- To develop leaders in working for peace at the grass roots level, to become involved in expressing the will of the people, and to work with NGOs and governments as the executors of the public will.

The objectives of Peacemakers groups are to have people get together to work for mankind's search for peace at a time when this is the main objective of all mankind. The threats to peace are increasing, placing the future of humanity at risk. Peacemakers know that mankind everywhere is yearning for peace, but ordinary citizens feel that there is nothing an individual can do under our present system to change society's drift toward a less peaceful world. To find a way out of this quicksand will require that steps be taken now to try yet another new and different solution. The first step is to activate individuals to tackle this problem in the time-honored way, by talking to friends, meeting frequently to discuss possible projects and strategies, and taking steps to do the best one can to bring all available thought and effort to bear on working toward solutions. Friends will share agreed bed-rock principles to guide the formation of a group; what specific problems do you want to explore, what do you want to do, and how do you want to do it? The first groups will have to feel their way, as there are no obvious answers or "quick fixes" to joining with others to start off on the road to peacemaking. Knowing how other small groups have started will be helpful. The examples of Peacemakers philosophy, principles, and organization procedures are presented to stir up ideas. The history of organizing peace groups shows frequent changes from first ideas in many cases. The process of forming a group and finding and starting meaningful projects is largely a "learn as you go" process.

It will be helpful to review the many lessons learned from the growth of the Nobel Peace Prize institutions and associations, most of which started on the same basis as our Peacemakers proposal—with a few friends forming a group to take action to work for peace. The following institutions are some examples of the peacemaking achievements of associations founded by one person and a few friends:

- Salvation Army;
- YMCA and YWCA;
- Red Cross and Red Crescent;
- Nansen International Office for Refugees (now part of UN);
- English and American Quakers;
- Amnesty International;

- International Physicians for the Prevention of Nuclear War;
- Pugwash Conferences on Science and World Affairs;
- International Campaign to Ban Landmines;
- Médicins Sans Frontières (Doctors Without Borders).

There are many lessons to be learned by looking at the "pilgrim's progress" of these institutions:

- It required just one person and a group of friends to decide something had to be done to remove obstacles to peace, and the time for action had arrived;
- The appeal to stop man's inhumanity to man has been deeply felt and universal, from the need to help one another to the need to stop nuclear arms. Great numbers of volunteers were ready to join causes to promote peace and welfare;
- Public indifference and political lethargy and obstruction was a prevailing problem. However, this did not stop the struggle for peace. A way around these difficulties was always found
- Many new efforts were necessary to get funding. The right appeal carried out in the right way has often been successful. Most groups have funded their start-up themselves, as done by Greenpeace founders;
- Grass roots flexibility and ingenuity can succeed where structured rigidities of governments have failed;
- The simpler the organization, the better the results. For example, the Salvation Army is described as the most efficient organization in the U.S., with a minimum of staff above the local unit level;
- Avoid being bought off by face-saving, political compromises, or so-called "quick solutions." The last fundamental cataclysm of destruction of world security went from bad to worse from, say, 1900. Any recovery from this trend could well take another hundred years for mankind to learn how to live in peace. All peacemaking is a gradual never-ending work-in-progress of succeeding generations. The long journeys of peacemaking societies have always started with one lonely person taking the

first step. Peacemaking is not for the timid, complacent, or impatient. The pioneers of volunteer movements attacked indifference, lethargy, and satisfaction with the status quo as diseases to be defeated;

- Three of the Peace Prize organizations involved scientists and doctors who had support from their professional facilities and colleagues, adding strength to their advocacy. Their volunteer work required considerable financial, professional, and personal sacrifice, as has been the case with a great many volunteers for a wide variety of missions for peace which were not projects of state governments or the UN. The future of peacemaking depends on individuals rearranging their personal priorities and being willing to make sacrifices. Surely every person concerned about peacemaking has the time to prepare for and attend at least one meeting a month as the start of a renewed effort to work for peace. The excuse of "I am too busy" should not be made by anyone concerned about world peace.

The idea that there is one group in possession of the truth has done great harm, especially in the last century. We now are facing up to the reality that mankind is destined to live together, with a great diversity of peoples and cultures. We have come to realize that peace depends on living in harmony with diversity. Also, as now more people are moving from nation to nation, realizing the many benefits of multiculturalism is gradually overcoming hatred or fear of strangers. Instead of endless misunderstanding and hostility, if we truly want peace our only alternative is to seek out and sustain the unity of mankind and the things we have in common. In every society one can find the universal values on which the unity of mankind has been sustained throughout history.

The question arises as to what the vast majority of people have in common respecting living together in peace: understanding of the moral principles that guide the living of a good and happy life; love for one's fellow man, as shown by the lives of countless workers for peace; love for peace; love for sharing; a belief in the healing power of forgiveness, as shown by Martin Luther King Jr. and Nelson Mandela; respect for leadership and good governance; respect for the integrity of an organized society. These reflect the values that will bring peace to the world.

It is a tragedy of history and sociology that all mankind has a natural instinct for what is peaceful, right, and good, but has repeatedly turned away from this to pursue conflict and war. It is useful to review the basic causes of war: the grasping for more territory, resources, or power; the lack of laws and legal institutions; lack of education, understanding, and tolerance; the seeking of revenge; allowing ethnic and religious differences to escalate into fears, hatreds, and violence. It need not be so. "Peoples of different religions and cultures live side by side in almost every part of the world . . . . We *can* love what we are without hating what—and who—we are not . . . . The notion that what is ours is necessarily in conflict with what is theirs is both false and dangerous. It has resulted in endless enmity and conflict, leading men to commit the greatest of crimes in the name of a higher power." (Kofi Annan, Appendix D.) The spirit of humanitarianism, as exemplified by the faith in non-violence of Mahatma Gandhi, Nelson Mandela, Bishop Tutu, Mother Teresa, and Martin Luther King Jr. has gradually prevailed in more and more parts of the world as peoples have learned to live in peace and respect for one another.

Following the proposal that small Peacemakers groups should be tried out as an added force for peace, many specific ideas that have helped strong existing peacemaking organizations can be guidance for future progress of new Peacemakers groups:

- Start with friends who are interested in the common cause of peacemaking;
- At all times welcome multiculturalism and minorities;
- Some existing groups organized for book lovers, investors, speakers, service clubs, veterans, recreation, hobbies—the list is endless—may want to expand their present interest with a new challenge to evolve into Peacemakers groups;
- Access to new contacts and friends will develop as today's e-mail and worldwide web contacts increase;

- Contacts for guest speakers will include people with wide national and international travel and speaking experience, and relations with special interest groups, minorities, etc.;
- Emphasis on group programs, not on large conferences or large consortiums that come and go and often specialize in the latest fads of professional speakers;
- Emphasis on volunteer contributions of time and money, with a bare minimum of overhead;
- Emphasis on "spreading the word" and outreach programs to demonstrate successful peace programs at home and abroad;
- Cultivate understanding, not confrontation;
- Cultivate two-way communication and open-mindedness, avoiding doctrinaire approaches—look at both sides of questions and problems;
- Cultivate contacts with local NGOs and other peacemaking groups of civil society, many of which will have had extensive experience in peacemaking.

The story of Amnesty International shows the importance and strength of enlisting individuals to carry out an initiative that could not be done by government. From the appeal in 1961 of one young British lawyer, Peter Benenson, and a group of friends, Amnesty has worked since its beginning for over 45,000 prisoners and has responded to 16,660 appeals on behalf of men, women, and children in immediate danger. Today, Amnesty International has more than one million members, subscribers, and regular donors in more than 140 countries. Its nerve center is in London, with 350 staff members and over one hundred volunteers from more than fifty countries. The Amnesty movement consists of 7,800 local, youth, specialist, and professional groups in more than one hundred countries. There are nationally-organized sections in fifty-six countries, and co-ordinating groups in another twenty-four countries. Amnesty is a democratic movement, self-governed by a nine-member Executive Committee whose members are elected every two years by an International Council.

Amnesty International's mission is to undertake research and action focussed on preventing and ending grave abuses of prisoners of conscience, of the rights of individuals to physical and mental integrity, freedom of conscience and expression, and freedom from discrimination, within the context of its work to promote all human rights. It is Amnesty's policy not to take credit for a prisoner's release, but letters of thanks have come from many of the former prisoners themselves. A labor organizer in the Dominican Republic wrote: *When the first two hundred letters came, the guards gave me back my clothes. Then the next two hundred letters came and the prison director came to see me. When the next pile of letters arrived, the director got in touch with his superior. The letters kept coming and coming: three thousand of them. The President was informed. The letters still kept arriving, and the President called the prison and told them to let me go.*

In addition to actions to secure the release of illegally detained political prisoners, Amnesty continues to campaign for international commitments to implement the UN Declaration of Human Rights, for the abolition of both torture and the death penalty, for the end of political killings and "disappearances," and for preventing governments from unlawful killings in armed conflicts. Amnesty opposes abuses by opposition groups, including hostage-taking, torture, and killings of prisoners and other deliberate and arbitrary killings; assists asylum-seekers; co-operates with other NGOs and the UN and with regional intergovernmental organizations; verifies control of international military, security, and police relations; organizes human rights education and awareness-raising programs.

Each year Amnesty International members from around the world join forces to campaign respecting one country or on a particular human rights issue. These major campaigns involve reporting on human rights issues, lobbying governments, and working closely with local human rights activists. Special programs in 2002 included a campaign by over 35,000 people from 188 countries against torture and ill-treatment of women and minorities. Recent programs include the following:

- Urgent Action Network, working for 2,813 named victims of human rights violations;

- Lawyers' Network, campaigning for the International Criminal Court, ratified in February, 2002;
- Military Security and Police Network;
- Company Approaches Network, campaign for controls on the international diamond trade;
- Children's Network, lobbying against using children in armed conflicts;
- Women's Network, campaigning against abuse of women and minorities;
- Medical Network, health professionals in more than thirty countries, helping ill prisoners who had been refused medical care.

Amnesty has scrupulously followed its basic commitment to remain neutral, impartial, and independent. They do not accept contributions from any source that might call into question their independence. No funds are accepted from governments. Donations come from members, the public, and organizations such as trusts, foundations, and medical supply companies. The budget for the year ending March 31, 2002, was about $21 million, including $5 million spent on Research and Action and $3 million spent on Research and Action Support. Administrative costs were seventeen percent—very low for the highly detailed investigative and legal research work required.

Even some of the most oppressive governments have not been immune to letter campaigns. Amnesty has earned such a reputation for integrity and accuracy that its public statements, the findings of its investigative missions, and its annual reports are widely respected. A recent Amnesty report gives a grim picture of the world's lack of observance of the Universal Declaration of Human Rights. The report tallies in detail documented violations, for example, the execution of persons under eighteen years of age and the mentally impaired, and incidents of police and prison-guard brutality, including sexual abuse and torture, much of it racially motivated.

The story of Amnesty gives reason for hope. Its work is done by individuals concerned about human suffering who act in the faith that an ordinary individual can make a difference. Mümtaz Soysal of Turkey, Amnesty International's Vice-Chairman, who with Thomas Hammarberg of Sweden represented the organization at the Peace Prize presentation ceremony, said in his Nobel lecture: "*It was upon this commitment of individual human beings to each other's welfare that Amnesty International was founded . . . . It began with the courage of one man who, when confronted with the plight of unjustly detained individuals, called on others to join with him to rouse international public opinion, to do something concrete, and, where human beings are at stake, to break down all barriers.*" The address was concluded with the words of a woman who had managed to send a letter from her prison cell:

> "*They are envious of us. They will envy us all.*
> *For it is an enviable but very difficult task*
> *to live through history as a human being,*
> *to complete a life as a human being.*
> *Soon the night will fall and they will close the doors of the cell.*
> *I feel lonely.*
> *No . . . . I am with the whole of mankind*
> *And the whole of mankind is with me.*"

The work of Amnesty continues with the dedication of individual volunteers. For example, a large local municipal library which was visited recently had a young woman volunteer of Amnesty International speaking to a constant stream of mainly young people, collecting names and addresses and handing out brochures asking for support of Amnesty's activist program. A summary of this program illustrates procedures that would be helpful for Peacemakers groups.

WRITE A LETTER, SAVE A LIFE—thousands of people write letters to stand up for the rights of others:

- Write when you have the time—sign up for The Activist magazine and act on the featured cases;
- Write on a regular basis—request our special Letter-Writing Package;
- Start now—call us or e-mail us.

STAY INFORMED—recent donors receive our annual 8-page newsletter, *The Candle*, our bimonthly *Amnesty E-News*, and *The Activist* (12-16 pages) for your response to priority cases by writing letters. Request our publication list of selected books and videos. Sign up for all Amnesty news releases (5-10 per week) or visit our website. Please select which services you wish to receive.

2002 WORLDWIDE CAMPAIGN AGAINST TORTURE—please request information.

TAKE HUMAN RIGHTS TO WORK—encourage your employer to make a gift to Amnesty or to set up a matching gift program—see our Workplace Giving Kit.

A GIFT FOR THE FUTURE—you can perpetuate your support by including a bequest to Amnesty in your will.

PLEASE SEND ME—information on the Youth & Student program and a VHS copy of Amnesty's TV program Cry for Justice.

BECOME A MONTHLY DONOR—through your bank account or credit card.

VISIT WWW.AMNESTY.CA

MEMBERSHIP OPTIONS

- Write letters;
- Join a group;
- Stay informed;
- Take action on-line;
- Tell a friend

The reader can see that Amnesty has covered the communication field, with volunteers in contact with one another, a national service office, and people needing help. They operate with minimum overhead and maximum exposure through all communication channels—including the best of all, word of mouth. A program such as this has something for everyone, with enough options to help people participate at any desired level of commitment. Like Amnesty, Peacemakers would never be at a loss to find projects to do. The Amnesty program gives a clear picture of the wide scope of issues and services that would be guides to helping Peacemakers groups get started, organize, commit to one or more of a wide variety of programs, follow through on specific action, and achieve concrete results. Peacemakers would get great personal and group satisfaction from action "with a human face" and activities that would enable Peacemakers to feel that they were making meaningful contributions to humanity.

It is hoped that Peacemakers would find that active participation in group activities would benefit both the givers and the receivers of peacemaking activities within one's country and overseas. Peacemaking is one of the main activities that relate to the "global village" and to citizens of all parts of the world. Peacemaking would expand one's horizons, create opportunities for personal contacts with NGO organizations and interesting travellers and experts in many fields, both domestic and overseas, and add to one's knowledge of the world and mankind. It would be an invaluable learning process in politics, motivation, and human relations, problem assessment, developing action programs, and improving organization efficiencies—in brief, helping one to become a more knowledgeable citizen, not only of your country but also of the world. One can travel and see the world, but participating actively in peacemaking projects would bring the world to you.

During the Second World War the civilians working on the home front of Great Britain were faced with new and difficult jobs, longer hours of work, sleep deprivation from bombing, and stringent food and petrol rationing. Even the elderly put in full days, working for organizations such as the Red Cross or home guard units. Due to food rationing calorie intake went down, but the government was amazed to find that for six long years people's health improved, there were fewer visits to the doctor, a sharp drop in pill usage, and many people felt better and happier to be working for a cause. Could this same moral and emotional outlook that enhances the lives of the volunteers who work for Amnesty International, inspire the lives of future Peacemakers?

Aid That Makes A Difference

One of the many ways for small groups to organize projects to provide help and make contacts with the most needy in every part of the less developed regions is to fund gifts organized by established aid and welfare groups. Examples from discussions with Canadian Food For the Hungry International show ways in which aid can go from donors to experienced foreign field representatives for direct distribution to aid recipients (prices in Canadian dollars).

- $10 provides a daily lunch for a hungry child for one month;
- $15 supplies enough seeds for a family to grow vegetables all year;
- $25* stocks medicines for a village pharmacy;
- $35* trains a health worker for isolated villagers;
- $50 teaches a person to read and write;
- $70 buys a weaving loom to help a mother learn a trade;
- $100* trains a Livestock Agent to keep village livestock healthy;
- $270* installs a clean water well, built for low cost local maintenance;
- $2,700 buys a motorcycle for a Village Health Worker to visit sick people in remote locations;
- $12,000 procures and ships a forty-foot container load of donated medicines or medical equipment (average value of $300,000) to a hospital with trained local medical staff.

* can qualify for a Canadian International Development Agency (CIDA) matching grant.

"Nuclear weapons pose an intolerable threat to all humanity and its habitat, yet tens of thousands of these weapons remain in arsenals built up at an extraordinary time of deep antagonism. That time has passed, yet assertions of the utility of nuclear weapons continue . . . . The proposition that nuclear weapons can be retained in perpetuity and never used—accidentally or by decision—defies credibility. *The only complete defence is the elimination of nuclear weapons and the assurance that they will never be produced again."*

The Canberra Commission on the Elimination
Of Nuclear Weapons, 1996

"The epidemic of world lawlessness is spreading. When an epidemic of physical disease starts to spread, the community approves and joins in a quarantine of the patients in order to protect the health of the community against the spread of the disease."

President F. D. Roosevelt
Speech—Chicago, 1937

Chapter 15

WHAT THE U.S. AND WORLD GOVERNMENTS CAN DO NOW.

The actions that the U.S., the leader of the free world, and other world governments can take to avoid war and build world peace are recommended in the book *Wilson's Ghost*, by Robert S. McNamara, former U.S. Defense Secretary, and Professor James G. Blight of Brown University. Their conclusions are paraphrased as follows:

- The traditional decisions and actions of world governments have resulted in the twentieth century being the most murderous century in history. The next century will be worse unless world governments develop a new agenda for world peacemaking;

- This requires new moral commitments to stop killing and to work on all matters in co-operation with other nations and the UN, called multilateralism;

- The new agenda of McNamara and Blight is based on their analysis of three major issues. First, the U.S. has failed to prevent Great Power conflict—to bring China and Russia in from the cold. Their message: *Empathy now!* Second, the U.S. has failed to reduce ethnic genocide (called "communal killing" in *Wilson's Ghost*). Their message: *Resolve conflict without violence now!* Third, the U.S. has failed to move decisively to reduce nuclear danger. Their message: *Radical reductions—and ultimate elimination—beginning now!*

McNamara and Blight stress that there are two imperatives that must be honored by governments if the world is to find the road to peace:

The Moral Imperative: An unprecedented moral commitment to stop killing, to stop armed conflict. Establish that a major goal of the U.S., and other governments, is to stop the carnage of war.

The moral imperative and the various alternatives that must be considered are debated at length in *Wilson's Ghost*, with arguments from many points of view. The Swiss theologian and philospher Hans Kung states that morality is based on an ethical principle that has guided humanity for thousands of years:

"This is a fundamental demand: every human being must be treated humanely . . . What you wish done to yourself, do unto others . . . This should be the irrevocable, unconditional norm for all areas of life, for families and communities, for races, nations, and religions."

Leading philosophers and ordinary citizens have many different views with respect to the moral precept *Thou shalt not kill.* A moral decision is faced with many moral complexities, such as—*love may require force to protect the innocent,* and *sometimes killing is justified in order to halt the killing.* This is expressed again as—*it may be necessary to commit an evil in order to save mankind from a greater evil.* If a despot is destroying his people, acting like the leader of a pack of mad dogs, there is a responsibility to destroy this evil. The moral imperative must be debated carefully before a decision is made to carry out an immoral act—*which is the lesser of two evils?* Society has decided that policemen may have to kill in the line of duty, to prevent a greater evil. By the same logic, there may be times when a state may have to kill to prevent a greater evil. This is not to say that Quakers and pacifists are wrong, as they have every right to be guided by their principles. When the state faces a moral dilemma, it obviously must ponder long and hard for a moral decision, *made only on a multilateral basis,* after consulting with the states affected by the issue and with the UN.

McNamara writes that during the Cuban crisis the question of the morality of a U.S. first strike against Cuba, with inevitable escalation to a nuclear war, was raised many times. President Kennedy and his advisers were challenged to define who they were as a people, and what were the moral limits of the actions that the U.S. should be prepared to take. "In the end, President Kennedy acted on the belief that 'victory' without the preservation of moral imperatives would be hollow."[1] McNamara concludes that the Cuban missile crisis was a good example of the art of preserving the national interest while also holding fast to the essence of one's moral convictions. Robert Kennedy posed the question in these terms: "What, if any, circumstance or justification gives this government or any government the moral right to bring . . . possibly all people under the shadow of nuclear devastation?"

The Multilateral Imperative: Collective Decision-making, Collective Security. One must recognize that while the U.S. must provide world leadership to achieve the objective of reducing the risk of conflict, it will not apply its power—economic, political, or military—other than in a multilateral context, subject to multilateral decision-making processes.

Preventing Great Power Conflict: Bringing Russia and China in from the Cold.

McNamara and Blight conclude as follows: "What is needed most in the West, especially in the U.S., is a conceptual shift from deterrence—or even 'competition'—to reassurance . . . . We emphatically warn those who may wish to approach the Russians and Chinese in the roles of obvious victors, complacent rationalists, or pugnacious realists that these views are counterproductive and uninformed about the true nature of the issues now dividing Russia and China from the West."[2]

Reducing Communal Killing: Intervention in "Dangerous, Troubled, Failed, Murderous States."

McNamara and Blight examined the question of U.S. intervention to stop communal killing within states. (This question is now before the UN—see Chapter 7 on *The Responsibility to Protect—Report of the International Commission on Intervention and State Sovereignty, December 2001.* This Commission was established in response to the urging of Kofi Annan.) The authors of *Wilson's Ghost* recommend a policy of "zero-tolerance multilateralism." "This means that in no case should the U.S. intervene on its own: via a unilateral decision, using U.S. motives alone, and on behalf of U.S. interests, without consultation with others who have similar values or interests, and some capacity to participate constructively in the decision of whether to intervene and in the intervention itself . . . . Even if the U.S. cannot convince others of the need to intervene, and thus is unable to demonstrate to others that the intervention will probably accomplish whatever its objective may be, it should not intervene unilaterally."[3] When the U.S. takes the lead to observe this policy as a member of the UN, other nations will find it necessary to follow.

Does any informed and thinking person anywhere doubt that today's "global village" is faced with monumental problems that cross all boundaries and affect all people? Many of today's most urgent and critical challenges to securing international peace, and economic and human rights for all people, are summarized as follows:

- Nuclear weapons, a continuing arms race, and weapons of mass destruction
- Population explosion
- International terrorism
- Environmental non-sustainability and global warming
- Over twenty-three million refugees, many of long-standing
- Increasing Muslim/West hostility
- Lack of funds to fight diseases and malnutrition
- The growing cancer of the drug trade, both in producing and consuming countries
- Widening gap between rich and poor both in and between nations. "The industrialized world has not yet made the commitment to share with others an appreciable part of our excessive wealth." (Jimmy Carter, Nobel lecture, December, 2002.)
- Growing barbarity of ethnic warfare, crimes against humanity, and genocide
- Lack of progress to eliminate human rights abuses
- Great advances in technology in many areas but with very few agreements for controls to benefit all society. A few examples are the continuing escalation of militarization of space,

experiments in animal and human cloning, and experiments with genetically modified organisms.

It is significant to note that most of the above challenges faced in 2003 were not significant in the year 1900. It confirms the analysis of many historians today who predict that the century ahead will be wholly different from today, just as the last century was wholly different from the nineteenth century.

Just as this host of challenges crosses all boundaries, the approach to solutions must cross all boundaries. *Great and small powers today have no alternative but to address all international problems multilaterally, in co-operation with other states. A unilateral, go-it-alone approach cannot be an option if a future of peace and world co-operation is to be realized.*

With respect to avoiding nuclear catastrophe, the message of McNamara and Blight is basic: "Say no to nuclear weapons, arms races, and nuclear danger." The authors quote from the *Report of the Canberra Commission on the Elimination of Nuclear Weapons (1996).*[4] Its essential elements are as follows:

- *The Commitment.* "The political will must be found to undertake a process of radical, rapid denuclearisation leading ultimately to the elimination of nuclear weapons. The U.S. must lead the way in this effort."[5]
- *The Immediate U.S.-Russian Program.* (a) Reduce the many thousands of U.S. and Russian nuclear arms to roughly the number held by China, France, and Britain—around 500 or so. (b) Other Nuclear Weapons States—after (a), begin multilateral talks to negotiate zero nuclear weapons on all sides. (c) Getting to Zero—Negotiate a fool-proof verification regime now. "We believe that problems along these lines can be solved if the nations really want to solve them."[6]

Will We Tend to the Details in Time?

The authors of *Wilson's Ghost* conclude as follows: "The actions recommended . . . can be accomplished if we set out to do so. But the first step is to stimulate public debate—of which there has been very little—on the problems and possible solutions."[7]

The Dilemma.

The above words, *if we set out to do so,* bring us back to the problem discussed throughout this book. These crucial actions recommended by McNamara and Blight *will not be taken until state governments develop the will to do so.* There is no evidence that democratic lawmakers are changing—they are generally most concerned in being re-elected, and often do not favor long-term public interests that conflict with their short-term prospects to get re-elected, or that are not the "partisan politics position" of one's party. There is evidence that the public often do not respect politicians, fail increasingly to vote, and are not interested in becoming more involved in civic, social, and political issues. There is also much evidence that our politicians generally reflect the same good and bad performances of citizenship as the public they represent—that we have the politicians we deserve, and that "they" are "us."

In matters of peace or war, a nation's responsibility to have good governance must start at the beginning, with civic-minded and well-informed individuals joining together in groups that grow, gain strong support of public opinion, and work as partners with government to build stronger and better foundations of peace. The time for public debate and action is now, and the only available reinforcements that can work for more effective peacemaking are the women and men who are the grass roots of our society.

Gunnar Berge, Chairman of the Norwegian Nobel Committee, made a statement at the Peace Prize award ceremony in 2001 that highlights the essence of the fundamental UN problem of preventing war and ensuring peace. "But it is not the veto [of the five permanent members of the Security Council] itself, of course, that explains the UN's inability to act, but rather the fact that the interests of the two super-powers diverged so radically throughout the many years of the cold war." There will always be international interests that diverge radically, and hostilities between the Great Powers. If they learn that goodwill, co-operation, and peace must grow before these hostilities are allowed to escalate into armed conflict, the world can gradually become more peaceful. Most leading "middle powers" have had to learn this. Finally, the nations of Europe have been forced by their tragic history to learn this. There will always be threats to peace until all nations learn this, and hopefully before more tragic lessons of history exact their toll from victors and vanquished. If the members of the Security Council and leading state governments can learn that armed hostilities are no longer an option, and the costs of war, armaments and the neglect of the poor can be replaced by investments in progressive living standards and human rights for all mankind, then progress will be made toward peace. To learn this the Security Council must be made more democratic, and must show enlightened leadership for peace, to ensure a peaceful future for all humanity.

"Hold on to dreams
For if dreams die,
Life is a broken winged bird
And cannot fly."

Langston Hughes

American poet

"Idealism is the highest form of realism."

John Polanyi

Nobel Prize in Chemistry, 1986

"We do not inherit the world from our parents, but rather we are lent it by our children."

Swahili saying

Chapter 16

"I WANT TO HELP, WHAT CAN I DO NOW?"

During the preparation of this book I have had many discussions on the problems of world peace with serious men and women, young and old. They are very concerned about the constant threat of wars, big and small, with barbaric carnage continuing to take its deadly toll. They are alarmed at the recurrent murders by terrorist groups, with no one safe any time, anywhere, and with no end in sight. Parents have a new fear after the terrorist killings and destruction of September 11, 2001, and feel helpless to do anything about it. Even where wars, killing, and destruction stop, the aftermath is often worse than conditions before the wars started. The legacy of war is still death and despair, broken homes, rampant crime and brutality, disease, starvation, and destruction of resources and the means to support a family. Many recent books and the electronic media have made people more knowledgeable about the desperate need of war-ravaged people for help to rebuild their lives. The individual has no power to bring wars to an end, but has the power to join with others to help the victims of wars, and to remove the causes of future wars, starting with saying—"I understand the threats to peace we are facing. I want to help."

There are thousands of different ways to help, depending on one's experience and capabilities. The start of individual peacemaking is to *know about the need*, and to *care enough to do something about it*. There are literally hundreds of sources of information about the need for more aid for the less developed world; the Internet, the library, magazines, media, local and visiting travellers and speakers, contacts with other peacemakers and peacemaking groups. There are many needs for aid to the poor in one's home country. However, as this book is about world peace, the attention herein is on the overall world situation. Today the greatest need is in the less developed world, for whom the only access to substantive and timely help is from the more developed world.

There are many kinds of foreign aid for the purpose of assisting countries to stabilize their society and raise their standard of living. One separate category is industrial development aid, which is an important adjunct of social, humanitarian, and economic aid. Industrial development aid is usually initiated by government or business. Most other kinds of aid are initiated and implemented by government or by volunteer groups of civil society. This latter category of aid is the objective of this proposal, involving small peacemaking groups of volunteers to add to the work for world peace. This is the area that addresses the question of a concerned citizen—"*I want to help, what can I do now?*"

There are many ways for an individual who is concerned about the increasing threats of war and the failure of governments to find the road to peace, to become an activist volunteer peacemaker in an NGO or peace society that is already established. The other option is to have new peacemakers get together with a group of a few friends who want to bring new reinforcements into the work for peace. Over the past 140 years there have been many such beginnings of individuals discussing the problem with friends, leading to regular meetings of a small organized group of peacemakers. The next step is to search for the ways to give help. There is access to information about all active NGO's and peacemaking societies available from governments, the UN, thousands of peacemaking organizations of civil society, and thousands of individuals experienced in a multitude of peacemaking projects. The main step is to contact the resources who are experienced in your field of interest, and start a dialogue that will help you decide on your specific program. Further contacts should be made with individuals and groups that have experience in your area of interest. In many cases new peacemakers make contact with the best available information at home, augmented by group members going out to a destitute country and making contact with the actual receivers of aid and the administrators of all the legalities and logistics involved. The start-up group could be open to the merit of an alliance with other groups which might be experienced in a common cause. There is an old saying in business—"You don't know until you go"—that cannot be stressed too much in any endeavour to work with individuals and the overall society of a foreign country. Travel in foreign countries is usually very popular and enjoyable in this age of "one world," and gives individuals the kind of background and experience that can not only be very rewarding personally, but also an essential part of one's education and extended family of friends.

The search for information could start with government sources. Canadian government resources are an example: Canadian International Development Agency (CIDA), which has a registry of large NGOs; Department of Foreign Affairs; Department of Finance; International Research Centre; Export Development Corporation—all have had many years of experience in providing foreign humanitarian and development aid to people in need of help. Miscellaneous agencies of the Canadian government, or supported by government, give foreign aid to over one hundred countries each year. The Canadian Council for International Co-operation is a coalition of over ninety large non-profit organizations.

There are over 80,000 registered charities, plus thousands of informal, non-profit organizations, in Canada—most of them giving foreign aid. Canada is only one of the many UN members funding international aid agencies and organizations. Over 185 NGOs, plus many non-governmental institutions, receive funding from CIDA and other government sources. All of these organizations have facilities to provide information to peacemaker groups.

The problem is not the lack of available information on the process and administration of providing and receiving foreign aid, but the amount of time and effort needed to search out the specific aid programs which have the greatest need of more support from grass roots volunteer groups. As most aid programs are always in great need, an alternative approach for new groups is to focus on existing active small group aid programs, and find examples of the most practical program for the particular interests of a new peacemakers group. One way to get started on this is to search out and talk to people in one's home city or province who have aid staff located in less developed regions and can advise on potential projects most suitable for peacemakers groups' areas of interest. Many local peacemakers will have had field experience in various foreign countries of interest. Person-to-person contact with experienced aid administrators of field staff is much better than a printed page or phone calls.

Assuming a potential peacemaker is talking to concerned friends, the next step is for the friends to meet and explore the idea of forming a Peacemakers group. This will be a very important first step, requiring a meeting at least once a month, probably in the evening. Most new groups of peacemakers are "single purpose" to start with. Some peacemakers will enjoy going to seminars, workshops, and public lectures. Experience shows that these should not replace the first group meetings, but could add to the knowledge that team members bring back to the group. It is important to follow up the meetings and start organizing in a very business-like way as a group—to have rotating chairmen, meeting agendas, brief minutes, a treasurer/accountant, and a secretary—all volunteers. A non-profit charitable organization could be registered to give income tax deductibility for financial donations, as appropriate. Without this all the "busy" people would not continue to be involved, for all the familiar reasons.

It is often asked, "Why are many people under, say, forty, not interested and activist peacemakers now?" One reason may be that they will not get involved until something new and different is tried and appeals to them. Most of them have not joined existing peace societies up to now, and probably would not do so in future until they realize that something different must be done to advance the cause of peace before it is too late. The challenge to repair the destruction of warfare and remove the causes must be faced now by today's generation, guided only by the degree to which they have learned the ways of peace in a peacemaking family, in a peaceful society.

Before September 11, 2001, most persons left it up to governments to handle the problems of peace and war. But that has now changed. The problems of war affect whole populations directly. Peacemaking has now become a matter of serious public concern. We face the probability that future internal wars and terrorism may carry on for generations. Parents today know that the many threats to peace on the horizon will affect future generations. To face in the future another *last chance* for peace, as in the Cuban nuclear crisis, would be intolerable. Peace-loving peoples must find ways to disarm the threat of another September 11 crisis, or of an attack with weapons of mass destruction by unknown enemies. Making today's peacemaking more effective would be a good first step. It is obvious that the more new peacemakers recruited at the grass roots, the greater the ability of the grass roots to meet their responsibility to be a new partner in peacemaking. The successful history of the new role of many peacemaking groups at the grass roots level confirms the importance of individuals forming activist groups rather than "going it alone." Personal financial donations are, of course, helpful, but these will not meet the mountain of needs for hands-on contacts and support of the less developed world.

All of the peacemaking groups described in Chapters 6 to 9 started as small groups. They have grown to large organizations and are continuing to do all that they can in their respective fields of interest. Peace is increasingly under attack today, and peacemaking needs major reinforcements now—new teams that can make a difference and add to the power of the grass roots. The only entity that can *add* to existing peacemaking is the *individual,* so here is where we must look for new reinforcements. Individuals can maximize their strength by working in small groups that stimulate ideas, energy, action, and enhanced results. Anyone will be welcome to join existing peace groups which are already in the field and fully engaged. However, the compelling requirement now is to meet the increasing need for peacemakers who will be a wholly new force of reinforcements—much like the initial fourteen young Greenpeace volunteers.

Many "young people" today—of whatever age—are attracted to activist peacemaking groups, such as Amnesty International, Doctors Without Borders, and Campaign to Ban Landmines, and they keep these associations for many years. A common experience is to make many friends both at home and abroad, and to develop a life-time interest in peacemaking. It is not a commitment to the fad of the year, but to a work that gives the great satisfaction of making a difference to the future of humanity.

Governments have come to realize that large financial grants for foreign aid between governments, and between governments and big business, have generally not worked satisfactorily. Young people can look forward to many active years of new and interesting work in a rapidly-expanding endeavor, quite different from the rigidity and red tape common to "big government" aid grants. A prime example is the career of Fridtjof Nansen of Norway, Peace Laureate of 1922, who was a "one man" initiator and leader in organizing large scale programs for the repatriation of prisoners of war after 1918, and the resettlement of refugees uprooted by wars, famine, and revolution. In 1922, he created the "Nansen Passport" which enabled many millions of refugees to be resettled legally, with documentation. He persuaded the League of Nations to support his work for refugees until his death in 1930. Today, the UN High Commissioner for Refugees carries on Nansen's work, and is responsible for about twenty-one million refugees. Nansen showed that one man could organize to do a tremendous job, leading the way ahead of governments. As foreign aid expands to a major degree, so will the role of the individual helper, entrepreneur, organizer, and manager.

While foreign aid now covers a very wide range of specific projects and programs, the increasing need of more aid to the less developed regions is so great that deciding which program should be first for a start-up group should not be difficult, as long as a specific focus is agreed. As one example, the need for better children's education in sub-Saharan Africa is one of the highest priorities to remove causes of future wars. Education is a vital need for all children—they will be the parents who train the children of tomorrow. There are many adults in Canada who have taught in African schools and could have an interest in supporting children's education programs.

There are many successful world aid programs that could be considered, depending on the background and interests of group members, the need of the receiving nation, and the kind of education aid requested. Some examples of specific programs are well within the capability of any new group of peacemakers to provide, such as the following:

- Kindergarten leaders and services;
- Teachers for one or two years;
- Used school books, computers, laboratory equipment, dictionaries;
- Essential schoolroom supplies;
- Used audio and video projectors, tapes, radios, and CD players;
- Equipment and supplies needed by staff;
- Maintenance of used school buildings, equipment, and facilities—new school buildings if needed, built at very low cost with local labor and materials;
- Used equipment for extra-curricular activities such as music, athletics, art, plays, handicrafts, photography, and copying machines for staff;
- Used equipment could be provided to assist post-school students needing help to start cottage industries;
- Provide special child development needs, such as used eye glasses, and aids for handicapped children;
- Used school library books and magazines such as National Geographic and Popular Mechanics;
- Support school lunch programs;
- Suitable teacher housing and facilities;
- Field trips or awards for outstanding students;
- Provide supplies needed to encourage "pen pals" and communication outreach.

Some advantages of a program to send aid to African children's education up to Grade 6 in the first instance, and up to Grade 12 when best to phase in, are:

- Aid would go directly from the donor group to the recipient school, giving efficient communication and administration, and getting the most value for the dollar;

- If the program succeeds, it could be expanded easily to other peacemakers groups and other schools;
- Success of the program is measurable;
- Good supply procedures could be arranged, procuring used equipment to the best advantage in many cities in the developed world;
- A good program for a "learn as you go" approach by the aid sender and receiver;
- Many opportunities to have donor groups relate on a one-to-one basis with African staff and students, expanding horizons for both;
- Explore the possibility of each primary school in a city or municipality "adopting" a school in a receiving nation;
- Excellent opportunity for children and adults in a donor country to become friends on an individual basis with children and teachers in the receiving country.

There is an endless number of projects for future Peacemakers groups. Examples are: special clubs for the blind; special clubs for physically handicapped children; and for those suffering from injuries due to landmines. These would be projects which physically handicapped children and adults of the more developed world could support. Young people with skills in engineering, transportation, sanitation and water supply, communications, lighting equipment, and farming could do "service corps" work in rural and urban locations.

The world of 2003 is facing a great chasm between the armed world of today and the disarmed world which we must have on some near tomorrow. Humanity must now take a journey that has never been taken before—we must find the road to world peace, no matter how long the journey and how heavy the load mankind must carry. We must advance along the road to peace, to emerge from the swamp of violence and despair into the sunshine of the broad uplands of peace and goodwill to all mankind. We can advance along that road only by the efforts of all men and women who will be dedicated peacemakers. We can all do our part, inspired by the words of the brave heroes on the doomed flight over Pennsylvania on September 11, 2001—"Let's Roll."

HOW TO ORDER AND FIND OUT MORE ABOUT THIS BOOK

This book was printed from a computer disk, using a new method of publishing called "print-on-demand"—the production of books for sale and delivery to anyone, anywhere, and shipment within two to three weeks.

You may order hardbacks or paperbacks directly from the publisher—Xlibris Corporation—an affiliate of Random House, the world's largest trade book publisher; from over 200 online retailers; or from traditional retail bookstores.

To order directly from Xlibris:

- Tel. 215-923-4686
- Fax 215-923-4685
- U.S. only, telephone toll free — 888-795-4274
- Mail — Xlibris Corp., 436 Walnut Street, 11th Floor, Philadelphia, P.A. 19106-3703, U.S.A.
- Web sites and Email:
    - to order by Email: orders@xlibris.com
    - for more information, Email: info@xlibris.com
    - Website: www.xlibris.com
    - www.chapters.ca (in Canada)

Books can also be ordered from online bookstores such as:

- www.amazon.com   www.bn.com
- www.borders.com   www.chapters.ca

You may order single or multiple copies for delivery to your home or to the addresses of family members or friends. There is a discount of 15 percent off retail price for orders placed directly with Xlibris, due to print-on-demand cost savings. Normal shipping costs are added, plus sales tax where applicable. Payment is in U.S. dollars by credit card or check.

To learn more about this book, go online to www.xlibris.com and click "Bookstore" to search for Grass Roots Peacemakers.

Appendix A

ALFRED NOBEL'S WILL—AN EXCERPT.

"The whole of my remaining realizable estate shall be dealt with in the following way: the capital, invested in safe securities by my executors, shall constitute a fund, the interest on which shall be annually distributed in the form of prizes to those who, during the preceding year, shall have conferred the greatest benefit on mankind. The said interest shall be divided into five equal parts, which shall be apportioned as follows: one part to the person who shall have made the most important discovery or invention within the field of physics; one part to the person who shall have made the most important chemical discovery or improvement; one part to the person who shall have made the most important discovery within the domain of physiology or medicine; one part to the person who shall have produced in the field of literature the most outstanding work of an idealistic tendency; and one part to the person who shall have done the most or the best work for fraternity between nations, for the abolition or reduction of standing armies and for the holding and promotion of peace congresses. The prizes for physics and chemistry shall be awarded by the Swedish Academy of Sciences; that for physiological or medical works by the Karolinska Institute in Stockholm; that for literature by the Academy in Stockholm; and that for champions of peace by a committee of five persons to be elected by the Norwegian Storting. It is my express wish that in awarding the prizes no consideration whatever shall be given to the nationality of the candidates, but that the most worthy shall receive the prize, whether he be a Scandinavian or not."

Paris, 27 November 1895.

Appendix B

NOBEL PEACE PRIZE WINNERS—from first Peace Prize awarded in 1901, to 2002.

Year	Laureate	Year	Laureate
1901	H. Dunant (Swi)	1921	K. H. Branting (Swe)
	F. Passy (F)		
1902	E. Ducommun (Swi)		C. L. Lange (N)
	A. Gobat (Swi)	1922	F. Nansen (N)
1903	W. R. Cremer (GB)		
		1923	None
1904	Institute for Int'l Law, Ghent	1924	None
1905	Bertha von Suttner (Au)	1925	C. G. Dawes (US)
1906	T. Roosevelt (US)		A. Chamberlain (GB)
1907	E. T. Moneta (I)	1926	A. Briand (F)
	L. Renault (F)		G. Stresemann (G)
1908	P. Arnoldson (Swe)	1927	F. Buisson (F)
	F. Bajer (D)		L. Quidde (G)
1909	A. M. F. Beernaert (B)	1928	None
		1929	F. B. Kellogg (US)
	P. H. d'Estournelles de Constant (F)	1930	N. Söderblom (Swe)
1910	Int'l Peace Bureau, Berne	1931	N. M. Butler (US)
			J. Addams (US)
1911	T. M. C. Asser (Nl)	1932	None
		1933	N. Angell (GB)
	A. H. Fried (Au)		
		1934	A. Henderson (GB)
1912	Elihu Root (US)	1935	C. von Ossietzky (G)
		1936	C. Saavedra Lamas (Ar)
1913	H. La Fontaine (B)	1937	E. A. R. G. Cecil (GB)
1914	None	1938	Nansen Int'l Office for Refugees, Geneva
		1939	None
1915	None	1940	None
		1941	None
1916	None	1942	None
		1943	None
1917	Int'l Red Cross, Geneva	1944	Int'l Committee of the Red Cross, Geneva
		1945	C. Hull (US)
1918	None	1946	E. G. Balch (US)
			J. R. Mott (US)
1919	T. W. Wilson (US)	1947	The Friends Service Council (GB)
			The American Friends Service Committee (US)
1920	L. Bourgeois (F)	1948	None

Year	Laureate	Year	Laureate
1949	J. Boyd Orr (GB)	1979	Mother Teresa (In)
1950	Ralph Bunche (US)	1980	A. Pérez Esquivel (Ar)
1951	L. Jouhaux (F)		
1952	A. Schweitzer (F)	1981	Office of the High Commissioner for Refugees, Geneva
1953	G. C. Marshall (US)		
1954	Office of the UN High Commissioner for Refugees, Geneva	1982	A. Myrdal (Swe)
			A. Garcia Robles (Mexico)
1955	None	1983	L.Walesa (Pol)
1956	None	1984	D. Tutu (SA)
1957	L. B. Pearson (Ca)	1985	Int'l Physicians for the Prevention of Nuclear War
1958	G. Pire (B)		
1959	P. J. Noel-Baker (GB)	1986	E. Wiesel (US)
1960	A. J. Lutuli (SA)		
1961	D. Hammarskjöld (Swe)	1987	O. Arias Sanchez (CR)
1962	L. C. Pauling (US)	1988	United Nations Peacekeeping Forces
1963	Int'l Committee of the Red Cross, Geneva	1989	The 14th Dalai Lama (T)
	League of Red Cross Societies, Geneva	1990	M. Gorbachev (USSR)
1964	M. L. King, Jr. (US)	1991	Aung San Suu Kyi (Bur)
1965	UN Children's Fund (UNICEF)+D14	1992	R. Menchú (Guat)
1966	None	1993	N. Mandela (SA)
1967	None		F. W. de Klerk (SA)
1968	R. Cassin (F)	1994	Y. Arafat (PNA)
1969	Int'l Labor Organization, Geneva		S. Peres (Is)
1970	N. E. Borlaug (US)		Y. Rabin (Is)
1971	W. Brandt (G)	1995	J. Rotblat (GB)
1972	None		Pugwash Conferences
1973	H. A. Kissinger (US)	1996	C. Belo (ET)
	[Le Duc Tho (N. Vietnam) (declined the prize)]		J. Ramos-Horta (ET)
		1997	J. Williams (US)
1974	S. MacBride (Ir)		International Campaign to Ban Landmines
	E. Sato (J)	1998	D. Trimble (GB)
1975	A. Sakharov (USSR)		J. Hume (GB)
1976	M. Corrigan (GB)	1999	Doctors Without Borders/Médicins Sans Frontières
	B. Williams (GB)	2000	Kim Dae-jung (RK)
		2001	Kofi Annan (Gh)
1977	Amnesty Int'l		United Nations
		2002	J. Carter (US)
1978	M. Begin (Is)		
	A. Sadat (Egypt)		

Country abbreviations: (Au)-Austria (Ar)-Argentina; (B)-Belgium; (Bur)-Burma (Myanmar); (Ca)-Canada; (CR)-Costa Rica; (D)-Denmark; (ET)-East Timor; (F)-France; (G)-Germany; (GB)-Great Britain; (Gh)-Ghana; (Guat)-Guatemala; (In)-India; (Ir)-Ireland; (Is)-Israel; (I)-Italy; (J)-Japan; (NL)-Netherlands; (N)-Norway; (PNA) Palestinian National Authority; (Pol)-Poland; (RK)-Republic of Korea; (Swe)-Sweden; (Swi)-Switzerland; (T)-Tibet; (SA)-Union of South Africa; (US)-United States; (USSR)-Soviet Union-now Russia.

Appendix C

TABLES

TABLE 1. Prize Winners by Category.

Category	I. 1901-18	II. 1919-39	III. 1940-59	IV. 1960-87	V. 1988-2002	Total: 1901-2002
The Organized Peace Movement	Passy Ducommun Gobat Cremer von Suttner Moneta Arnoldson Bajer D'Estournelles Int'l Peace Bur. Fried La Fontaine	Lange Quidde Buisson Addams Butler Angell Ossietzky Cecil	Balch Noel-Baker	Pauling Williams, B. Corrigan Myrdal IPPNW	Pugwash Rotblat ICBL Williams, J.	31
Humanitarian	Dunant Int'l Red Cross	Nansen Nansen Office For Refugees Söderblom	Int'l Red Cross Mott English Quakers Amer. Quakers Boyd Orr Jouhaux Schweitzer H. C. Refugees Pire	Int'l Red Cross League Red Cr. UNICEF ILO Borlaug M. Teresa H. C. Refugees UN Peacekeeping Forces	Doctors Without Borders	23
International Jurist	Inst. Int'l Law Renault Beernaert Asser	None	None	None	None	4
Statesman and Political Leaders	T. Roosevelt Root	Wilson Bourgeois Branting Chamberlain Dawes Briand Stresemann Kellogg Henderson C. S. Lamas	Hull Bunche Marshall Pearson	Hammarskjöld Brandt Sato Kissinger [Le Duc Tho*] Sadat Begin Robles Arias	Gorbachev Mandela de Klerk Arafat Peres Rabin Hume Trimble Kim Dae-jung Kofi Annan United Nations J. Carter	37
Human Rights	None	None	None	Lutuli King Cassin MacBride Sakharov Amnesty Int'l Pérez Esquivel Walesa Tutu Wiesel	Dalai Lama Aung San Suu Kyi Rigoberta Menchú Belo Ramos-Horta	15
Total	20	21	15	32	22	110

*   declined.

TABLE 2. Prize Winners by Country, Excluding Institutions and Associations

Nation	I. 1901-18	II. 1919-39	III. 1940-59	IV. 1960-87	V. 1988-2002	Total: 1901-2002
Switzerland	4***		1***	1***		6
France	3	2	2			7
Great Britain	1	4	3**	3****	3****	14
Austria	2					2
United States	2	5	7**	4	2	20
Italy	1					1
Denmark	1					1
Belgium	2		1			3
Netherlands	1					1
Sweden	1	2	1	1		5
Norway		2				2
Germany (and West Germany)		3		1		4
Argentina		1		1		2
Canada			1			1
South Africa				2	2	4
(North Vietnam)*				(1)*		(1)*
Ireland				1		1
Japan				1		1
USSR				1	1	2
Egypt				1		1
Israel				1	2	3
India				1		1
Mexico				1		1
Poland				1		1
Costa Rica					1	1
Tibet					1	1
Palestinian Authority					1	1
Burma (Myanmar)					1	1
Guatemala					1	1
East Timor					2	2
South Korea					1	1
Ghana					1	1
Total Countries (incl. North Vietnam): 32	10	7	7	16	13	

* Declined the prize

** Includes one institution, the Quakers

*** Includes one institution, the International Committee of the Red Cross

*** Includes Northern Ireland

TABLE 3. Awards to Institutions and Associations

I. 1901-18	II. 1919-39	III. 1940-59	IV. 1960-87	V. 1988-2002	Total: 1901-2002
Institute of Int'l Law (1904) Permanent Int'l Peace Bur. (1910) Int'l Committee of the Red Cross (1917)	Nansen Int'l Office for Refugees (1938)	Int'l Committee of the Red Cross (1944) English Quakers* American Quakers (1947)* UN High Comm. for Refugees (1954)	Int'l Committee of the Red Cross* League of Red Cross Soc.(1963)* UNICEF (1965) Int'l Labor Org. (1969) Amnesty Int'l (1977) UN High Comm. For Refugees (1981) Int'l Physicians For the Prevention Of Nuclear War (1985)	The United Nations Peacekeeping Forces (1988) Pugwash Conferences on Science and World Affairs (1995)* International Campaign to Ban Landmines (1997)* Doctors Without Borders (1999) United Nations (2001)*	
Total: 3	1	4	7	5	20

*Divided prize

TABLE 4. Women Peace Laureates

I. 1901-18	II. 1919-39	III. 1940-59	IV. 1960-87	V. 1988-2002	Total: 1901-2002
Suttner (1905)	Addams* (1931)	Balch* (1946)	B. Williams/ Corrigan* (1976) Mother Teresa (1979) Myrdal* (1982)	Aung San Suu Kyi (1991) Menchú (1992) J. Williams* (1997)	

*Divided prize

Appendix D-1

SPEECH BY GUNNAR BERGE, CHAIRMAN OF THE NORWEGIAN
NOBEL COMMITTEE; OSLO, NORWAY, DECEMBER 10, 2001.

Your Majesty, Your Royal Highnesses, Excellencies, Ladies and
Gentlemen, and, not least, this year's and past years' Peace Prize
Laureates

Let me begin by extending a warm welcome to this year's special
Peace Prize award ceremony.

The Nobel Peace Prize for 2001 is awarded to the United Nations
(the UN) and its Secretary-General Kofi Annan for their work for a
better organized and more peaceful world.

This year we are celebrating the centenary of the Nobel Prizes,
including the Peace Prize. That makes it natural to consider historical
continuities where both the better organized world and the Nobel
Peace Prize are concerned. The idea that mankind has common
interests, and that this should find expression in some form or other
of shared government or rules, can be traced back to the Roman
Empire. In the twentieth century, Woodrow Wilson was a vigorous
early spokesman for the belief that we people need each other. Such
a belief means that, whether as states or as individuals, we should
treat one another in ways that do not make us less able to live together.
Tolerance, justice and humanity are essential to the unity of mankind.

Alfred Nobel had no self-evident place in this tradition. At one
time, he believed that dynamite, his great invention, could do more
to prevent war than any peace movement. Nevertheless, the will he
made in 1895 was inspired by belief in the community of man. The
Peace Prize was to be awarded to the person who had done most for

"fraternity between nations, for the abolition or reduction of standing armies and for the holding and promotion of peace congresses."

Over the one hundred years that have passed since the first Peace Prize was awarded in 1901, the foremost sustained intention of the Norwegian Nobel Committee has been precisely that: of strengthening international co-operation between states. In the period before World War One, the majority of the Peace Prizes went to representatives of the organized peace movement, either at the parliamentary level through the Inter-Parliamentary Union, or at the more popular level through the International Peace Bureau. But the prizes do not seem to have helped much. The First World War broke out in 1914.

In the words of Woodrow Wilson, the First World War was to be "the war to end wars," and should "make the world safe for democracy." The new League of Nations was to be the body that resolved conflicts before they led to war. Once again, the Norwegian Nobel Committee sought to promote this greater commitment in international co-operation. In the years between the wars, at least eight Peace Prize Laureates had clear connections with the League of Nations, although the League as such never in fact received the prize.

Again the world, and not least Wilson himself, was to be disappointed. The 1919 Peace Prize Laureate was unable to persuade his own United States to join the League of Nations. For would not binding obligations to an international organization also limit American sovereignty?

Practically all of us wish to avoid the horrors of war. But we have different notions about how this can come about. All non-pacifists seek other things in addition to peace. There is not necessarily anything wrong with that. Nor can peace be absolute. That was why so many took up arms against Hitler Germany and the Emperor's Japan.

The horrors of World War II made the hopes people pinned on the new world organization, the United Nations, all the greater. The new organization was set even higher targets than the League of Nations. The preamble to the UN Charter thus speaks of "We the peoples of the United Nations determined to save succeeding generations from the scourge of war, which twice in our lifetime has brought untold sorrow to mankind . . . . ." There were many points of organizational similarity between the League of Nations and the UN. But the League of Nations had failed. The answer was to give the Security Council a much more prominent role than the corresponding council had had in the League of Nations. Universal membership would be combined with special rights exercised by the Great Powers. The Security Council could use military force to maintain peace. It was even to have standing armed forces at its disposal, to be established by member states in cooperation. We have not reached that goal even today, fifty-six years on.

The UN has achieved many successes, not least in the humanitarian and social fields, where its various special organizations have done such important work. In some respects, the UN achieved more than its founders believed possible. It found itself in the thick of the process of decolonization which in a few short decades swept away centuries-old colonial empires. The UN set important standards, which influenced developments for the majority of people all over the world. The Universal Declaration of Human Rights, adopted by the UN in 1948, became one of the major documents of our time. Article 1 gives clear expression to the hope for a better organized and more peaceful world; "All human beings are born free and equal in dignity and human rights. They are endowed with reason and conscience and should act towards one another in a spirit of brotherhood."

The Norwegian Nobel Committee has sought to give these successes the credit they deserve. Since 1945, at least 13 of the Peace Prizes have had links to the UN. Some have gone to UN organizations such as the High Commissioner for Refugees, winner of two awards, UNICEF, the ILO, or the UN's peacekeeping forces. Others have gone to individuals like Cordell Hull, reputed to have provided the inspiration underlying the UN, John Boyd Orr, the first head of the FAO, Ralph Bunche, first of many UN mediators in the Middle East and, in 1950, the first non-white Peace Prize Laureate, Dag Hammarskjöld, the UN's second Secretary-General, or René Cassin, main author of the Declaration of Human Rights.

In its most important area, however, preventing war and ensuring peace, the UN did not turn out to be all that its supporters had hoped for. In many serious conflicts, the organization remained on the sidelines or was used as a tool by one of the parties. The five Great Powers had all agreed that they had to have a veto. But it is not the veto itself, of course, that explains the UN's inability to act, but rather the fact that the interests of the two super-powers diverged so radically throughout the many years of cold war.

Seeing that the main theme in the history of the Peace Prize has been the wish for a better organized and more peaceful world, it is surprising that the UN as such has not been awarded the Peace Prize before. One reason may be disappointment that the UN did not quite live up to all the expectations of 1945. Another may be the many UN-related prizes, which made it less necessary to given the award to the organization itself. A good deal can be attributed to chance: the UN could have won the award so often that in the end it never did. Until a suitably important occasion arrived. In connection with this year's centenary, the Committee once again felt a need to emphasize the continuous theme of the history of the Peace Prize, the hope for a better—organized and more peaceful world. Nothing symbolizes that hope, or represents that reality, better than the United Nations.

The end of the cold war meant that the UN became able to play more of the role in security policy for which it was originally intended. The Great Powers still had diverging interests; so, too, of course, had the smaller states, but they had less impact on the international climate. Although the U.S.A. provides the clearest illustration, all countries are more or less selective in their attitudes to the UN. They favour an active UN when they need and see opportunities to obtain its support; but when the UN takes a different stance, they seek to limit its influence. Since the cold war, however, greater and smaller powers have to a significant extent been able to unite in meeting the most serious common challenges: to prevent wars and conflicts; to stimulate economic development, especially in poor countries; to strengthen fundamental human rights; to promote a better environment; to fight epidemics; and, in the most recent common endeavour, to prevent international terrorism.

No one has done more than Kofi Annan to revitalize the UN. After taking office as the UN's seventh Secretary-General in January, 1997, he managed in a very short time to give the UN an external prestige and an internal morale the likes of which the organization had hardly seen in its over fifty-year history, with the possible exception of its very first optimistic years. His position within the organization has no doubt benefited from his having devoted almost all his working life to the UN. Experience in a bureaucracy is not always the best springboard for action and fresh approaches to the outside world, but Annan has brought about both. The UN structure has been tightened up and made more efficient. The Secretary-General has figured prominently in the efforts to resolve a whole series of international disputes: the repercussions of the Gulf War, the wars in the former Yugoslavia and especially in Kosovo, the status of East Timor, the war in the Congo, and the implementation of the UN resolutions concerning the Middle East and "land for peace."

On the basis of renewed emphasis on the Declaration of Human Rights, Annan has given the Secretary-General a more active part to play as a protector of those rights. Time and again, he has maintained that sovereignty is not a shield behind which member countries can hide their violations. He has shown the same activist approach to the struggle against HIV/AIDS, a struggle which he has called his "personal priority." Since the terrorist attack on New York and Washington on the 11th of September, he has urged that the UN must be given a leading part to play in the fight against international terrorism. The Secretary-General's report on the role of the UN in the 21st Century formed the basis for the UN's Millennium Declaration. Here, too, the agenda is ambitious: to put an end to poverty, to provide better education for the world's billions of people, to reduce HIV/AIDS, to protect the environment, and to prevent war and armed conflict.

The only one of the UN's previous six Secretaries-General who can be compared to Annan in personal force and historical importance is Dag Hammarskjöld, the organization's second Secretary-General and the recipient of the Nobel Peace Prize in 1961. For Kofi Annan, Dag Hammarskjöld has been a model. In his Hammarskjöld Memorial Lecture in September this year, Annan said, "There can be no better rule of thumb for a Secretary-General, as he approaches each new challenge or crisis, than to ask himself, 'how would Hammarskjöld have handled this?" Annan is nevertheless more of a team player than Hammarskjöld was. In other respects, too, Annan goes further than Hammarskjöld could: "I suspect he would envy me the discretion I enjoy in deciding what to say, and what topics to comment on." This can occasionally be a bit much, however, even for Annan: "I find myself called on to make official statements on almost everything that happens in the world today, from royal marriages to the possibility of human cloning!"

Wars between states have grown quite rare in recent decades. This can be regarded as a victory for norms which the UN has stood for throughout its existence. But many wars are still fought in our time. The new development is that wars within states, civil wars, have become relatively more frequent. This is confronting the UN with major challenges. The UN has traditionally been a defender of the sovereignty of individual states. The principle of state sovereignty is laid down in the UN Charter, especially in Article 2.7. but even that Article contains a qualification: "this principle shall not prejudice the application of enforcement measures under Chapter VII" (the chapter on action to preserve peace.) Now that we are attaching ever-increasing importance to "human security" and not just to the security of states, it makes little difference whether a life is lost in an international or a civil war.

If the UN is to prevent civil war, the question soon arises of intervention from outside. Many see intervention as equivalent to invasion. Small states are naturally afraid that big states will use it as a pretext for interfering in their domestic affairs. The policies of colonial powers in Africa and Asia, the Soviet Union's entries into Eastern Europe, and the U.S.A.'s various interventions in the Western hemisphere all illustrate the need to protect the sovereignty of small states. On the other hand, the present situation, with civil wars in numerous countries, is a high price to pay for regarding state sovereignty as absolute. The massacres in Rwanda taught us all, and not least Annan, that the world does not necessarily get any better if one refrains from intervening. As Annan himself has said, we applaud the policeman who "intervenes" to stop a fight, or the teacher who tries to prevent bullying and fighting; and a doctor "intervenes" to save patients' lives. "A doctor who never intervenes has few admirers and probably even fewer patients." Where humanitarian concerns are uppermost, Doctors without Borders (MSF) in particular, the 1999 Laureate, has argued that the global community has "a duty to intervene," a principle which the UN General Assembly has accepted in several important resolutions.

The debate on "humanitarian intervention" raises difficult questions to which there are no pat answers, especially when the debate shifts from purely humanitarian to more political ground. Under Annan's leadership, the UN has shown itself willing to participate in this difficult discussion, with significant results in the last few years. Developments have taken a favourable turn in Kosovo, though there is still a long way to go. The UN played a leading part in the process which in a short space of time advanced East Timor from the status of a colony to, before long, that of an independent state. Maybe the 1996 Peace Prize awarded to Belo and Ramos-Horta also contributed. Today large and small states alike are almost competing in urging the UN to take the lead in developing Afghanistan away from a Taliban regime that has been a leading supporter of international terrorism, and towards a broadly-based government that can lead the country back into the international community.

So we have already moved well into the discussion of what steps to take to achieve a better organized and more peaceful world in the next hundred years. It has been repeated again and again that the UN can not become anything more than the world's ever so multifarious governments wish to make it. But in the light of the many common tasks that lie ahead, we must at least see to it that the very slowest movers among the nations are not allowed to set too much of the future pace. As globalization expands, the question will be asked even more loudly than at present of who is to manage this development and by what means. In the view of the Nobel Committee, that will be a task for the UN, if not in the form of a centralized world government then at least as the more efficient global instrument which the world so sorely needs.

For that to come about, it will help if nations as far as possible have a shared platform. Democracy is stronger today than at any time in history; over half of the world's population lives under democratic government. This marks a great victory for the principles in the Human Rights Declaration. One need go no further than back to the interwar years, when democracy was a threatened species of government, to realize how dramatic this progress has been. Democracies rarely if ever go to war with each other.

The strong position of democracy today gives grounds for optimism. But much remains to be done, not least in the economic field. We have made very few advances in solidarity between countries that are growing ever richer, and the many countries and individuals who either are not benefiting to the same extent from globalization or are even suffering from its economic and social consequences. The number of poor people in the world is ever-increasing.

There were many reverses in the twentieth century, for the world as a whole and for the idea of a better-organized and more peaceful world. Two world wars, and a cold war that lasted more than forty years and spread into every corner of the world, set a limit to how optimistic we can feel about the future. On the other hand, we have witnessed a remarkable development, from the scattered and rather private peace initiatives at the previous turn of the century to the ever stronger and more efficient United Nations we have today. The Norwegian Nobel Committee wishes both to honour the work that the UN and its Secretary-General Kofi Annan have already done, and to encourage them to go ahead along the road to a still more forceful and dynamic United Nations.

Appendix D-2

LECTURE BY KOFI ANNAN, SECRETARY-GENERAL OF THE
UNITED NATIONS AND 2001 NOBEL PEACE PRIZE LAUREATE;
OSLO, NORWAY, DECEMBER 10, 2001.

Your Majesties, Your Royal Highnesses, Excellencies, Members of
the Norwegian Nobel Committee, Ladies and Gentlemen,

Today, in Afghanistan, a girl will be born. Her mother will hold
her and feed her, comfort her and care for her—just as any mother
would anywhere in the world. In these most basic acts of human nature,
humanity knows no divisions. But to be born a girl in today's
Afghanistan is to begin life centuries away from the prosperity that
one small part of humanity has achieved. It is to live under conditions
that many of us in this hall would consider inhuman.

I speak of a girl in Afghanistan, but I might equally well have
mentioned a baby boy or girl in Sierra Leone. No one today is unaware
of this divide between the world's rich and poor. No one today can
claim ignorance of the cost that this divide imposes on the poor and
dispossessed who are no less deserving of human dignity,
fundamental freedoms, security, food and education than any of us.
The cost, however, is not borne by them alone. Ultimately, it is borne
by all of us—North and South, rich and poor, men and women of all
races and religions.

Today's real borders are not between nations, but between
powerful and powerless, free and fettered, privileged and humiliated.
Today, no walls can separate humanitarian or human rights crises in
one part of the world from national security crises in another.

Scientists tell us that the world of nature is so small and
interdependent that a butterfly flapping its wings in the Amazon
rainforest can generate a violent storm on the other side of the earth.
This principle is known as the "Butterfly Effect." Today, we realize,

perhaps more than ever, that the world of human activity also has its own "Butterfly Effect"—for better or for worse.

Ladies and Gentlemen,

We have entered the third millennium through a gate of fire. If today, after the horror of 11 September, we see better, and we see further—we will realize that humanity is indivisible. New threats make no distinction between races, nations or regions. A new insecurity has entered every mind, regardless of wealth or status. A deeper awareness of the bonds that bind us all—in pain as in prosperity—has gripped young and old.

In the early beginnings of the 21st century—a century already violently disabused of any hopes that progress towards global peace and prosperity is inevitable—this new reality can no longer be ignored. It must be confronted.

The 20th century was perhaps the deadliest in human history, devastated by innumerable conflicts, untold suffering, and unimaginable crimes. Time after time, a group or a nation inflicted extreme violence on another, often driven by irrational hatred and suspicion, or unbounded arrogance and thirst for power and resources. In response to these cataclysms, the leaders of the world came together at mid-century to unite the nations as never before.'

A forum was created—the United Nations—where all nations could join forces to affirm the dignity and worth of every person, and to secure peace and development for all peoples. Here States could unite to strengthen the rule of law, recognize and address the needs of the poor, restrain man's brutality and greed, conserve the resources and beauty of nature, sustain the equal rights of men and women, and provide for the safety of future generations.

We thus inherit from the 20th Century the political, as well as the scientific and technological power, which—if only we have the will to use them—give us the chance to vanquish poverty, ignorance and disease.

In the 21st Century I believe the mission of the United Nations will be defined by a new, more profound, awareness of the sanctity and dignity of every human life, regardless of race or religion. This will require us to look beyond the framework of States, and beneath the surface of nations or communities. We must focus, as never before, on improving the conditions of the individual men and women who give the state or nation its richness and character. We must begin with the young Afghan girl, recognizing that saving that one life is to save humanity itself.

Over the past five years, I have often recalled that the United Nations' Charter begins with the words: "We the peoples." What is not always recognized is that "we the peoples" are made up of individuals whose claims to the most fundamental rights have too often been sacrificed in the supposed interests of the state or the nation.

A genocide begins with the killing of one man— not for what he has done, but because of who he is. A campaign of 'ethnic cleansing' begins with one neighbour turning on another. Poverty begins when even one child is denied his or her fundamental right to education. What begins with the failure to uphold the dignity of one life, all too often ends with a calamity for entire nations.

In this new century, we must start from the understanding that peace belongs not only to states or peoples, but to each and every member of those communities. The sovereignty of States must no longer be used as a shield for gross violations of human rights. Peace must be made real and tangible in the daily existence of every individual in need. Peace must be sought, above all, because it is the condition for every member of the human family to live a life of dignity and security.

The rights of the individual are of no less importance to immigrants and minorities in Europe and the Americas than to women in Afghanistan or children in Africa. They are as fundamental to the poor as to the rich; they are as necessary to the security of the developed world as to that of the developing world.

From this vision of the role of the United nations in the next century flow three key priorities for the future: eradicating poverty, preventing conflict, and promoting democracy. Only in a world that is rid of poverty can all men and women make the most of their abilities. Only where individual rights are respected can differences be channelled politically and resolved peacefully. Only in a democratic environment, based on respect for diversity and dialogue, can individual self-expression and self-government be secured, and freedom of association be upheld.

Throughout my term as Secretary-General, I have sought to place human beings at the centre of everything we do, from conflict prevention to development, to human rights. Securing real and lasting improvement in the lives of individual men and women is the measure of all we do at the United Nations.

It is in this spirit that I humbly accept the Centennial Nobel Peace Prize. Forty years ago today, the Prize for 1961 was awarded for the first time to a Secretary-General of the United Nations— posthumously, because Dag Hammarskjöld had already given his life for peace in Central Africa. And on the same day, the Prize for 1960 was awarded for the first time to an African—Albert Lutuli, one of the earliest leaders of the struggle against apartheid in South Africa. For me, as a young African beginning his career in the United Nations a few months later, those two men set a standard that I have sought to follow throughout my working life.

This award belongs not just to me. I do not stand here alone. On behalf of all my colleagues in every part of the United Nations, in every corner of the globe, who have devoted their lives—and in many instances risked or given their lives in the cause of peace—I thank the Members of the Nobel Committee for this high honour. My own path to service at the United Nations was made possible by the sacrifice and commitment of my family and many friends from all continents—some of whom have passed away—who taught me and guided me. To them, I offer my most profound gratitude.

In a world filled with weapons of war and all too often words of war, the Nobel Committee has become a vital agent for peace. Sadly, a prize for peace is a rarity in this world. Most nations have monuments or memorials to war, bronze salutations to heroic battles, archways of triumph. But peace has no parade, no pantheon of victory.

What it does have is the Nobel Prize—a statement of hope and courage with unique resonance and authority. Only by understanding and addressing the needs of individuals for peace, for dignity, and for security can we at the United Nations hope to live up to the honour conferred today, and fulfil the vision of our founders. This is the broad mission of peace that United Nations staff members carry out every day in every part of the world.

A few of them, women and men, are with us in this hall today. Among them, for instance, are a Military

Observer from Senegal who is helping to provide basic security in the Democratic Republic of the Congo; a Civilian Police Adviser from the United States who is helping to improve the rule of law in Kosovo; a UNICEF Child Protection Officer from Ecuador who is helping to secure the rights of Colombia's most vulnerable citizens; and a World Food Programme Officer from China who is helping to feed the people of North Korea.

Distinguished guests,

The idea that there is one people in possession of the truth, one answer to the world's ills, or one solution to humanity's needs, has done untold harm throughout history—especially in the last century. Today, however, even amidst continuing ethnic conflict around the world, there is a growing understanding that human diversity is both the reality that makes dialogue necessary, and the very basis for that dialogue.

We understand, as never before, that each of us is fully worthy of the respect and dignity essential to our common humanity. We recognize that we are the products of many cultures, traditions and memories; that mutual respect allows us to study and learn from other cultures; and that we gain strength by combining the foreign with the familiar.

In every great faith and tradition one can find the values of tolerance and mutual understanding. The Qur'an, for example, tells us that "We created you from a single pair of male and female and made you into nations and tribes, that you may know each other." Confucius urged his followers: "when the good way prevails in the state, speak boldly and act boldly. When the state has lost the way, act boldly and speak softly." In the Jewish tradition, the injunction to "love thy neighbour as thyself," is considered to be the very essence of the Torah.

This thought is reflected in the Christian Gospel, which also teaches us to love our enemies and pray for those who wish to persecute us. Hindus are taught that "truth is one, the sages give it various names." And in the Buddhist tradition, individuals are urged to act with compassion in every facet of life.

Each of us has the right to take pride in our particular faith or heritage. But the notion that what is ours is necessarily in conflict with what is theirs is both false and dangerous. It has resulted in endless enmity and conflict, leading men to commit the greatest of crimes in the name of a higher power.

It need not be so. People of different religions and cultures live side by side in almost every part of the world, and most of us have overlapping identities which unite us with very different groups. We *can* love what we are, without hating what—and who—we are *not*. We can thrive in our own tradition, even as we learn from others, and come to respect their teachings.

This will not be possible, however, without freedom of religion, of expression, of assembly, and basic equality under the law. Indeed, the lesson of the past century has been that where the dignity of the individual has been trampled or threatened—where citizens have not enjoyed the basic right to choose their government, or the right to change it regularly—conflict has too often followed, with innocent civilians paying the price, in lives cut short and communities destroyed.

The obstacles to democracy have little to do with culture or religion, and much more to do with the desire of those in power to maintain their position at any cost. This is neither a new phenomenon nor one confined to any particular part of the world.

People of all cultures value their freedom of choice, and feel the need to have a say in decisions affecting their lives.

The United Nations, whose membership comprises almost all the States in the world, is founded on the principle of the equal worth of every human being. It is the nearest thing we have to a representative institution that can address the interests of all states, and all peoples. Through this universal, indispensable instrument of human progress, States can serve the interests of their citizens by recognizing common interests and pursuing them in unity. No doubt, that is why the Nobel Committee says that it "wishes, in its centenary year, to proclaim that the only negotiable route to global peace and cooperation goes by way of the United Nations."

I believe the Committee also recognized that this era of global challenges leaves no choice but cooperation at the global level. When States undermine the rule of law and violate the rights of their individual citizens, they become a menace not only to their own people, but also to their neighbours, and indeed the world. What we need today is better governance—legitimate, democratic governance that allows each individual to flourish, and each State to thrive.

Your Majesties, Excellencies, Ladies and Gentlemen,

You will recall that I began my address with a reference to the girl born in Afghanistan today. Even though her mother will do all in her power to protect and sustain her, there is a one-in-four risk that she will not live to see her fifth birthday. Whether she does is just one test of our common humanity—of our belief in our individual responsibility for our fellow men and women. But it is the only test that matters.

Remember this girl and then our larger aims—to fight poverty, prevent conflict, or cure disease—will not seem distant, or impossible. Indeed, those aims will seem very near, and very achievable—as they should. Because beneath the surface of states and nations, ideas and language, lies the fate of individual human beings in need. Answering their needs will be the mission of the United Nations in the century to come.

Thank you very much.

Appendix E

LECTURE BY ALBERT SCHWEITZER, NOBEL PEACE PRIZE
LAUREATE OF 1952, AT THE PRIZE AWARD CEREMONY IN OSLO,
NORWAY, NOVEMBER 4, 1954.

The Problem of Peace

For the subject of my lecture, a redoubtable honor imposed by the
award of the Nobel Peace Prize, I have chosen the problem of peace
as it is today. In so doing, I believe that I have acted in the spirit of the
founder of this prize who devoted himself to the study of the problem
as it existed in his own day and age, and who expected his Foundation
to encourage consideration of ways to serve the cause of peace.

I shall begin with an account of the situation at the end of the two
wars through which we have recently passed.

The statesmen who were responsible for shaping the world of
today through the negotiations which followed each of these two wars
found the cards stacked against them. Their aim was not so much to
create situations which might give rise to widespread and prosperous
development as it was to establish the results of victory on a permanent
basis. Even if their judgment had been unerring, they could not have
used it as a guide. They were obliged to regard themselves as the
executors of the will of the conquering peoples. They could not aspire
to establishing relations between peoples on a just and proper basis;
all their efforts were taken up by the necessity of preventing the most
unreasonable of the demands made by the victors from becoming
reality; they had, moreover, to convince the conquering nations to
compromise with each other whenever their respective views and
interests conflicted.

The true source of what is untenable in our present situation—

and the victors are beginning to suffer from it as well as the vanquished—lies in the fact that not enough thought was given to the realities of historical fact and, consequently, to what is just and beneficial.

The historical problem of Europe is conditioned by the fact that in past centuries, particularly in the so-called era of the great invasions, the peoples from the East penetrated farther and farther into the West and Southwest, taking possession of the land. So it came about that the later immigrants intermingled with the earlier already established immigrants.

A partial fusion of these peoples took place during this time, and new relatively homogeneous political societies were formed within the new frontiers. In western and central Europe, this evolution led to a situation which may be said to have crystallized and become definitive in its main features in the course of the nineteenth century.

In the East and Southeast, on the other hand, the evolution did not reach this stage; it stopped with the coexistence of nationalities which failed to merge. Each could lay some claim to rightful ownership of the land. One might claim territorial rights by virtue of longer possession or superiority of numbers, while another might point to its contribution in developing the land. The only practical solution would have been for the two groups to agree to live together in the same territory and in a single political society, in accordance with a compromise acceptable to both. It would have been necessary, however, for this state of affairs to have been reached before the second third of the nineteenth century. For, from then on, there was increasingly vigorous development of national consciousness which brought with it serious consequences. This development no longer allowed peoples to be guided by historical realities and by reason.

The First World War, then, had its origins in the conditions which prevailed in eastern and south eastern Europe. The new order created after both world wars bears in its turn the seeds of a future conflict.

Any new postwar structure is bound to contain the seeds of conflict unless it takes account of historical fact and is designed to provide a just and objective solution to problems in the light of that fact. Only such a solution can be really permanent.

Historical reality is trampled underfoot if, when two peoples have rival historical claims to the same country, the claims of only one are recognized. The titles which two nations hold to disputed parts of Europe never have more than a relative value since the peoples of both are, in effect, immigrants.

Similarly, we are guilty of contempt for history if, in establishing a new order, we fail to take economic realities into consideration when fixing frontiers. Such is the case if we draw a boundary so as to deprive a port of its natural hinterland or raise a barrier between a region rich in raw materials and another particularly suited to exploiting them. By such measures do we create states which cannot survive economically.

The most flagrant violation of historical rights, and indeed of human rights, consists in depriving certain peoples of their right to the land on which they live, thus forcing them to move to other territories. At the end of the Second World War, the victorious powers decided to impose this fate on hundreds of thousands of people, and under the most harsh conditions; from this we can judge how little aware they were of any mission to work toward a reorganization which would be reasonably equitable and which would guarantee a propitious future.

Our situation ever since the Second World War has been characterized essentially by the fact that no peace treaty has yet been signed. It was only through agreements of a truce-like nature that the war came to an end; and it is indeed because of our inability to effect a reorganization, however elemental, that we are obliged to be content with these truces which, dictated by the needs of the moment, can have no foreseeable future.

This then is the present situation. How do we perceive the problem of peace now?

In quite a new light—different to the same extent that modern war is different from war in the past. War now employs weapons of death and destruction incomparably more effective than those of the past and is consequently a worse evil than ever before. Heretofore war could be regarded as an evil to which men must resign themselves because it served progress and was even necessary to it. One could argue that thanks to war the peoples with the strongest virtues survived; thus determining the course of history.

It could be claimed, for example, that the victory of Cyrus over the Babylonians created an empire in the Near East with a civilization higher than that which it supplanted, and that Alexander the Great's victory in its turn opened the way, from the Nile to the Indus, for Greek civilization. The reverse, however, sometimes occurred when war led to the replacement of a superior civilization by an inferior one, as it did, for instance, in the seventh century and at the beginning of the eighth when the Arabs gained mastery over Persia, Asia Minor, Palestine, North Africa, and Spain, countries that had hitherto flourished under a Greco-Roman civilization.

It would seem then that, in the past, war could operate just as well in favor of progress as against it. It is with much less conviction that we can claim modern war to be an agent of progress. The evil that it embodies weighs more heavily on us than ever before.

It is pertinent to recall that the generation preceding 1914 approved the enormous stockpiling of armaments. The argument was that a military decision would be reached with rapidity and that very brief wars could be expected. This opinion was accepted without contradiction.

Because they anticipated the progressive humanization of the methods of war, people also believed that the evils resulting from future conflicts would be relatively slight. This supposition grew out of the obligations accepted by nations under the terms of the Geneva Convention of 1864, following the efforts of the Red Cross. Mutual guarantees were exchanged concerning care for the wounded, the humane treatment of prisoners of war, and the welfare of the civilian population. This convention did indeed achieve some significant results for which hundreds of thousands of combatants and civilians were to be thankful in the wars to come. But, compared to the miseries of war, which have grown beyond all proportion with the introduction of modern weapons of death and destruction, they are trivial indeed. Truly, it cannot be a question of humanizing war.

The concept of the brief war and that of the humanization of its methods, propounded as they were on the eve of war in 1914, led people to take the war less seriously than they should have. They regarded it as a storm which was to clear the political air and as an event which was to end the arms race that was ruining nations.

While some lightheartedly supported the war on account of the profits they expected to gain from it, others did so from a more noble motive: this war must be the war to end all wars. Many a brave man set out for battle in the belief that he was fighting for a day when war would no longer exist.

In this conflict, just as in that of 1939, these two concepts proved to be completely wrong. Slaughter and destruction continued year after year and were carried on in the most inhumane way. In contrast to the war of 1870, the duel was not between two isolated nations, but between two great groups of nations, so that a large share of mankind became embroiled, thus compounding the tragedy.

Since we now know what a terrible evil war is, we must spare no effort to prevent its recurrence. To this reason must also be added an ethical one: in the course of the last two wars, we have been guilty of acts of inhumanity which make one shudder, and in any future war we would certainly be guilty of even worse. This must not happen!

Let us dare to face the situation. Man has become superman. He is a superman because he not only has at his disposal innate physical forces, but also commands, thanks to scientific and technological advances, the latent forces of nature which he can now put to his own use. To kill at a distance, man used to rely solely on his own physical strength; he used it to bend the bow and to release the arrow. The superman has progressed to the stage where, thanks to a device designed for the purpose, he can use the energy released by the combustion of a given combination of chemical products. This enables him to employ a much more effective projectile and to propel it over far greater distances.

However, the superman suffers from a fatal flaw. He has failed to rise to the level of superhuman reason which should match that of his superhuman strength. He requires such reason to put this vast power to solely reasonable and useful ends and not to destructive and murderous ones. Because he lacks it, the conquests of science and technology become a mortal danger to him rather than a blessing.

In this context is it not significant that the first great scientific discovery, the harnessing of the force resulting from the combustion of gunpowder, was seen at first only as a means of killing at a distance?

The conquest of the air, thanks to the internal-combustion engine, marked a decisive advance for humanity. Yet men grasped at once the opportunity it offered to kill and destroy from the skies. This invention underlined a fact which had hitherto been steadfastly denied: the more the superman gains in strength, the poorer he becomes. To avoid exposing himself completely to the destruction unleashed from the skies, he is obliged to seek refuge underground like a hunted animal. At the same time he must resign himself to abetting the unprecedented destruction of cultural values.

A new stage was reached with the discovery and subsequent utilization of the vast forces liberated by the splitting of the atom. After a time, it was found that the destructive potential of a bomb armed with such was incalculable, and that even large-scale tests could unleash catastrophes threatening the very existence of the human race. Only now has the full horror of our position become obvious. No longer can we evade the question of the future of mankind.

But the essential fact which we should acknowledge in our conscience, and which we should have acknowledged a long time ago, is that we are becoming inhuman to the extent that we become supermen. We have learned to tolerate the facts of war: that men are killed en masse—some twenty million in the Second World War— that whole cities and their inhabitants are annihilated by the atomic bomb, that men are turned into living torches by incendiary bombs. We learn of these things from the radio or newspapers and we judge them according to whether they signify success for the group of peoples to which we belong, or for our enemies. When we do admit to ourselves that such acts are the results of inhuman conduct, our admission is accompanied by the thought that the very fact of war itself leaves us no option but to accept them. In resigning ourselves to our fate without a struggle, we are guilty of inhumanity.

What really matters is that we should all of us realize that we are guilty of inhumanity. The horror of this realization should shake us out of our lethargy so that we can direct our hopes and our intentions to the coming of an era in which war will have no place.

This hope and this will can have but one aim: to attain, through a change in spirit, that superior reason which will dissuade us from misusing the power at our disposal.

The first to have the courage to advance purely ethical arguments against war and to stress the necessity for reason governed by an ethical will was the great humanist Erasmus of Rotterdam in his *Querela pacis (The Complaint of Peace)* which appeared in 1517. In this book he depicts Peace on stage seeking an audience.

Erasmus found few adherents to his way of thinking. To expect the affirmation of an ethical necessity to point the way to peace was considered a utopian ideal. Kant share this opinion. In his essay on "Perpetual Peace", which appeared in 1795, and in other publications in which he touches upon the problem of peace, he states his belief that peace will come only with the increasing authority of an international code of law, in accordance with which an international court of arbitration would settle disputes between nations. This authority, he maintains, should be based entirely on the increasing respect which in time, and for purely practical motives, men will hold for the law as such. Kant is unremitting in his insistence that the idea of a league of nations cannot be hoped for as the outcome of ethical argument, but only as the result of the perfecting of law. He believes that this process of perfecting will come of itself. In his opinion "nature, that great artist" with lead men, very gradually, it is true, and over a very long period of time, through the march of history and the misery of wars, to agree on an international code of law which will guarantee perpetual peace.

A plan for a league of nations having powers of arbitration was first formulated with some precision by Sully, the friend and minister of Henry IV. It was given detailed treatment by the Abbé Castel de Saint-Pierre in three works, the most important of which bears the title *Projet de paix perpétuelle entre les souverains chrétiens* (Plan for Perpetual Peace between Christian Sovereigns). Kant was aware of the views it developed, probably from an extract which Rousseau published in 1761.

Today we can judge the efficacy of international institutions by the experience we have had with the League of Nations in Geneva and with the United Nations. Such institutions can render important services by offering to mediate conflicts at their very inception, by taking the initiative in setting up international projects, and by other actions of a similar nature, depending on the circumstances. One of the League of Nations' most important achievements was the creation in 1922 of an internationally valid passport for the benefit of those who became stateless as a consequence of war. What a position those people would have been in if this travel document had not been devised through Nansen's initiative! What would have been the fate of displaced persons after 1945 if the United Nations had not existed!

Nevertheless these two institutions have been unable to bring about peace. Their efforts were doomed to fail since they were obliged to undertake them in a world in which there was no prevailing spirit directed toward peace. And being only legal institutions, they were unable to create such a spirit. The ethical spirit alone has the power to generate it. Kant deceived himself in thinking that he could dispense with it in his search for peace. We must follow the road on which he turned his back.

What is more, we just cannot wait the extremely long time he deemed necessary for this movement toward peace to mature. War today means annihilation, a fact that Kant did not foresee. Decisive steps must be taken to ensure peace, and decisive results obtained without delay. Only through the spirit can all this be done.

Is the spirit capable of achieving what we in our distress must expect of it?

Let us not underestimate its power, the evidence of which can be seen throughout the history of mankind. The spirit created this humanitarianism which is the origin of all progress toward some form of higher existence. Inspired by humanitarianism we are true to ourselves and capable of creating. Inspired by a contrary spirit we are unfaithful to ourselves and fall prey to all manner of error.

The height to which the spirit can ascend was revealed in the seventeenth and eighteenth centuries. It led those peoples of Europe who possessed it out of the Middle Ages, putting an end to superstition, witch hunts, torture, and a multitude of other forms of cruelty or traditional folly. It replaced the old with the new in an evolutionary way that never ceases to astonish those who observe it. All that we have ever possessed of true civilization, and indeed all that we still possess, can be traced to a manifestation of this spirit.

Later, its power waned because the spirit failed to find support for its ethical character in a world preoccupied with scientific pursuits. It has been replaced by a spirit less sure of the course humanity should take and more content with lesser ideals. Today if we are to avoid our own downfall, we must commit ourselves to this spirit once again. It must bring forth a new miracle just as it did in the Middle Ages, an even greater miracle than the first.

The spirit is not dead; it lives in isolation. It has overcome the difficulty of having to exist in a world out of harmony with its ethical character. It has come to realize that it can find no home other than in the basic nature of man. The independence acquired through its acceptance of this realization is an additional asset.

It is convinced that compassion, in which ethics takes root, does not assume its true proportions until it embraces not only man but every living being. To the old ethics, which lacked this depth and force of conviction, has been added the ethics of reverence for life, and its validity is steadily gaining in recognition.

Once more we dare to appeal to the whole man, to his capacity to think and feel, exhorting him to know himself and to be true to himself. We reaffirm our trust in the profound qualities of his nature. And our living experiences are proving us right.

In 1950, there appeared a book entitled *Témoignages d'humanité (Documents of Humanity)*, published by some professors from the University of Göttingen who had been brought together by the frightful mass expulsion of the eastern Germans in 1945. The refugees tell in simple words of the help they received in their distress from men belonging to the enemy nations, men who might well have been moved to hate them. Rarely have I been so gripped by a book as I was by this one. It is a wonderful tonic for anyone who has lost faith in humanity.

Whether peace comes or not depends on the direction in which the mentality of individuals develops and then, in turn, on that of their nations. This truth holds more meaning for us today than it did for the past. Erasmus, Sully, the Abbé Castel de Saint-Pierre, and the others who in their time were engrossed in the problem of peace dealt with princes and not with peoples. Their efforts tended to be concentrated on the establishment of a supranational authority vested with the power of arbitrating any difficulties which might arise between princes. Kant, in his essay on "Perpetual Peace", was the first to foresee an age when peoples would govern themselves and when they, no less than the sovereigns, would be concerned with the problem of peace. He thought of this evolution as progress. In his opinion, peoples would be more inclined than princes to maintain peace because it is they who bear the miseries of war.

The time has come, certainly, when governments must look on themselves as the executors of the will of the people. But Kant's reliance on the people's innate love for peace has not been justified. Because the will of the people, being the will of the crowd, has not avoided the danger of instability and the risk of emotional distraction from the path of true reason, it has failed to demonstrate a vital sense of responsibility. Nationalism of the worst sort was displayed in the last two wars, and it may be regarded today as the greatest obstacle to mutual understanding between peoples.

Such nationalism can be repulsed only through the rebirth of a humanitarian ideal among men which will make their allegiance to their country a natural one inspired by genuine ideals.

Spurious nationalism is rampant in countries across the seas too, especially among those peoples who formerly lived under white domination and who have recently gained their independence. They are in danger of allowing nationalism to become their one and only ideal. Indeed, peace, which had prevailed until now in many areas, is today in jeopardy.

These peoples, too, can overcome their naïve nationalism only by adopting a humanitarian ideal. But how is such a change to be brought about? Only when the spirit becomes a living force within us and leads us to a civilization based on the humanitarian ideal, will it act, through us, upon these peoples. All men, even the semi-civilized and the primitive, are, as beings capable of compassion, able to develop a humanitarian spirit. It abides within them like tinder ready to be lit, waiting only for a spark.

The idea that the reign of peace must come one day has been given expression by a number of peoples who have attained a certain level of civilization. In Palestine it appeared for the first time in the words of the prophet Amos in the eighth century B.C., and it continues to live in the Jewish and Christian religions as the belief in the Kingdom of God. It figures in the doctrine taught by the great Chinese thinkers: Confucius and Lao-tse in the sixth century B.C., Mi-tse in the fifth, and Meng-tse in the fourth. It reappears in Tolstoy and in other contemporary European thinkers. People have labelled it a utopia. But the situation today is such that it must become reality in one way or another; otherwise mankind will perish.

I am well aware that what I have had to say on the problem of peace is not essentially new. It is my profound conviction that the solution lies in our rejecting war for an ethical reason; namely, that war makes us guilty of the crime of inhumanity. Erasmus of Rotterdam and several others after him have already proclaimed this as the truth around which we should rally.

The only originality I claim is that for me this truth goes hand in hand with the intellectual certainty that the human spirit is capable of creating in our time a new mentality, an ethical mentality. Inspired by this certainty, I too proclaim this truth in the hope that my testimony may help to prevent its rejection as an admirable sentiment but a practical impossibility. Many a truth has lain unnoticed for a long time, ignored simply because no one perceived its potential for becoming reality.

Only when an ideal of peace is born in the minds of the peoples will the institutions set up to maintain this peace effectively fulfill the function expected of them.

Even today, we live in an age characterized by the absence of peace;

even today, nations can feel themselves threatened by other nations; even today, we must concede to each nation the right to stand ready to defend itself with the terrible weapons now at its disposal.

Such is the predicament in which we seek the first sign of the spirit in which we must place our trust. This sign can be none other than an effort on the part of peoples to atone as far as possible for the wrongs they inflicted upon each other during the last war. Hundreds of thousands of prisoners and deportees are waiting to return to their homes; other, unjustly condemned by a foreign power, await their acquittal; innumerable other injustices still await reparation.

In the name of all who toil in the cause of peace, I beg the peoples to take the first step along this new highway. Not one of them will lose a fraction of the power necessary for their own defence.

If we take this step to liquidate the injustices of the war which we have just experienced, we will instill a little confidence in all people. For any enterprise, confidence is the capital without which no effective work can be carried on. It creates in every sphere of activity conditions favoring fruitful growth. In such an atmosphere of confidence thus created we can begin to seek an equitable settlement of the problems caused by the two wars.

I believe that I have expressed the thoughts and hopes of millions of men who, in our part of the world, live in fear of war to come. May my words convey their intended meaning if they penetrate to the other part of the world—the other side of the trench—to those who live there in the same fear.

May the men who hold the destiny of peoples in their hands, studiously avoid anything that might cause the present situation to deteriorate and become even more dangerous. May they take to heart the words of the Apostle Paul: "If it be possible, as much as lieth in you, live peaceably with all men". These words are valid not only for individuals, but for nations as well. May these nations, in their efforts to maintain peace, do their utmost to give the spirit time to grow and to act.

Appendix F

UN WORLD URBANIZATION PROSPECTS: THE 1999 REVISION.

The UN Population Division presented estimates and projections of world population size and growth, 2000 to 2030.

Table 1.

DISTRIBUTION OF THE WORLD POPULATION BY URBAN OR RURAL PLACE OF RESIDENCE, YEARS 2000 AND 2030

	Population (in billions) year 2000	Population (in billions) year 2030	The average annual growth rate per year (%) 2000-2030	Doubling time (years) 2000-2030
A—Total world population	6.06	8.11	.97	71
• more developed regions	1.19	1.21	.06	1,158
• less developed regions	4.87	6.9	1.16	60
B—Total urban population—world	2.85	4.89	1.80	38
• more developed regions	.90	1.01	.37	186
• less developed regions	1.94	3.88	2.31	30
C—Total rural population—world	3.21	3.22	.01	5,313
• more developed regions	.28	.20	-1.19	-
• less developed regions	2.93	3.02	.11	632

KEY FINDINGS:

1. World

    - the world had 6.1 billion people in 2000, and is expected to have 8.1 billion in 2030, an increase of 2 billion, or 33%
    - more developed regions had 1.2 billion in 2000, and are expected to have the same in 2030

- less developed regions had 4.9 billion in 2000 and 6.9 in 2030, an increase of 2 billion.

  All of this world population increase from 2000 to 2030 will occur in the less developed regions group urban population.

2. More Developed Regions Group—world

- urban population increased slightly from .9 billion to 1.0
- rural population decreased from .3 billion to .2

3. Less Developed Regions Group – world

- urban population increased by 2 billion, from 1.9 billion to 3.9 billion, a total increase of 2 billion
- rural population increased slightly from 2.9 billion to 3 billion. This raises the major problem of an increase of urban population in the less developed regions of 2 billion being fed by an almost static rural population. Either farm productivity will have to double, or more costly imports will be needed.

4. Virtually all the population growth expected during 2000-2030 will be concentrated in the urban areas of the world. During that period the urban population is expected to increase by 2 billion persons, the same number that will be added to the whole population of the world. In terms of population size, there are 2.9 billion inhabitants in urban areas today and 4.9 billion are expected in 2030.

5. Less developed regions are expected to have all of the world population increase from 2000 to 2030, an increase of 2 billion. All of this increase is expected to be in urban regions.

6. More developed regions are expected to have no increase in population.

7. Growth will be particularly rapid in the urban areas of less developed regions, from 1.9 billion to 3.9 billion, averaging 2.3

percent growth per year during 2000 to 2030, consistent with a doubling time of thirty years.

8. The rural population of the less developed regions is expected to grow very slowly, at just .11 percent per year.

9. Rural to urban migration and the transformation of rural settlements into cities are important determinants of the high population growth expected in urban areas of the less developed regions over the next thirty years.

10. As of 2030 the rural populations of less developed regions will begin to experience a steady decline to a growth rate of .11 percent per year, similar to that characterizing the rural population of more developed regions since 1950.

11. The rapid increase of the world's urban population coupled with the lack of growth of the rural population will lead to a major redistribution of the population. In 1950 thirty percent of the world's population lived in urban areas; this is expected to reach sixty percent by 2030.

12. By 2030, eighty-three percent of the inhabitants of more developed countries will be urban dwellers

Appendix G

THE RESPONSIBILITY TO PROTECT

Report of the International Commission on Intervention and State Sovereignty—December 2001[1]

(*ad verbatim* extracts from the Report).

FOREWARD

This report is about the so-called "right of humanitarian intervention": the question of when, if ever, it is appropriate for states to take coercive—and in particular military—action, against another state for the purpose of protecting people at risk in that other state. At least until the horrifying events of 11 September 2001 brought to center stage the international response to terrorism, the issue of intervention for human protection purposes has been seen as one of the most controversial and difficult of all international relations questions. With the end of the Cold War, it became a live issue as never before. Many calls for intervention have been made over the last decade—some of them answered and some of them ignored. But there continues to be disagreement as to whether, if there is a right of intervention, how and when it should be exercised, and under whose authority.

The Policy Challenge and the Commission's Report

External military intervention for human protection purposes has been controversial both when it has happened—as in Somalia, Bosnia and Kosovo—and when it has failed to happen, as in Rwanda. For some the new activism has been a long overdue internationalization of the human conscience; for others it has been an alarming breach of an international state order dependent on the sovereignty of states and the inviolability of their territory. For some, again, the only real issue is ensuring that coercive interventions are effective; for others, questions about legality, process and the possible misuse of precedent loom much larger.

NATO's intervention in Kosovo in 1999 brought the controversy to its most intense head. Security Council members were divided; the legal justification for military action without new Security Council authority was asserted but largely unargued; the moral or humanitarian justification for the action, which on the face of it was much stronger, was clouded by allegations that the intervention generated more carnage than it averted; and there were many criticisms of the way in which the NATO allies conducted the operation.

At the United Nations General Assembly in 1999, and again in 2000, Secretary-General Kofi Annan made compelling pleas to the international community to try to find, once and for all, a new consensus on how to approach these issues, to "forge unity" around the basic questions of principle and process involved. He posed the central question starkly and directly:

> . . . if humanitarian intervention is, indeed, an unacceptable assault on sovereignty, how should we respond to a Rwanda, to a Srebrenica—to gross and systematic violations of human rights that affect every precept of our common humanity?

It was in response to this challenge that the Government of Canada, together with a group of major foundations, announced at the General Assembly in September 2000 the establishment of the International Commission on Intervention and State Sovereignty (ICISS). Our Commission was asked to wrestle with the whole range of questions—legal, moral, operational and political—rolled up in this debate, to consult with the widest possible range of opinion around the world, and to bring back a report that would help the Secretary-General and everyone else find some new common ground.

The report which we now present has been unanimously agreed by the twelve Commissioners. Its central theme, reflected in the title, is "The Responsibility to Protect", the idea that sovereign states have a responsibility to protect their own citizens from avoidable catastrophe—from mass murder and rape, from starvation—but that when they are unwilling or unable to do so, that responsibility must be borne by the broader community of states. The nature and dimensions of that responsibility are argued out, as are all the questions that must be answered about who should exercise it, under whose authority, and when, where and how. We hope very much that the report will break new ground in a way that helps generate a new international consensus on these issues. It is desperately needed.

However, the text on which we have found consensus does reflect the shared views of all Commissioners as to what is politically achievable in the world as we know it today. We want no more Rwandas, and we believe that the adoption of the proposals in our report is the best way of ensuring that. We share a belief that it is critical to move the international consensus forward, and we know that we cannot begin to achieve that if we cannot find consensus among ourselves. We simply hope that what we have achieved can now be mirrored in the wider international community.

SYNOPSIS

The Responsibility to Protect: Core Principles

(1)   Basic Principles

    A.   State sovereignty implies responsibility, and the primary responsibility for the protection of its people lies with the state itself.

    B.   Where a population is suffering serious harm, as a result of internal war, insurgency, repression or state failure, and the state in question is unwilling or unable to halt or avert it, the principle of non-intervention yields to the international responsibility to protect.

(2)   Foundations

    A.   The foundations of the responsibility to protect, as a guiding principle for the international community of states, lie in: obligations inherent in the concept of sovereignty; the responsibility of the Security Council, under Article 24 of the UN Charter, for the maintenance of international peace and security; specific legal obligations under human rights and human protection declarations, covenants and treaties, international humanitarian law and national law; the developing practice of states, regional organizations and the Security Council itself.

(3) Elements

The responsibility to protect embraces three specific responsibilities:

A. The responsibility to prevent: to address both the root causes and direct causes of internal conflict and other man-made crises putting populations at risk.

B. The responsibility to react: to respond to situations of compelling human need with appropriate measures, which may include coercive measures like sanctions and international prosecution, and in extreme cases military intervention.

C. The responsibility to rebuild: to provide, particularly after a military intervention, full assistance with recovery, reconstruction and reconciliation, addressing the causes of the harm the intervention was designed to halt or avert.

(4) Priorities

A. Prevention is the single most important dimension of the responsibility to protect: prevention options should always be exhausted before intervention is contemplated, and more commitment and resources must be devoted to it.

B. The exercise of the responsibility to both prevent and react should always involve less intrusive and coercive measures being considered before more coercive and intrusive ones are applied.

The Responsibility to Protect: Principles for Military Intervention

(1)   The Just Cause Threshold

A. Military intervention for human protection purposes is an exceptional and extraordinary measure. To be warranted, there must be serious and irreparable harm occurring to human beings, or imminently likely to occur, of the following kind: large scale loss of life, actual or apprehended, with genocidal intent or not, which is the product either of deliberate state action, or state neglect or inability to act, or a failed state situation; or large scale 'ethnic cleansing', actual or apprehended, whether carried out by killing, forced expulsion, acts of terror or rape.

(2)   The Precautionary Principles

A. Right intention: The primary purpose of the intervention, whatever other motives intervening states may have, must be to halt or avert human suffering. Right intention is better assured with multilateral operations, clearly supported by regional opinion and the victims concerned.

B. Last resort: Military intervention can only be justified when every non-military option for the prevention or peaceful resolution of the crisis has been explored, with reasonable grounds for believing lesser measures would not have succeeded.

C. Proportional means: The scale, duration and intensity of the planned military intervention should be the minimum necessary to secure the defined human protection objective.

D. Reasonable prospects: There must be a reasonable chance of success in halting or averting the suffering which has justified the intervention, with the consequences of action not likely to be worse than the consequences of inaction.

(3) Right Authority

A. There is no better or more appropriate body than the United Nations Security Council to authorize military intervention for human protection purposes. The task is not to find alternatives to the Security Council as a source of authority, but to make the Security Council work better than it has.

B. Security Council authorization should in all cases be sought prior to any military intervention action being carried out. Those calling for an intervention should formally request such authorization, or have the Council raise the matter on its own initiative, or have the Secretary-General raise it under Article 99 of the UN Charter.

C. The Security Council should deal promptly with any request for authority to intervene where there are allegations of large scale loss of human life or ethnic cleansing. It should in this context seek adequate verification of facts or conditions on the ground that might support a military intervention.

D. The Permanent Five members of the Security Council should agree not to apply their veto power, in matters where their vital state interests are not involved, to obstruct the passage of resolutions authorizing military intervention for human protection purposes for which there is otherwise majority support.

I. If the Security Council rejects a proposal or fails to deal with it in a reasonable time, alternative options are: consideration of the matter by the General Assembly in Emergency Special Session under the "Uniting for Peace" procedure; and action within area of jurisdiction by regional or sub-regional organizations under Chapter VIII of the Charter, subject to their seeking subsequent authorization from the Security Council.

E. The Security Council should take into account in all its deliberations that, if it fails to discharge its responsibility to protect in conscience-shocking situations crying out for action, concerned states may not rule out other means to meet the gravity and urgency of that situation—and that the stature and credibility of the United Nations may suffer thereby.

(4)   Operational Principles

A. Clear objectives; clear and unambiguous mandate at all times; and resources to match.

B. Common military approach among involved partners; unity of command; clear and unequivocal communications and chain of command.

C. Acceptance of limitations, incrementalism and gradualism in the application of force, the objective being protection of a population, not defeat of a state.

D. Rules of engagement which fit the operational concept; are precise; reflect the principle of proportionality; and involve total adherence to international humanitarian law.

E. Acceptance that force protection cannot become the principal objective.

F. Maximum possible coordination with humanitarian organizations.

Appendix H

UN PEACEKEEPING MISSIONS—COMPLETED/OR STILL
ACTIVE

A. *Completed Missions*   *Period of Mission*

Africa

Angola I	1988-1991
Angola II	1991-1995
Angola III	1995-1997
Angola	1997-1999
Central Africa Republic	1998-2000
Chad/Libya	1994-1994
Congo	1960-1964
Liberia	1993-1997
Mozambique	1992-1994
Namibia	1989-1990
Rwanda	1993-1996
Rwanda/Uganda	1993-1994
Sierra Leone	1998-1999
Somalia I	1992-1993
Somalia II	1993-1995

Americas

Central America	1989-1992
Dominican Republic	1965-1966
El Salvador	1991-1995
Guatemala	1997-1997
Haiti	1993-1996
Haiti	1996-1997
Haiti	1997-1997
Haiti	1997-2000

Asia

Afghanistan/Pakistan	1988-1990
Cambodia	1991-1992
Cambodia	1992-1993
East Timor	1999-2002
India/Pakistan	1965-1966
Tajikistan	1994-2000
West New Guinea	1962-1963

Europe

Croatia	1995-1996
Croatia	1996-1998
Croatia	1998-1998
Former Yugoslavia	1992-1995
Former Yugoslav Republic of Macedonia	1995-1999

Middle East

Iran/Iraq	1988-1991
Lebanon	1958-1958
Middle East I	1956-1967
Middle East II	1973-1979
Yemen	1963-1964

B. *Still Active as of May, 2002*   *Date Commenced*

Africa

Democratic Republic of the Congo	1999—
Ethiopia and Eritrea	2000—
Sierra Leone	1999—
Western Sahara	1991—

Asia

East Timor	2002—
India—Pakistan	1949—

Europe

Bosnia and Herzegovina	1995—
Cyprus	1964—
Georgia	1993—
Kosovo	1999—
Croatia	1996—

Middle East

Golan Heights	1974—
Iraq/Kuwait	1991—
Lebanon	1978—
Middle East	1948—

Source—UN website—www.un.org

Appendix I

MAIN SUBJECTS OF UN ACTIVITY LISTED IN THE INDEX
OF THE BRITANNICA YEAR BOOK OF 2002

Afghanistan
Anthropology
China
Declaration of Commitment
Election (of Kofi Annan to a second term as Secretary-General of the
UN)
Eritrea
Ethiopia
Georgia
Iraq
Switzerland
U.S.
West Timor
World Conference Against Racism
Yugoslavia
UN Children's Fund
Food risks, genetic modification
UN Commission on Human Rights
UN Conference on Trade and Development (UNCTAD)
UN Conference on the Illicit Trade in Small Arms and Light Weapons
UN Educational, Scientific and Cultural Organization (UNESCO)
UN Environment Program
UN Framework Convention on Climate Change
UN General Assembly

Human Rights
- death penalty
- religion
- slavery

Human Rights Commission
Human Rights: The Status of Women
Human Rights Violation Investigation Commission
Human trafficking
Humanitarian Aid
- Afghanistan
- Burundi
- Liberia
- Sierra Leone
- South Korea

Appendix J

MAIN TREATIES ON NUCLEAR AND STRATEGIC BALLISTIC
MISSILES DISARMAMENT
(Based on Internet data as of the 2nd quarter of 2002.)

1967 Outer Space Treaty

Parties agree that their activities in space will be for the benefit of all humanity. The treaty includes the specification that parties shall not place in orbit around the earth any object carrying nuclear weapons or any other kind of weapons of mass destruction, install such weapons on celestial bodies, or station such weapons in outer space in any other manner.

Opened for Signature January 27, 1967. Entered into force, October 10, 1967.

1970 Nuclear Non-Proliferation Treaty (NPT)

This treaty is perhaps the most far-ranging disarmament agreement. Only five states were permitted to enter the treaty as nuclear-weapons states, and in signing the treaty they agreed to work to eliminate their nuclear arsenals. Nations who have not signed the treaty include: Israel, India, Pakistan, and North Korea. Under the treaty, each nuclear-weapon State Party to the Treaty undertakes not to transfer to any recipient whatsoever nuclear weapons or other nuclear explosive devices or control over such weapons or explosive devices directly, or indirectly; and not in any way to assist, encourage, or induce any non-nuclear-weapon State to manufacture or otherwise acquire nuclear weapons or other nuclear explosive devices, or control over such weapons or explosive devices. Each non-nuclear-weapon State party to the Treaty undertakes not to receive the transfer from any transferor whatsoever of nuclear weapons or other nuclear explosive devices or of control over such weapons or explosive devices directly, or indirectly; not to manufacture or otherwise acquire nuclear weapons or other nuclear explosive devices; and not to seek or receive any assistance in the manufacture of nuclear weapons or other nuclear explosive devices. Nuclear weapons states have agreed to negotiate a global ban on all nuclear weapons. The next conference to review progress will be in 2005.

Signed July, 1968. Entered into force March 5, 1970.

1972 Anti-Ballistic Missile Treaty (ABM Treaty)

The two parties agreed to deploy only one anti-ballistic missile system defending an individual region, either an ICBM site or the national capital. (The original treaty allowed both sites to be protected, but a 1976 amendment limited it to one site. The Soviet Union chose to protect Moscow. The United States protected a site in North Dakota for a short while, but the system was dismantled in 1976.) In this way, each remains vulnerable to the other's nuclear explosive devices, and arsenal. This tends to stabilize relations by avoiding the need for a further arms race involving defensive systems and countermeasures. The treaty is intended to ensure that deterrence, through mutually assured destruction, keeps the peace by rendering each party equally vulnerable.

Entered into force October 3, 1972

(Note—ballistic missile—powered and guided but falls by gravity.)

1972 Strategic Arms Limitation Talks (SALT I)

This pact between the United States and the Soviet Union included an interim agreement on offensive forces in an effort to find a point at which the two nations were evenly matched.

Entered into force in 1972 for a period of five years.

1979 SALT II

Like SALT I, SALT II placed further limits on the number of offensive missiles and also limited multiple warhead missile and delivery systems.

Signed in 1979. Although it was never ratified, it was adhered to by both nations throughout the 1980s.

1988 Intermediate-Range Nuclear Forces Treaty (INF Treaty)

The two parties agree to eliminate their intermediate and shorter-range missiles and not have such systems hereafter.

Signed at Washington December 8, 1987. Ratification advised by U.S. Senate May 27, 1988. Entered into force June 1, 1988.

1994 Strategic Arms Reduction Treaty (START I)

The two parties agree to reductions to equal aggregate levels in strategic offensive arms, carried out in three phases over seven years from the date the treaty enters into force. Central limits include: 1,600 strategic nuclear delivery vehicles; 6,000 accountable warheads; 4,900 ballistic missile warheads; 1,540 warheads on 154 heavy intercontinental ballistic missiles for the Soviet side. The Soviets also agreed in a side letter to eliminate 22 SS-18 launchers every year for seven years to achieve this level; 1,100 warheads on deployed mobile ICBMs; throw-weight ceiling of 3,600 metric tons.

Signed in Moscow on July 31, 1991. Entered into force 1994.

Not in force. START II

Like its predecessor, START II aims to further limit the number of deployed weapons to 3,000 to 3,500 deployed nuclear weapons each.

Signed January 3, 1993. Ratified by the United States in 1996. Ratified by Russia in March 2000, but with an amendment that must be approved by the United States before entry into force.

Not in force. Comprehensive Test Ban Treaty (CTBT)

The treaty bans all nuclear weapons tests.

Signed September 1996. Not yet in force; the treaty requires the ratification of the 44 nations that are members of the UN Conference on Disarmament. The U.S. Senate rejected ratification 51 to 48 in October 1999. (President George W. Bush said recently he will not ask the senate to reconsider its action.)

Other Relevant Treaties and Agreements:

1961 Antarctic Treaty

This treaty mandated that Antarctica be used for peaceful purposes only. It prohibited any nuclear explosions and the disposal of radioactive waste there. It is considered a model for nations working together to prevent conflict before it develops and it served as a precedent for later treaties excluding nuclear weapons from various zones.

Signed at Washington December 1, 1959.

1963 Hot-Line Agreement between the United States and the Soviet Union

For use in time of emergency, the government of the United States of America and the government of the Union of Soviet Socialist Republics established a direct communications link between the two governments. Although the idea and drafts of a possible hotline system had existed since 1954, the Cuban Missile Crisis of October 1962 provided a final, compelling impetus for the hot-line.

Signed at Geneva on June 20, 1963. Entered into force June 20, 1963.

1963 Treaty Banning Nuclear Weapon Tests in the Atmosphere, in Outer Space and Under Water (Partial Test Ban Treaty)

Each party agrees to prohibit, prevent, and not carry out any nuclear explosion at any place under its jurisdiction or control in the atmosphere, in outer space, under water, or in any other environment if such an explosion causes radioactive debris to be present outside the limits of the state which is conducting the test. The parties will also refrain from causing, encouraging, or in any way participating in such a test. Public interest in a test ban dated from a 1952 incident in which tests conducted by the United States accidentally contaminated a Japanese fishing vessel. A major sticking point, one that would resurface during debate on the Comprehensive Test Ban Treaty, was verification. A 1958 report of experts in Geneva on the ability of an international system to effectively detect a test in violation of the treaty succeeded in paving the way for the completion of the treaty. The treaty applies to peaceful explosions as well because of the difficulty in differentiating between a peaceful and a military test.

Opened for signature August 5, 1963. Entered into force October 10, 1963.

1968 Convention on Third Party Liability in the Field of Nuclear Energy

The operator of a nuclear installation shall be liable for damage to or loss of life of any person and damage to or loss of any property upon proof that such loss or damage was caused by a nuclear incident involving either nuclear fuel or radioactive products or waste in, or nuclear substances coming from, such an installation.

Adopted in Paris, July 7, 1960. Entered into force, April 1, 1968.

1968 Treaty for the Prohibition of Nuclear Weapons in Latin America (Treaty of Tlatelolco)

The parties promise to use exclusively for peaceful purposes the nuclear material and facilities which are under their jurisdiction. No testing, use, manufacture, production, acquisition, receipt, storage, installation, or deployment of nuclear weapons, and no encouraging of those actions. The area covered includes Mexico, the Caribbean, Central America, and South America.

Signed at Mexico City on February 14, 1967. Entered into force April 22, 1968.

1971 Agreement on Measures to Reduce the Risk of Outbreak of Nuclear War Between the United States and the Union of Soviet Socialist Republics

The agreement featured: a pledge by each party to take measures each considers necessary to maintain and improve its organizational and technical safeguards against accidental or unauthorized use of nuclear weapons; arrangements for immediate notification should a risk of nuclear war arise from such incidents, from detection of unidentified objects on early warning systems, or from any accidental, unauthorized, or other unexplained incident involving a possible detonation of a nuclear weapon; and advance notification of any planned missile launches beyond the territory of the launching party and in the direction of the other party.

Signed and entered into force, September 30, 1971.

1972 Treaty on the Prohibition of the Emplacement of Nuclear Weapons and Other Weapons of Mass Destruction on the Seabed and the Ocean Floor and in the Subsoil Thereof

This treaty follows in the tradition of the Antarctica and Outer Space treaties. Parties undertake not to place on the sea-bed, on the ocean floor or in the subsoil thereof, nuclear weapons or other weapons of mass destruction, or structures for launching, storing, testing or using such weapons.

Opened for signature February 11, 1971. Entered into force May 18, 1972.

1973 Agreement Between the United States of America and the Union of Soviet Socialist Republics on the Prevention of Nuclear War

The United States and the Soviet Union agreed that an objective of their policies is to remove the danger of nuclear war and of the use of nuclear weapons. They further agreed that they would act in such a manner as to prevent the development of situations capable of causing a dangerous exacerbation of their relations, as to avoid military confrontations, and as to exclude the outbreak of nuclear war between them and between either of the Parties and other countries.

Signed at Washington and entered into force June 22, 1973.

1975 Nuclear Suppliers Group

The NSG exists to ensure that nuclear exports are made under appropriate safeguards, physical protection, and nonproliferation conditions.

It first met in November 1975 and consists of 34 member states:

Argentina, Australia, Austria, Belgium, Bulgaria, Canada, Czech Republic, Denmark, Finland, France, Germany, Greece, Hungary, Ireland, Italy, Japan, Republic of Korea, Luxembourg, Netherlands, New Zealand, Norway, Poland, Portugal, Romania, Russian Federation, Slovak Republic, South Africa, Spain, Sweden, Switzerland, Ukraine, United Kingdom, United States.

1977 Convention on Civil Liability for Nuclear Damage

Established minimum standards to provide financial protection against damage resulting from peaceful uses of nuclear energy.

Adopted in Vienna, May 21, 1963. Entered into force, November 11, 1977.

1979 Conference on Disarmament

The Conference on Disarmament was formed in 1979 as the multilateral disarmament negotiating forum of the international community. Membership includes 61 members and 33 observers.

Members: Algeria, Argentina, Australia, Bangladesh, Belarus, Belgium, Brazil, Bulgaria, Cameroon, Canada, Chile, China, Colombia, Cuba, Democratic People's Republic of Korea, Egypt, Ethiopia, Finland, France, Germany, Hungary, India, Indonesia, Iran, Iraq, Israel, Italy, Japan, Kenya, Mexico, Mongolia, Morocco, Myanmar, Netherlands, New Zealand, Nigeria, Norway, Pakistan, Peru, Poland, Republic of Korea, Romania, Russian Federation, Senegal, Slovak Republic, South Africa, Spain, Sri Lanka, Sweden, Switzerland, Syria, Turkey, Ukraine, United Kingdom, United States, Venezuela, Viet Nam, Yugoslavia, Zimbabwe.

1986 South Pacific Nuclear-Free Zone Treaty (Treaty of Rarotonga)

The zone covers Australia, New Zealand, and the South Pacific. Production, acquisition, possession, testing, or control of any nuclear device is prohibited, as is the encouragement of the same. There can also be no fissile material or related equipment, or any radioactive dumping or storage. The United States opposes the zone on the grounds that it would impede the passage of nuclear powered and nuclear armed United States naval vessels and has signed but not ratified the protocols.

Signed August 6, 1985. Entered into force December 11, 1986.

1986 Convention on Early Notification of a Nuclear Accident

In the event of a nuclear accident, the party shall notify (directly or through the International Atomic Energy Agency) those states which are or may be physically affected. Both those states and the IAEA shall be informed about the nature of the accident, the time of its occurrence, and the exact location where appropriate.

Adopted on September 26, 1986 in Vienna. Entered into force October 27, 1986.

1987 Convention on the Physical Protection of Nuclear Material

Provides for the protection of nuclear material during international transport.

Signed at New York March 3, 1980. Ratification advised by U.S. Senate July 30, 1981. Ratified by U.S. President September 4, 1981. Entered into force February 8, 1987.

1987 Missile Technology Control Regime

The regime was established formally by the G-7 states on April 16, 1987. It controls the proliferation of nuclear-capable ballistic missiles (one capable of delivering at least 500 kg to a range of 300 km or more).

Members: Argentina, Australia, Austria, Belgium, Brazil, Canada, Denmark, Finland, France, Germany, Greece, Hungary, Iceland, Ireland, Italy, Japan, Luxembourg, the Netherlands, New Zealand, Norway, Portugal, Russian Federation, South Africa, Spain, Sweden, Switzerland, Turkey, the United Kingdom, and the United States. The following states have pledged to abide by MTCR guidelines: China, Israel, Romania, Slovakia, and Ukraine.

1987 Convention on Assistance in the Case of a Nuclear Accident or Radiological Emergency

The convention sets up a framework through which any state can request help of other states and of the International Atomic Energy Agency in case of a nuclear accident or radiological emergency, whether or not the state needing help is the cause of the accident or emergency.

Adopted in Vienna on September 26, 1986. Entered into force February 26, 1987.

1988 Agreement Between the United States and the Soviet Union on Notifications of Launches of Intercontinental Ballistic Missiles and Submarine-Launched Ballistic Missiles

The two parties agree to notify one another no less than twenty-four hours in advance of the planned date, launch area, and area of impact for any launch of a strategic ballistic missile.

Signed at Moscow and entered into force May 31, 1988.

1990 Treaty between the United States and the Soviet Union on the Limitation of Underground Nuclear Weapons Tests (Threshold Test Ban Treaty)

Signed July 3, 1974. The Treaty Between the United States and the Union of Soviet Socialist Republics on Underground Nuclear Explosions for Peaceful Purposes was signed May 28, 1976. The two parties undertook to prohibit, to prevent, and not to carry out any underground nuclear weapon test having a yield exceeding 150 kilotons at any place under its control, and to limit the number of its underground nuclear tests to a minimum while continuing negotiations with a view toward achieving a cessation of all underground nuclear weapon tests.

Entered into force December 11, 1990.

1995 No First Use Policy of the Declared Nuclear Weapons States (Negative Security Assurance)

France, the United States, Russia, and the United Kingdom affirm that they will not use nuclear weapons against a non-nuclear state unless that state invades or attacks them in conjunction with a nuclear state. China affirms that it will not be the first to use nuclear weapons under any circumstances.

Adopted April 5-6, 1995.

1995 Treaty on the South-East Asia Nuclear Weapon-Free Zone (Bangkok Treaty)

The treaty creates a nuclear weapon free zone covering the territories and continental shelves and exclusive economic zones of Brunei Darussalam, Cambodia, Indonesia, Laos, Malaysia, Myanmar, Philippines, Singapore, Thailand, and Vietnam. The treaty prohibits production, acquisition, possession, testing, transporting, stationing, or control of nuclear weapons and encouragement of those acts. In addition, there can be no fissile material or related equipment and no dumping or storage of radioactive material.

Signed in Bangkok on December 15, 1995, by all the above states.

1996 Convention on Nuclear Safety

The convention calls for the upgrading of national nuclear installations to ensure their continued safety.

Opened for signature September 20, 1994. Entered into force October 24, 1996.

1996 Cairo Declaration

The signatories to the African Nuclear-Weapon Free Zone Treaty make a general statement of opinion, including a call upon all states to adhere to the NPT and move toward a nuclear-free world.

Adopted April 11, 1996.

Joint Protocol Relating to the Application of the Vienna Convention and the Paris Convention— Not yet in Force.

The protocol links the Convention on Civil Liability for Nuclear Damage (1963; see above) and the Convention on Third Party Liability in the Field of Nuclear Energy (1960; see above) and eliminates possible conflicts arising from the simultaneous application of both conventions.

Adopted in Vienna, September 21, 1988.

African Nuclear-Weapon Free Zone (Pelindaba Treaty)—Not yet in Force.

The treaty creates a nuclear weapon free zone comprising the territory of Africa, including territorial seas, archipelagic waters and the airspace above them as well as the sea bed and soil beneath of the continent of Africa, the island states and all islands considered by the Organization of African Unity to be part of Africa. The treaty prohibits research, development, production, acquisition, assistance, control, or testing of nuclear devices and encouragement of those acts. It also mandates reversal of nuclear capabilities and adherence to IAEA physical protection procedures. The armed attack of nuclear installations is prohibited.

Signed April 11, 1996. Twenty-eight parties needed for entry into force.

(Source—Gobal Security Institute, www.gsinstitute.org).

Appendix K

UN HUMAN RIGHTS INSTRUMENTS (INCLUDING TREATIES AND OTHER DOCUMENTATION RELATED TO HUMAN RIGHTS).

(Note—The UN website for information on all Human Rights Instruments is www.un.org)

- International Bill of Human Rights.
- Universal Declaration of Human Rights.
- International Covenant on Economic, Social and Cultural Rights.
- International Covenant on Civil and Political Rights.
- Optional Protocol to the International Covenant on Civil and Political Rights.
- Second Optional Protocol to the International Covenant on Civil and Political Rights, aiming at the abolition of the death penalty.
- Declaration on the Right and Responsibility of Individuals, Groups and Organs of Society to Promote and Protect Universally Recognized Human Rights and Fundamental Freedoms.
- Proclamation of Teheran.
- Declaration on the Granting of Independence to Colonial Countries and Peoples.
- General Assembly resolution 1803 (XVII) of 14 December 1962, "Permanent sovereignty over natural resources".
- United Nations Declaration on the Elimination of All Forms of Racial Discrimination.
- International Convention on the Elimination of All Forms of Racial Discrimination.

- International Convention on the Suppression and Punishment of the Crime of Apartheid.
- International Convention against Apartheid in Sports.
- Discrimination (Employment and Occupation) Convention.
- Convention against Discrimination in Education.
- Protocol Instituting a Conciliation and Good Offices Commission to be responsible for seeking a settlement of any disputes which may arise between States Parties to the Convention against Discrimination in Education.
- Equal Remuneration Convention.
- Declaration on the Elimination of All Forms of Intolerance and of Discrimination based on Religion or Belief.
- Declaration on Fundamental Principles concerning the Contribution of the Mass Media to Strengthening Peace and International Understanding, to the Promotion of Human Rights and to Countering Racialism, Apartheid and Incitement to War.
- Declaration on Race and Racial Prejudice.
- Declaration on the Rights of Persons Belonging to National or Ethnic, Religious and Linguistic Minorities.
- Declaration on the Elimination of All Forms of Discrimination against Women.
- Convention on the Elimination of All Forms of Discrimination against Women.
- Declaration on the Elimination of Violence against Women.
- Convention on the Political Rights of Women.
- Declaration on the Protection of Women and Children in Emergency and Armed Conflict.
- Optional Protocol to the Convention on the Elimination of Discrimination against Women.
- Declaration on the Rights of the Child.
- Convention on the Rights of the Child.
- Optional protocol to the Convention on the Rights of the Child on the involvement of children in armed conflict.
- Optional protocol to the Convention on the Rights of the Child on the sale of children, child prostitution and child pornography.

- Declaration on Social and Legal Principles relating to the Protection and Welfare of Children, with Special Reference to Foster Placement and Adoption Nationally and Internationally.
- Slavery Convention.
- Protocol amending the Slavery Convention.
- Supplementary Convention on the Abolition of Slavery, the Slave Trade, and Institutions and Practices Similar to Slavery.
- Forced Labor Convention.
- Abolition of Forced Labor Convention.
- Convention for the Suppression of the Traffic in Persons and of the Exploitation of the Prostitution of Others.
- Standard Minimum Rules for the Treatment of Prisoners.
- Basic Principles for the Treatment of Prisoners.
- Body of Principles for the Protection of All Persons under Any Form of Detention or Imprisonment.
- United Nations Rules for the Protection of Juveniles Deprived of their Liberty.
- Declaration on the Protection of All Persons from Being Subjected to Torture and Other Cruel, Inhuman or Degrading Treatment or Punishment.
- Convention against Torture and Other Cruel, Inhuman or Degrading Treatment or Punishment.
- Principles on the Effective Investigation and Documentation of Torture and Other Cruel, Inhuman or Degrading Treatment or Punishment.
- Principles of Medical Ethics relevant to the Role of Health Personnel, particularly Physicians, in the Protection of Prisoners and Detainees against Torture and Other Cruel, Inhuman or Degrading Treatment or Punishment.
- Safeguards guaranteeing protection of the rights of those facing the death penalty.
- Code of Conduct for Law Enforcement Officials.
- Basic Principles on the Use of Force and Firearms by Law Enforcement Officials.
- Basic Principles on the Role of Lawyers.
- Guidelines on the Role of Prosecutors.

- United Nations Standard Minimum Rules for Non-custodial Measures (The Tokyo Rules).
- United Nations Guidelines for the Prevention of Juvenile Delinquency (The Riyadh Guidelines).
- United Nations Standard Minimum Rules for the Administration of Juvenile Justice ("The Beijing Rules").
- Declaration of Basic Principles of Justice for Victims of Crime and Abuse of Power.
- Basic Principles on the Independence of the Judiciary.
- Model Treaty on the Transfer of Proceedings in Criminal Matters.
- Model Treaty on the Transfer of Supervision of Offenders Conditionally Sentenced or Conditionally Released.
- Declaration on the Protection of All Persons from Enforced Disappearances.
- Principles on the Effective Prevention and Investigation of Extra-legal, Arbitrary and Summary Executions.
- Convention on the International Right of Correction.
- Freedom of Association and Protection of the Right to Organize Convention.
- Right to Organize and Collective Bargaining Convention.
- Workers' Representatives Convention.
- Labour Relations (Public Service) Convention.
- Employment Policy Convention.
- Convention (No. 154) concerning the Promotion of Collective Bargaining.
- Convention (No. 168) concerning Employment Promotion and Protection against Unemployment.
- Convention (No. 169) concerning Indigenous and Tribal Peoples in Independent Countries.
- Convention on Consent to Marriage, Minimum Age for Marriage and Registration of Marriages.
- Recommendation on Consent to Marriage, Minimum Age for Marriage and Registration of Marriages.
- Declaration on the Promotion among Youth of the Ideals of Peace, Mutual Respect and Understanding between Peoples.

- Declaration on Social Progress and Development.
- Declaration on the Rights of Mentally Retarded Persons.
- Principles for the protection of persons with mental illness and the improvement of mental health care.
- Universal Declaration on the Eradication of Hunger and Malnutrition.
- Declaration on the Use of Scientific and Technological Progress in the Interests of Peace and for the Benefit of Mankind.
- Guidelines for the Regulation of Computerized Personal Data Files.
- Declaration on the Rights of Disabled Persons.
- Declaration on the Right of Peoples to Peace.
- Declaration on the Right to Development.
- International Convention on the Protection of the Rights of All Migrant Workers and Members of Their Families.
- Universal Declaration on the Human Genome and Human Rights (UNESCO).
- Declaration of the Principles of International Cultural Co-operation.
- Recommendation concerning Education for International Understanding, Co-operation and Peace and Education relating to Human Rights and Fundamental Freedoms.
- Convention on the Nationality of Married Women.
- Convention on the Reduction of Statelessness.
- Convention relating to the Status of Stateless Persons.
- Convention relating to the Status of Refugees.
- Protocol relating to the Status of Refugees.
- Statute of the Office of the United Nations High Commissioner for Refugees.
- Declaration on Territorial Asylum.
- Declaration on the Human Rights of Individuals Who are not Nationals of the Country in which They Live.
- Convention on the Prevention and Punishment of the Crime of Genocide.
- Convention on the Non-Applicability of Statutory Limitations to War Crimes and Crimes against Humanity.

- Principles of international co-operation in the detection, arrest, extradition and punishment of persons guilty of war crimes and crimes against humanity.
- Geneva Convention for the Amelioration of the Condition of the Wounded and Sick in Armed Forces in the Field.
- Geneva Convention for the Amelioration of the Condition of Wounded, Sick and Shipwrecked Members of Armed Forces at Sea.
- Geneva Convention relative to the Treatment of Prisoners of War.
- Geneva Convention relative to the Protection of Civilian Persons in Time of War.
- Protocol Additional to the Geneva Conventions of 12 August 1949, and relating to the Protection of Victims of International Armed Conflicts (Protocol 1).
- Protocol Additional to the Geneva Conventions of 12 August 1949, and relating to the Protection of Victims of Non-International Armed Conflicts (Protocol II).

Appendix L

STATEMENT BY 100 NOBEL LAUREATES ON THE 100ᵀᴴ ANNIVERSARY OF THE NOBEL PRIZE, WARNING THAT THE WORLD'S SECURITY HANGS ON ENVIRONMENTAL AND SOCIAL REFORM.

The most profound danger to world peace in the coming years will stem not from the irrational acts of states or individuals but from the legitimate demands of the world's dispossessed. Of these poor and disenfranchised, the majority live a marginal existence in equatorial climates. Global warming, not of their making but originating with the wealthy few, will affect their fragile ecologies most. Their situation will be desperate and manifestly unjust.

> *It cannot be expected, therefore, that in all cases they will be content to await the beneficence of the rich. If then we permit the devastating power of modern weaponry to spread through this combustible human landscape, we invite a conflagration that can engulf both rich and poor. The only hope for the future lies in co-operative international action, legitimized by democracy.*

It is time to turn our backs on the unilateral search for security, in which we seek to shelter behind walls. Instead, we must persist in the quest for united action to counter both global warming and a weaponized world.

These twin goals will constitute vital components of stability as we move toward the wider degree of social justice that alone gives hope of peace.

Some of the needed legal instruments are already at hand, such as the Anti-Ballistic Missile Treaty, the Convention on Climate Change, the Strategic Arms Reduction Treaties and the Comprehensive Test

Ban Treaty. As concerned citizens, we urge all governments to commit to these goals that constitute steps on the way to replacement of war by law.

To survive in the world we have transformed, we must learn to think in a new way. As never before, the future of each depends on the good of all.

(Source—*Globe and Mail,* Toronto, Canada, December 7, 2001.)

Appendix M

STATEMENT BY JOHN POLANYI, CANADIAN UNIVERSITY
PROFESSOR, NOBEL LAUREATE, CHEMISTRY, 1986.

"STUPIDITY IS THE ENEMY; IDEALISM IS OUR ONLY HOPE"

Canadian laureate John Polanyi tells why he and his colleagues have issued their challenge. (See Appendix L.)

Nobel Prize winners are presumed to be intelligent. But why pay attention to the views of the 100 who have supported the statement above, issued to coincide with the 100th anniversary of the Nobel Prize? Because one's perception of truth comes not from intelligence but from a sense of values. Scholarship embodies values: This was evident to Alfred Nobel, the Swedish tycoon and explosives manufacturer. In his will, he stipulated that his prizes recognize *idealisk riktning*—idealistic tendencies.

And what led to the Nobel Prize winners' statement? Not a sense of oracular wisdom but of obligation. Individuals who had shared the experience of discovery would likely be able to agree on a great deal more. Alfred Nobel was right; science engenders "idealistic tendencies".

Why? Because the pursuit of discovery is shot through with idealism. Discovery originates in the unsupported belief that the book of creation is open to being read. So deep is this idealism that many are willing to devote the best years of their lives to the quest for discovery, though the odds against success are huge.

Idealism must also triumph over the painful fact that the first to read nature's story may well be someone other than oneself. But the truth must be acknowledged whatever the hands that uncover it. Christian truth cannot be elevated over Muslim truth. Nor can accepted truth, backed by the massed armies of orthodoxy, be protected against the claims of upstart facts. One can trace the sense of "Nobel-esse oblige" to these idealistic origins.

What, then, do these 100 voices say? The opening sentence is bold enough to claim that the dominant forces shaping history are rational. This was contentious when written in early July, and appeared still more so following Sept. 11. The ferocity of that attack led Americans to believe that the attackers were insane. But it came to be recognized that the sustained terrorism has its causes and purposes.

The question is important, because what lies (to a large extent) within the realm of reason can (to a large extent) be countered by policies grounded in reason.

Of course, the statement is as much about threats from states as from non-state groups, and about threats of mass destruction as about conventional threats. The dominant setting for conflict in each case, it claims, is a world in which the rich and the poor live in full sight of one another.

If, in addition, the poor are voiceless, they may well be induced to speak through violence. Particularly so if their predicament is aggravated by the environmental carelessness of the rich.

It is peculiar folly, under these circumstances, for the rich to seek greater riches by selling weapons to the poor. Even without this, the prosperous grow ever more vulnerable. Advanced societies are complex and fragile. They operate efficiently by being open, not guarded. Like any complex mechanism, they are, therefore, vulnerable to the wrecker's ball.

To avoid a tragic outcome, the statement says, we shall be forced to do what we should have done previously. That is to recognize abroad what we have long recognized domestically: the right of all to food, shelter, education and freedom of expression. This is a revolution in thinking that is already under way. What is lacking, in this country as elsewhere, is a sense of urgency.

A Chinese leader, asked whether the French Revolution was a success, reportedly replied that it was too soon to tell. But it's not too early to identify its origins: the wilful blindness of the French ruling class of the 18th century. Possessed of wealth and power, they offered only promises to the poor.

Unless we recognize that the future of each depends on the good of all, the coming years will bring escalating conflict. One need not be a rocket scientist to see that.

But the recognition that science has thrived on change could persuade us to behave more like rocket scientists. We might even come to realize that idealism is the highest form of realism.

Nobel laureate John Polanyi, a University of Toronto chemistry professor, was involved in framing the Nobel statement.

(Source—*Globe and Mail,* Toronto, Canada, December 7, 2001.)

Notes

Chapter 1: Humanity At The Crossroads

[1.] Abrams, Irwin, *The Words of Peace*, Newmarket Press, New York, N.Y., 1990, p. 3, 4.

[2.] Abrams, Irwin, The Nobel Peace Prize and the Laureates, Watson Publishing International, Nantucket, MA, 2001.

[3.] Palmer, R. R., and Colton, Joel, *A History of the Modern World*, Alfred A. Knopf, New York, N.Y., 1992, p. 723.

[4.] *Britannica Book of the Year, 2001*, p. 277.

[5.] *Britannica Book of the Year, 2001*, p. 302.

[6.] Heilbroner, Robert F., *An Enquiry Into The Human Prospect*, W. W. Norton & Co., Inc., New York, N.Y., 1975, p. 13.

[7.] Commoner, Barry, *The Closing Circle*, Knopf, New York, N.Y., 1971, p.p. 84-93.

[8.] *The Gobe and Mail*, Toronto, Canada, from the *Manchester Guardian*, 26 March, 2002.

[9.] Heilbroner, p. 38.

[10.] Heilbroner, p. 43.

[11.] *Federal Reserve Flow of Funds Statistics*, September 15, 1999.

[12.] Heilbroner, p. 47.

[13.] Heilbroner, p. 48.

[14.] Heilbroner, p. 50.

[15.] Frisken, W. R., *Extended Industrial Revolution and Climate Change*, E&S, American Geophysical Union, Vol. 52 (July 1971), p. 505.

[16.] Ayres, Robert U. and Kneese, Allen V., *Economic and Ecological Effects of a Stationary State, Resources For The Future*, Reprint No. 99, December, 1972.

[17.] Ayres and Kneese, as above, p. 16.

[18.] Frisken, as above, p. 505.

[19.] Heilbroner, p. 55.

[20.] Heilbroner, p. 127.

[21.] Heilbroner, p. 57 and 58.

22. Hobsbawm, Eric, *The Age of Extremes*, Random House, New York, N.Y., 1994, p. 403.

23. Heilbroner, p. 168.

24. *Britannica Book of the Year, 2002*, p. 276 to p. 280, and by individual countries.

Chapter 2: Story of the Nobel Peace Prize

1. Abrams, Irwin, *The Nobel Peace Prize and the Laureates*, p. 335, 338.

    Information on Alfred Nobel's life came mainly from books by Irwin Abrams, Tony Gray (note 2), and on information from the library of the Norwegian Nobel Institute.

2. Gray, Tony, *Champions of Peace*, Paddington Press Ltd., The Two Continents Publishing Group, London, U.K., 1976.

3. Abrams, Irwin, *The Nobel Peace Prize and the Laureates*, p. 335 to 338.

4. Abrams, Irwin, p. 21-32.

Chapter 3: Lives of the Nobel Peace Laureates

1. Gray, Tony, *Champions of Peace*, as above, p. 111.

2. Gray, Tony, as above, p. 121.

3. Gray, Tony, as above, p. 232.

4. Abrams, Irwin, p. 202.

5. Abrams, Irwin, p. 311.

6. Abrams, Irwin, p. 311.

7. Abrams, Irwin, p. 317.

Chapter 4: The Laureates' Legacy of Peacemaking

1. Abrams, Irwin, p. 32.

Chapter 5: Obstacles To Peace

1. Holsti, K. J., *The State, War, and the State of War*, Cambridge University Press, 1996, p. 21, 22.

2. Holsti, p. 121.

3. Holsti, p. 124.

4. Holsti, p. 136.

5. Nelson Mandela lecture at his Peace Prize presentation ceremony, Oslo, December 10, 1993.

Chapter 6: Building An Enduring World Peace

1. *Britannica, Book of the Year, 2002*, p. 302.

2. Suzuki, David, *Earth Time: Essays*, Stoddart Publishing Co., Toronto, Canada, 1998, p. 132.

3. All of this paragraph is an extract from a booklet presenting the key issues of The Hague Agenda for Peace and Justice for the 21st Century, May 1999, The Hague, The Netherlands. www.haguepeace.org

Chapter 7: Peacemaking By State Governments

1. Britannica, 2002, p. 160, *Cultural Anthropology*, p. 159 and 160—Fadwa El Guindi.

2. Britannica, 2001, p. 191, *Globalization—Why All the Fuss?* Geza Feketekuty.

Chapter 8: United Nations, World Peacemaker

1. Bruntland, Ms. Gro Harlem, article, Britannica, 1998, p. 6.

2. Urquhart, Brian, article, *For a UN Volunteer Military Force*, The New York Review of Books, New York, N.Y., 10 June, 1994.

3. Human Development Report 1992, UN Development Program, New York, N.Y.

Chapter 9: Volunteer Partners In Peacemaking

1. Abrams, Irwin, *The Nobel Peace Prize and the Laureates*, p. 160.

2. Abrams, Irwin, p. 161.

3. Childers, Erskine, *Challenges to the United Nations*, St. Martin's Press, New York, N.Y., 1995.

4. Edwards, Michael, *The Globe and Mail*, Toronto, Canada, January 3, 2002.

Chapter 10: World Peace and Democracy

1. Annan, Kofi, Appendix D-2.

2. Churchill, Winston, House of Commons, 13 May, 1940.

3. Mandela, Nelson, Peace Prize acceptance lecture, 1993.

4. Hunter, Robert, *Warriors of the Rainbow*, Holt, Rinehart, and Winston, New York, N.Y., 1979, p. 104.

Chapter 11: World Peace, Social Free Enterprise, and the Market Economy

1. Thurow, Lester, *The Future of Capitalism*, Penguin Books U.S.A. Inc., New York, N.Y., p. 1 to p. 5.

2.   Olson, Mancur, *Power and Prosperity*, Basic Books, New York, N.Y., 2000, pp. 195 to 198.

3.   Sources:

   (a) Secretary-General Warns World Falling Short of Millenium Summit Commitments, *New York Times*, N.Y., October 1st, 2002.

   (b) World Bank Human Development Network Research Paper 2819, April 2002, www.un.org/news/press/docs/2002/dev2385

4.   Thurow, Lester, p. 277.

Chapter 12: New Approach To Peacemaking

1.   Heilbroner, p. 168.

2.   Heilbroner, p. 137, 138.

3.   Schweitzer, Albert, *Out of My Life and Thought*, New American Library, New York, N.Y., 1963, p. 74.

Chapter 13: The Greenpeace Story

1.   Hunter, Robert, *Warriors of the Rainbow, A Chronicle of the Greenpeace Movement*, Holt, Rinehart and Winston, New York, N.Y., 1979, p. 4.

   All quotations and text reprints in this chapter are from this excellent book—fascinating reading for all environmental enthusiasts—and from the Greenpeace Annual Report of year 2000.

2.   Ecology—the great systems of order underlying the complex flow of life on our planet—the study of the relations of organisms to one another and to their surroundings: the study of the interaction of people with their environment.

3.   CFC—usually a gaseous compound of carbon, hydrogen, chlorine, and fluorine, used in refrigerators, aerosol propellants, etc., and indicated to harm the ozone layer.

Chapter 14: Grass Roots Peacemakers Groups

1.   Extracts from Peace Laureate Albert Schweitzer's lecture at the Peace Prize presentation ceremony in Oslo, on November, 1954—see Appendix E.

Chapter 15: What the U.S. and World Governments Can Do Now

[1] McNamara, R.S., and Blight, J.G., *Wilson's Ghost*, Public Affairs Press, New York, N.Y., 2001, p. 48.

[2] As above, p. 221.

[3] As above, p. 222.

[4] As above, p. 223.

[5] As above, p. 224.

[6] As above, p. 224.

[7] As above, p. 225.

Chapter 16: "I Want To Help, What Can I Do Now?"

This chapter lists some main references on Canadian foreign peacemaking aid. Most other developed states will have comparable aid programs.

Bibliography

Abrams, Irwin—*The Nobel Peace Prize and the Laureates*, Watson Publishing International, Nantucket, Mass., U.S., 2001.

Abrams, Irwin, *Words of Peace*, Newmarket Press, New York, N.Y., 1990, 1995.

Axworthy, Lloyd, *The Responsibility To Protect*

- Report of the International Commission on Intervention and State Sovereignty published in 2001 by International Development Research Centre, Ottawa, Ont., Canada, K1G 3H9.

Ayres, Robert U., Kneese, Allen V., *Economic and Ecological Effects of a Stationary State*, Resources for the Future, Reprint No. 99, December 1972.

Britannica, *Book of the Year*

- recent years including 2002—by Encyclopaedia Britannica, Chicago, U.S.

Bok, Sissela, *A Strategy For Peace*, Pantheon Books, New York, N.Y., 1989.

Bruntland, Ms. Gro Harlem, *Madam Prime Minister*, Farrar, Straus and Giroux, New York, N.Y., 2002.

Childers, Erskine, *Challenges To The United Nations*, St. Martin's Press, London, U.K., 1994.

Commoner, Barry, *The Closing Circle*, Knopf, New York, N.Y., 1971.

Derber, Charles, *Corporation Nation*, St. Martin's Press, New York, N.Y., 1998.

Diamond, Jared, *Guns, Germs, and Steel*, W. W. Norton and Co., New York, N.Y., 1997.

Erlich, Paul and Anne, *Population, Resources, Environment*, W. H. Freeman, New York, N.Y., 1972.

Economist, The—*The World In 2002*, 25 St. James Street, London, U.K., 2002.

Economist, The—Weekly copies back to 2001.

Edwards, Michael, *Future Positive*, Earthscan Publications, London, U.K., 1999.

Fukuyama, Francis, *The End of History and the Last Man*, Maxwell, MacMillan, Toronto, Canada, 1992.

Frisken, W. R., *Extended Industrial Revolution and Climate Change*, E. & S., American Geophysical Union, Vol. 52, July 1971.

Gray, Tony, *Champions of Peace*, Paddington Press, The Two Continents Publishing Group, London, U.K., 1976.

Heilbroner, Robert L., *An Inquiry Into The Human Prospect*, W. W. Norton, New York, N. Y., 1974.

Hobsbawm, Eric, *The Age of Extremes*, Random House, New York, N. Y., 1994.

Holsti, Kalevi J., *The State, War, and the State of War*, Cambridge University Press, 1996.

Homer-Dixon, Thomas, *Wake-up Call to a Complacent World*, Vancouver Sun, Canada, June 14, 2002, page A1.

Hunter, Robert, *Warriors of the Rainbow, A Chronicle of the Greenpeace Movement*, Holt, Rinehart, and Winston, New York, N. Y., 1979.

Huntington, Samuel P., *The Clash of Civilizations and the Remaking of World Order*, Simon and Schuster, New York, N. Y., 1996.

Kaplan, Robert, *The Coming Anarchy*, Random House, New York, N. Y., 2000.

Kaplan, Robert, *Balkan Ghosts*, St. Martin's Press, New York, N.Y., 1993.

Katz, S. M.; Debay, Y., *The Blue Helmets Under Fire*, Concord Publications, New Territories, Hong Kong, 1996.

Kennedy, Paul, *The Rise and Fall of Great Powers*, Random House, New York, N. Y., 1987.

Langdon, Steven, *Global Poverty, Democracy, and the North-South Change*, Garamond Publishing, Toronto, Ont., 1999.

Machan, Tibor R., Editor, *Business Ethics in the Global Market*, Hoover Institution Press, Stanford, Calif., U.S., 1999.

MacMillan, Margaret, *Paris 1919*, Random House, Inc., New York, N.Y., 2001.

McNamara, Robert S., and Blight, James G., *Wilson's Ghost*, Public Affairs Press, New York, N.Y., 2001.

Olson, Mancur, *Power and Prosperity*, Basic Books, New York, N. Y., 2000.

Palmer, R. R., and Colton, Joel, *A History of the Modern World*, eighth edition, Alfred A. Knopf, New York, N. Y., 1995.

Robertson, Geoffrey, *Crimes Against Humanity*, New Press, New York, N. Y., 2000.

Roche, Douglas, *A Bargain For Humanity*, University of Alberta Press, Edmonton, Canada, 1993.

Spencer, R.; Kirton, John; Nossal, K., *International Joint Commission, Seventy Years On*, Centre for International Studies, University of Toronto, Canada, 1981.

Schweitzer, Albert, *Out of My Life and Thought*, New American Library, New York, N. Y., 1963.

The Simons Foundation, University of British Columbia, Vancouver, Canada, Documentaries on VHS Video Cassettes

- *Peacemakers*—This documentary examines the positive and powerful new voices of those who are devoted to making the world a safer place.
- *Countdown to Hope*—The Abolition of Nuclear Weapons
- *Ruled By A Bullet*—Small Arms and Light Weapons
- *Random Terror*—Documentary On Landmines.

Suzuki, David, *Earth Time: Essays*, Stoddart Publishing Co., Toronto, Canada, 1998.

The Hague Appeal For Peace Conference—*Conference Brochure* and *The Hague Agenda for Peace and Justice for the 21ˢᵗ Century*, UN Reference A/54/98, The Hague, The Netherlands.

Thurow, Lester C., *The Future of Capitalism*, Penguin Books U.S.A. Inc., New York, N. Y., 1997.

Van Crefeld, Martin, *The Transformation of War*, Collier, MacMillan, Toronto, Canada, 1999.

Woog, Adam, *The United Nations*, Lucent Books, Inc., San Diego, Calif., U.S., 1994.

Index

Paperback: USA $25
              Canada $34

Hardback: USA $35
              Canada $47